SOUTH WIND RED

Our Hemispheric Crisis

South Wind Red

Our Hemispheric Crisis

by Philip A. Ray

HENRY REGNERY COMPANY

Chicago 1962

© Henry Regnery Company 1962

Manufactured in the United States of America

Library of Congress Catalog Card No. 62-17968

Preface

Wading thigh-deep, I had worked the gleaming tarpon to a point ten feet away from me when the shark struck — the tarpon, not me. I saw his swift gray shadow as he knifed into my catch, saw the water foaming first white then red in the brief struggle at my feet, and then I was on the shore, supernaturally propelled.

All that remained of the gamest fish on earth was the head on the end of my nylon spinning line. The waters of the Boca Paila were quiet again.

"Were you scared?" asked Dedee when I got back to the tent camp we had on the eastern shore of Mexico's Yucatan peninsula.

"No," I replied, "happened too swiftly."

"Like Cuba," she said.

We were on our way home to San Francisco from Washington where I had served as Undersecretary of Commerce under President Eisenhower. Now our pleasant vacation was drawing to a close, but the incident and my wife's remark set off a chain of reflection.

A few weeks before, during one of those Washington dinner debates about the state of affairs, a pretty dinner partner had fumed in my ear, "If I hear one more word about the Cold War without being able to enlist, I am going to be ill. After all, even Madame Lafarge could knit, they say, and mother did those USO dances in World War II."

This remark delivered up a memory of the wartime street signs of Uncle Sam pointing a stern finger at the passerby, fixing him with a flaming eye and saying, "I need you."

v

Pretty good point she had, I thought. Just how does one go about enlisting in a Cold War? Is the Cold War struggle chiefly or solely a matter of government-to-government action through grants, loans, Care Packages, Peace Corps, Point Four, Foreign Aid, Food for Peace? Since the communists have all these weapons and others besides, such a self-imposed limitation upon the quality of our effort seems particularly unjustifiable.

Is there nothing the citizen can do save wring his hands and wince as he reads of Laos, Chaos, Cuba and Confusion? Since our purpose must be to establish as a fact rather than a theory, especially in the uncommitted and less-developed areas of the free world where exploding population regularly outstrips new jobs, that a free capitalistic society with limited government intervention is superior to and better for all concerned than statism and totalitarianism, one would think that the first weapon to be unlimbered would be our private sector.

Our capacity, through new private capital formation, to create needed private jobs in private plants in these decisive areas is our unique developmental missile, not found in the communist arsenal at all. This is Russia's freedom gap.

It seems shocking that, despite the intensity of the Cold War, not one single new government program has been adopted for the purpose of enlisting our own private sector, our business and industry, in the struggle. In World War II, partly by means of the carrot approach (fast tax writeoffs and Victory Loan guarantees) and partly by means of the no-carrot approach (government allocation of materials) we channeled our industrial might into the winning of the military conflict.

Must we not find, I ask, analogous measures to inject the total resources of our modern, widely-shared capitalism into the Cold War conflict, particularly with respect to the world's developmental needs, carefully adjusting these measures so as to preserve the essential freedom of our private sector, lest our own governmental intervention result in the adoption of communist methodology rather than our own?

In this thesis, my chief enemy has been the friend who agrees but says, "We just don't have that kind of time." He is my friend because he supports my doctrine, my enemy because he has unwittingly succumbed to the idea that merely meeting the ever-present and immediate crisis created by communism must forever occupy our total attention. He does not realize that the man who feeds on crises alone will in due course starve to death.

As we sat around the campfire that night, between the jungle and the surf, the questions mounted in our minds. Is American industry fighting the good fight on its own in risky Latin America without government backing, creating jobs, widening the reach of our system, displaying a modern corporate conscience? What practices, if any, have been changed since the communist shark gobbled up $1 billion of U. S. private plant in Cuba? What is United States industry doing in the light, say, of the fact that in Chile the socialists and communists ran the same candidate for President of Chile last time, on a platform calling for the expropriation of all United States industry there, and nearly won?

Are our investments hated and resented in Latin America, as some of the so-called "prestige polls" taken by our Voice of America show? Is this because our firms cling to outmoded feudal practices, or is it a pure communist propaganda victory, or is it both? What is being done there by our government, by our businessmen, their local counterparts and the host governments, to repel the communist offensive and to create a climate for purposeful economic expansion?

How badly are we losing to communism, elsewhere than in Cuba, we asked ourselves? Shortly before, I happened to have received a letter from a friend in Venezuela telling me that a communist student-body president had been elected in every public high school there except two. Is their human crop being blighted?

/ "Not more than 30 per cent of the people in Chile are communists," a Chilean friend said to me last summer. Since I consider this frightening in the extreme, I could not understand his nonchalance which I thought worthy of the steeliest matador.

Could my wife and I become a food-for-thought corps, personally investigate the subject? That night we decided to try. It would not be our first time around in Latin America, by any means, but it would be better planned and more comprehensive. We laid out a systematic plan, went to twelve different countries in five months, did our level best to avoid the cocktail-party and after-dinner-speech routines, interviewed more than 250 informed personalities — national presidents, lesser politicians, priests, communists, editors and, of course, business leaders both indigenous and foreign.

Prefaces are ordinarily laced with multiple acknowledgements of assistance, and this one should be too, but let me only say as a compliment to my wife that having a lovely traveling companion able to speak Spanish and get by in Portuguese enormously increases one's level of accomplishment in such an affair as this.

We asked two questions, essentially: Does this particular society — a capitalistic, Western, Christian society if you please — have a fabric of strength and justice adequate to withstand the communist offensive? And if not, what should the United States do about it?

Contents

PREFACE v

I. OUR INFECTED HEMISPHERE 1

II. THE POSTFEUDAL REMNANTS 25
Pitfalls of Land Reform

III. SOCIALISM SUPERIMPOSED 49
The Major Commodity Problem: Socialism at
the International Level

IV. EDUCATION: A BLIGHTED CROP? 86

V. POPULATION A SURPLUS CROP? 100
The Marshall Plan Fallacy

VI. PAVLOV, WASHINGTON AND LATIN
AMERICA 111

VII. PRIVATE INVESTMENT: NEGLECTED
WEAPON OF THE COLD WAR? 134
My Company 'Tis of Thee

VIII. POLICY AND PROGRAM: THE EX-
PORTATION OF SUCCESSFUL CAPITALISM 182
A Financing For Freedom Act

IX. THE ULTIMATE TEST: A UNITY
OF INTEREST 209

APPENDIX: A COMMON SUPER-MARKET
FOR LATIN AMERICA 225

INDEX 231

CHAPTER ONE

Our Infected Hemisphere

Come with me to the hills outside Caracas in Venezuela. Pause with me along the dusty path to grin at the dark-eyed girl of eight, to wink and cluck and jab a friendly finger in her direction. Her eyes will follow yours with warmth and interest, but the chances are no smile will wreathe her pretty face for the reason that her smile muscles have never developed.

Recently a medical team found that many children who live in the immediate slums of Caracas have never had occasion to smile, and the facial muscles that produce smiles have atrophied away. They can learn to smile, but it takes time and practice and someone who will smile back.

In these hills, within hailing distance of smooth highways where Rolls Royces slip swiftly by, 400,000 people without sewers, toilets, running water or jobs live in a crowded, jumbled heap of huts, cynically called "little ranches" in Spanish.

Picture if you will the night, a sturdy Friar-Tuck of a nun on a rooftop with a searchlight and loudspeaker, crying out for community action against rape and robbery and unspeakable crime committed where no policeman dares to enter.

The roof is the top of a seven-story structure called Fe y Alegria, plunked down by charity into the middle of these "ranchitos."

Here some 2,000 children come each day, for meager schooling, learning of simple trades, medical help, occasional food and simple protection against the ugly environment that

lies outside the barred gates. Now the nuns can only afford meals for 500, and those who may eat are chosen each day by the degree of their hungriness. One day this particular week a ten-year-old boy thus chosen had meat to eat for the first time in his life.

Every once in a while, a maturing young woman doesn't leave the Fe y Alegria when night falls, usually because the family environment has become too unbearable. Whatever the reason, mother a prostitute or father a drunk, the nuns have sealed some 50 girls within the walls, most of whom, trained as teachers and social workers, will return to teach and work in an environment they know only too well.

When they do, they will be among the few non-communist teachers. In the lower-grade schools, the percentage of communist teachers ranges from a high of 86 per cent to a low of 33 per cent. In the spring of that year, when the public high schools held student elections — and this is an out-and-out political dry-run in Latin American schools — the communist student ticket won out in every school but two.

For the most part the people of the "ranchitos" live outside the money economy; they are not a part of the realm of politics nor welcome in the world of jobs. "Ordinary politicians rarely come to these areas even during the campaigns, but the communists campaign here night and day," a Venezuelan friend told me.

These conditions are not peculiar to Caracas. What are called "ranchitos" in Venezuela are the "barriadas" of Peru, the "favellas" of Rio, the "callampas" of Chile and the urban slums of Mexico City. From city to city and town to town, from tens of thousands of hand-made huts that rim the hills like bleachers, new arrivals peer down upon modern office buildings and fashionable residential districts.

Lima, with its great colonial squares and edifices, its monuments and narrow streets, its magnificent boulevards and resi-

dences, has one aspect that is coming to be a characteristic of the modern Latin American metropolis. Within the past five years, 300,000 Peruvian Indians have come to Lima Town to take up residence based on a kind of squatter's right. Their jumbled "barriadas" of mud, cardboard, sticks and stones draw an unsightly girdle of streetless and sewerless slums around the old colonial city.

"In Peru you can smell misery, and you need not sniff too hard," wrote a recent visitor. "Behind Lima where the arid Andean foothills slouch down towards the sea, there is a hill called San Cristobal, crowned with a cross of pilgrimage, that commands a famous view of the capital. Splendidly below you lies the City of Kings, huddled beneath its winter vapors.

"Immediately at your feet, however, clustered on the hillside like some nightmare belvedere, there lies a slum so festering, so filthy, so toad-like, so bestially congested, so utterly devoid of water, light, health or comfort, so deep in garbage and excrement that just to wander through its alleys makes you retch."[1]

Mexico City is experiencing a similar kind of rural-to-urban migration, and he who strays behind the fashionable facades of the Paseo de la Reforma encounters the same sights and smells of incredible human misery. Now 5,300,000 strong, Mexico City is the second city in our hemisphere.

From northern Brazil, from the dusty pampas of the south, from the Andean villages, millions more are daily marching to town to create new rings around the urban bathtub.

In Chile, some people who can are quietly getting out. The reason is summed up in the words of a Britisher who for 40 years has lived and done business in Chile. "The next time around, the communists will come into office at the polls, without having to march out of the hills." That engaging parlor game we played in the case of armed revolutionaires such as Mao Tse and Castro, called "Do you think he is a communist?" may come to be outmoded by its emerging non-violent counterpart. Of course, the danger of explosive communist takeovers along the Russian pattern, or of insurrections that succeed through seizure of the primitive hinterland, followed by expanding accumulation of strength and power, as in the case of Castro and Mao Tse, will ever remain clear and present. Nevertheless they may soon be replaced in substantial part by the more sophisticated, initially more democratic, route of popular elections, as in British Guiana today. It is characteristic of all gangsters that once they acquire enough power to gain a sort of immunity, they want to take on the veneer of respectability.

The Chilean speaker had reference to the presidential elections, the "next time around" being 1964. President Alessandri won in 1958 by only 30,000 votes against a socialist-communist coalition whose platform and program, along with Karl Marx's, called for expropriation of all industry, especially United States firms. In effect, the communists sat in the cafes while the socialists ran their campaign, but now the communists are losing their reticence all over Latin America because of success at the polls and in the ministries. Alessandri cannot run again and the shadow of 1958 lengthens as 1964 draws near.

Colombia is a magnificent and highly diversified country, rich in natural resources yielding coffee, oil, sugar, emeralds, bananas, and many other primary products. Sparsely settled, its 14,000,000 people occupy a land larger than Texas and California combined, much of it potentially rich but now inaccessible.

What, then, is the reason for being concerned?

One important reason is that the concentration of Colombia's wealth in relatively few hands makes her a prime target for the communists, who are now placing their emphasis in the agrarian sugar areas and industries related thereto, striving for a revolution along the Chinese pattern.

A construction worker gets about 70 cents a day, and a typical corporate payroll shows a small cluster of high salaries at the top, then a sheer and virtually uninterrupted drop to a uniform level of bare subsistence pay, ranging from 75 cents to $1.50 a day. Obviously most of these people can do little in the way of saving, consuming or acquiring property. Poverty in the mass lives in the midst of plenty for the few, creating frictions of deepening intensity.

Unquestionably, the conquest of Cuba is the most important communist triumph in the dozen years since China. There is no Cuba any place in Africa nor, indeed, anywhere at all in the sense that Cuba became the first communist state in the world having no common border with any other communist nation. And China never had been a part of the western world, never had known popular government, whereas Cuba is Latin America in miniature. The cultural ties to Spain and Europe, the Catholic religion, the rich land, all are there. Thus Cuba provides an almost ideal beachhead for the pursuit of a Red objective of highest world priority — the destruction of United States influence and interest throughout Latin America.

One measure of the initial impact of the successful Castro revolution is seen in the steadfast refusal of other Latin American politicians to denounce him. In South America only Peru, Venezuela and, more recently, Argentina and Ecuador have parted company with Castro diplomatically.[2] In the last two mentioned, the severance was the result of military pressures. In Argentina, the severance proved to be a factor in Red-supported Peronista victories at the polls in March 1962 which in turn led to the military ouster of President Frondizi.

At Punta del Este in September of 1961, while we were in the very act of giving definitive expression to our $20 billion

Latin American aid program, it proved impossible for our emissaries to gain even a mild group expression against Castro communism. Brazil led the opposition to a resolution — seemingly quite bland — favoring "honest and periodic elections," on the ground it would tend to isolate the Cubans.[3] Far from evoking more explicit anticommunism in Latin America, the Cuban affair has given rise to a wave of enhanced neutralism. Even Castro's gleeful announcement on December 2, 1961, that he had been a communist since his college days and his revolution had been communist-directed from the beginning, did little to engender opposition to his cause. As it happened, this declaration was made only two days prior to a scheduled vote, in the Organization of American States, on a Colombian proposal for a foreign ministers' conference to consider the communist threat posed by Cuba against other nations of the Western Hemisphere. While the vote technically favored the Colombian proposal, for the reason that under OAS practices each country has one vote regardless of size, the governments of nations under which three-fourths of all Latin Americans live failed to approve. Mexico actually voted with Cuba while Argentina, Brazil, Bolivia, Chile and Ecuador abstained.[4] The foreign policy fiasco was completed when these six countries — the so-called "Soft Six" — stood their ground when the conference was held in January 1962[5] and abstained from voting on a resolution to exclude the present government of Cuba from participation in the American System.

In his historic Freedom of Press speech of June 7, 1961, President Lopez Mateos of Mexico expressed his country's passion for an independent character in this way: "Nothing is more harmful to the well-being of the Republic and the organic peace which has cost so much effort to consolidate than the struggle between diametrically opposed political philosophies which are in world conflict. . . ." This studied neutralism offers, in practical fact, a fertile ground for communistic activity.

If Mexico says "a plague on both your houses," Brazil has repeatedly made it plain that she wants to do business with both. While negotiating new barter deals with the Soviets, supporting Red China's bid for a U. N. seat, and decorating Major "Che" Guevara of Cuba with the highest Brazilian award, she found no difficulty in 1961 in raising $200 million from the United States Treasury in new and extended credits, nor in plugging for $1 billion of string-free aid annually from the United States to Latin America.

Together, Mexico and Brazil with over 100 million people are the spearhead of a "third force" in our hemisphere, one which refuses to be linked either to the East or the West, and tolerates communist penetration while actively seeking increasing shares of United States foreign aid on a string-free basis.

The Castro revolution, quite apart from its meaning within the Marxist context, is viewed by the Latin American masses as a triumph for the little guy and a slap at Uncle Sam: land for all and nationalization of $1 billion of private United States property. As one official of a Latin American foreign ministry said to me, "People seem to be saying that if tiny Cuba can push the Yankees around and take away their valuable properties, why, we can too." Hence few politicians can openly oppose Castro.

By all available yardsticks, a majority of the Latin American peoples favored Castro even before our invasion of the island in April 1961. The impact of two emotional factors associated with that invasion have immeasurably swelled the pro-Castro element: historical hatred for intervenors and native contempt for paper tigers. The adherence of Latin America's smoldering masses to the cause of tiny communist Cuba seems all the more alarming because it exemplifies Marx's original theory of the way in which international communism would spread.

Eudacio Ravines, Peruvian publisher of the anticommunist magazine Vanguardia, is a former communist who might be described as the Whittaker Chambers of Peru. Cogently he points out that the existence of Castro is polarizing the communists and the parties of the extreme left. Unless Castro is destroyed, this joint leftist movement will prevail, and in the process will be captured by communists. Literally everywhere in moderate circles in Latin America, one can hear the phrase: "Three years more of Fidel and all Latin America will be communist."

The pervasive leftward influence of Castro is well stated by H. K. Silvert in a paper entitled "The Island and the Continent" of January 29, 1961:

> The stock of the Russian-oriented communist parties has risen, of course. Trotskyist groups have been tempted to make common cause with the now more activist left, and Popular Frontism is gaining a new lease on life. Great debates rage as to whether the Chinese Way is better than the Russian Way, whether Castro really likes Tito better than Nasser, whether Cuban nationalism can be reconciled with genuine social revolution, and so forth. This part of the left is being reinvigorated by dispute, example, and the unaccustomed scent of success.

Domingo Alberto Rangel, the head of Venezuela's radical leftist MIR party, openly plots a Castro-like takeover, and a subsequent "liquidation" of moderate elements that may initially be allied with the revolution. It is fashionable for leftists in Latin America everywhere now — students and adults as well — to believe that a violent, radical revolution is essential. All of them are willing to ally themselves with the communists — locally and internationally — to achieve their goals. Many, perhaps most of them, innocently believe such an alliance to be tactical and temporary in character. "We shall have a revolution," said a Peruvian newspaper man to me, "but it will be uniquely Peruvian while relying upon Castro techniques."

"Won't you come into my parlor?" said the spider to the fly.

Communism, the most powerful totalitarian force in the history of the world, sits in the saddle or rides hard on the flank of every potential revolution in Latin America today, ready to direct it openly or capture it from within, the moment it is launched. In recent years a key policy of the Communist Party in Latin America has been to carry communism to power on the backs of non-communist collaborators.

In addition to providing a bond between the left and communism in Latin America, the Castro revolution creates Spanish-speaking centers of communist subversion in every nation in the world to which Cuba sends a diplomatic representative. Most recently, it was disclosed that the Cuban Embassy in the Philippines has become an "active center of communist subversion."[6]

With communism on the rise in Latin America, how is the capitalism we export viewed now by the masses in Latin America? The best evidence is found in some of the so-called "prestige polls" taken by our Voice of America in Brazil.

The list of United States firms in Brazil looks like the yellow pages of your telephone book. Yet these billions of investment, which provide new wealth, technology, growth, and employment for Brazilians, have come to be resented more than they are admired as a result of the relentless communist campaign against capitalism.

The full impact was not appreciated until recently, when public opinion polls financed in part by United States business revealed that all was not well. For example, in Rio the answers to the question, "What is your opinion with respect to the investment of United States capital in Brazil?" were as follows:

Should have more 26%
Have enough 14%
Should have less 7%
Should stop 34%
Don't know, no opinion 19%
                                   ——————
                                   100%

On this and other questions, in Rio and other cities as well, two out of three of those sampled who expressed any opinion at all were adverse to our private investments — the primary illustration of our capitalistic system.[7]

This is a formidable showing, especially in view of the fact that one would think such foreign private investment would be our main instrument for assisting in the growth of the less-developed nations, more significant than our government aid because, in addition to being far larger in amount, it recreates abroad the very kind of private enterprise system we try to foster at home.

Indeed, the first necessity of the Cold War would seem to be to prove, in the uncommitted areas of the world, that the private enterprise system is more efficient and better for all than totalitarian communism or state ownership. Since this is a point which government aid has a hard time proving, it is no wonder that the communists center their principal fire on our private sector overseas.

The communist claims are clever, often require more than first-year accounting to refute. They charge that United States companies make exorbitant profits and cite out-of-context figures or isolated instances in support. They claim we take back to the United States far more each year in profits than our new investments, hammering away at so-called "hidden profits," payments made by subsidiary companies in Brazil to the United States parent company for patent rights, research and other home-office costs.

Moreover, many well-meaning people, innocently predisposed by the communist propaganda, have come to believe and endorse these allegations. A high official of a Brazilian quasi-governmental bank told me in all seriousness that "United States companies should stop making 30, 40, 50 and even 100 per cent profit per year in Brazil and sending it to the States." Unwittingly he was repeating communist propaganda in its rawest form.

What country of Latin America, one may ask, now has a fabric of capitalism adequate in strength and justice to resist the communist offensive?

Is it *Argentina,* where the cost of living increased more than four times since 1953? Where the labor unions are communist-dominated? Where totalitarianism recently made its hemispheric home? Where Red-backed Peronista candidates won decisive ballot victories in eleven provinces in March 1962, leading to the military ouster of moderate President Frondizi? Where productivity continues to decline and the distribution of wealth gets worse instead of better? While increased new investment and reduced inflation and better international balance seemed for a time to point to a way out, the case for an affirmative answer is not yet made?

Is it *Bolivia,* where the mines have been nationalized and the politicians helplessly watch declining productivity and rising wages price the products out of world markets? Where the primary plank of Marx's program, nationalization of industry, has been largely fulfilled, and the entire economy would have collapsed but for United States emergency grants that have exceeded $175 million in the past decade? Where communist-inspired riots, strikes and mass killings are common occurrences, necessitating frequent declarations of a state of siege by the government?

Is it *Chile* where private investment is so frustrated by state intervention that 75 per cent of new jobs are government jobs? Where the polarization of the left with communism was demonstrated even prior to Castro? Where, in 1961, the people of Chile elected forty-seven communist members to the Chilean parliament?[8] Heroic measures to salvage a private enterprise economy have been taken but the answer cannot now be yes.

Is it *Colombia,* where 14,000 were killed in the most recent leftist riots—250,000 to 500,000 estimated victims over the last 12 years in bloody civil wars? Where the government lives in a virtual state of seige to prevent a communist takeover or a rightist counter-coup?

Is it *Venezuela,* where, typically, only 10 per cent of the people have enough income to be consumers in the sense of buying things in the stores? Where despite great natural wealth, poverty and joblessness, illiteracy and Fidelismo are perhaps most prevalent?

Is it *Ecuador,* where far-left President Arosemena, upon taking office in 1961, openly espoused the Castro cause?

Is it *Brazil,* where private enterprise, i.e. capitalism, is polled down 2 to 1 even in industrial cities like Sao Paulo? Where the cost of living has quadrupled in the last eight years? Vice President Goulart, who succeeded the resigning President Quadros, is a Marxist and Castro sympathizer who has long been more critical of the United States than his predecessor; he is suspicious of United States business overseas and a warm friend of communists from Cuba to China. Just to make certain everyone understood Brazil's intent to continue romancing the Reds while panhandling the United States for more foreign aid, he promptly and simultaneously angled for an invitation to visit President Kennedy, planted the Order of the Southern Cross on communist Poland's visiting Foreign Minister Rapacki, had his own Foreign Minister announce that Brazil no longer considers herself a member of the Western bloc and was going to "stop playing with marked cards in the U. N."[9]

Is it *Panama*, where the communists have succeeded so well in selling the idea that our canal belongs to them that we recently conceded their right to fly their flag over it? Not long afterward, the new President of Panama came to Washington to demand that we "agree that the Panama Canal is an enterprise in which both are equally interested."[10] He had forgotten that there never was a Panama until we conspired with the "Panamanians" to create one out of part of what was then Colombia and that, in return, we paid $10 million in gold plus the cost of the canal. It is also convenient to forget that the canal has been of inestimable value in the economic life of Colombia and Panama and all of Latin America, not to mention our large and growing annual government outlays there and our fixed annual pension to Panama, which has increased under successive blackmailing from $430,000 to $1,930,000 a year. Based on past accommodations and the current fashion to avoid any conceivable injury to the feelings of any other nation, it would be reasonable to expect some fresh concession to pacify Panama once more.

Is it *Mexico*, perhaps, where a major, perhaps the majority, element of the only political party is pro-Castro? Where state expropriation started with oil in 1938 and continued in 1960 with motion pictures, power and light and trucks? Where the official policy is to find a non-United States oriented solution? Is there one, realistically, other than communism? Mexico, which during most of the postwar period has been the main operating center of Soviet subversion in Latin America, including espionage, terrorism, propaganda and political infiltration?[11] The place where Castro went to get ready? The home of the latest communist Peace Conference in this hemisphere sponsored by General Cárdenas, a former President of Mexico?

Since the Mexican revolution of 1910, a single political party, containing irrational elements held together by a desire for power and respect for the goals of the revolution, has held an iron grip on Mexican public life. If the communist fringe and the left-wing elements of the party headed by General Cárdenas, who espouses the Castro position, were to break away, much informed opinion would give them the leading position in Mexican political life today.

Is it tiny, socialistic, becalmed *Uruguay* perhaps? *British Guiana,* perchance, a British possession approaching independence which recently elected a communist majority to its parliament, and to which, some may have been surprised to read, millions of United States foreign aid had been given in recent years? When a United States senator suggested that perhaps under these circumstances our aid ought to cease, communist Prime Minister Cheddi Jagan of British Guiana came to Washington to protest. He held a press conference in October in which he characterized himself as a socialist rather than a communist. Describing himself as a neutral in the Cold War, "like Brazil and India," he staked out his claim to aid from both sides. When questioned about his attitude toward private ownership, he said he did not intend to nationalize industry, but to this latter assertion he quickly added the words, "at this time," evidently hoping thereby to remain on a good footing with the communist world. Jagan is a new kind of neutralist. Completely betrothed to communism, he halfway recants in order to keep the Western sector sending flowers. Why not, when this will bring no less powerful an organ than the *New York Times* to plug editorially for the continuance of foreign aid?[12]

Why not, when President Kennedy could feel it appropriate to say to the Russian people, in his famous off-the-cuff interview in Izvestia: "Mr. Jagan, who was recently elected Prime Minister in British Guiana is a Marxist, but the United States doesn't object—because that choice was made by an honest election, which he won. If the people of any country choose to follow a communist system in a free election, after a fair opportunity for a number of views to be presented, the United States would accept that."[13]

Do we really mean to tell the Russian people that the gulf between our philosophies is to be measured merely by a contest at the polls? Can we be so gullible as to believe that communism, once in the saddle via the election process, will maintain that process intact? And if they do not, how do we propose that freedom shall be regained?

Latin America's economic indicators, swamped by the world's fastest population growth, point clearly in the direction of increased joblessness—Latin America's fundamental problem—hence increased poverty in these unhappy lands. Free and democratic institutions cannot prevail against totalitarian forces when large sectors of the population, as in Latin America, are offered no reasonable avenue through which to alleviate their economic condition. Hence it is the communists who have most of the "rising expectations" in our hemisphere. Their outlook is further improved by the political and economic instability which prevails throughout Latin America, a condition they exploit at every opportunity.

According to reports of one United States newspaper for a single week in October 1961, Colombia declared a state of martial law to put down a rightist coup. Bolivia did the same because of riots in which at least six students were killed, resulting from an increase in the price of gasoline announced by the state-owned oil company. Press censorship was imposed and all educational institutions shut down. Ecuadorian lepers seized plantation land and divided it among themselves. Janio Quadros, who had resigned as President of Brazil a few weeks

earlier in an abortive effort to gain dictatorial control through
fresh popular support, announced an early return to put down
the "exploiters" of the people. Peru suspended constitutional
guarantees as 5,000 striking grammar and high school teachers
and students assailed the Presidential palace. The President of
Ecuador called on the people to keep his government in office.
The Latin-American Student Congress, held in Natal, Brazil,
ended in a brawl. No plenary sessions were held since twelve
of the delegations were said to represent democratic principles
while eight were called communist or pro-communist. A month
earlier, in Mexico, at least 30 persons were killed in a frustrated series of peasant uprisings. Hundreds were arrested in
connection with the antigovernment demonstrations, shootings
and uprisings allegedly backed and directed by the Cuban
embassy in Mexico.[14] During this period, President Dorticos,
puppet President of Cuba, was touring Red China speaking on
the theme of regaining Formosa and Guantanamo Bay.

In the thirties the Communist Party was just another radical fringe under alien direction. Prior to World War II, only
we and Uruguay allowed the Soviet Russian Export Monopoly,
Amtorg, to come in to trade and spy; and only she and three
others—Mexico, Argentina and Colombia—had given formal
recognition to Russia's Soviet regime. President Roosevelt's
insistence for purposes of unity in World War II caused the
others "to take the Soviet serpent to our bosom officially," as
the Brazilian Foreign Minister once said.

After World War II, the communists entered the arena
openly and in force but soon again lost ground by overplaying
their role as puppets of an alien dictatorship. In fact, by 1955
fifteen Latin American nations had severed all diplomatic relations with Russia; this time only Mexico, Ecuador, Uruguay,
and Argentina followed our example of maintaining diplomatic relations with the Soviets.

Today, the Communist Party is now completely legal in

nine* countries and operates more or less openly in most of the other eleven.[15] The communists' dramatic and pervasive return to strength is a consequence of years of careful underground work, resulting in an infiltration of governments, labor unions, education, and left wing organizations, but it also gained additional impetus through the Cuban victory. Their present position of dominance is due to the kind of critical failure of capitalism that Marx prophesied, and to the continued presence of a communist showcase in Cuba.

The communists control labor organizations embracing perhaps one million rank-and-file members, most of whom are not communists but are subject to communist leadership. In other labor organizations the communists have varying degrees of influence through strategically placed officials. While communist membership is negligible among the 12 million rank-and-file union members in Latin America, infiltration at the top gives communist leaders an influence far out of proportion to the size of the party membership.[16]

"The most recent ILO** meeting in Buenos Aires (April 1961) satisfied me," said one of our labor union delegates to me, "that the commies control the labor movement in Latin America. I have been around long enough to know by their motions and resolutions when a labor leader is a communist. The place was full of them," he added.

At the end of 1958 there were 316 known communist or pro-communist publications in Latin America, the largest number being 55 in Mexico. About one half are newspapers and other periodicals. At the time there were more than 150

---

*These nine countries are Argentina, Bolivia, Brazil, Chile, Colombia, Ecuador, Mexico, Uruguay, and Venezuela, approximately 90 per cent of Latin America in population.

**ILO means International Labor Organization, the only vestigial remainder of the post-World War I League of Nations.

communist publishing houses and bookstores. These activities have increased sharply since 1958.

A 75-man Soviet mission in Montevideo, Uruguay, one of Latin America's smallest nations, supervises the distribution of 12 different weekly and bi-monthly magazines, including glossy publications from East Germany and Poland, and vast flocks of gaily colored children's comics.[17]

Recently in the United Nations, Ambassador Stevenson revealed that the only Latin American press represented in the world press corps at the United Nations is La Prensa Latina, which is a pro-Castro newspaper operating more or less freely in several Latin American countries.[18]

"Through their control of public media and their extensive infiltration of newspapers, radio, libraries and schools, the communists now control public opinion in Brazil and can sway it almost any way they wish," I was told in September 1961 by a prominent Brazilian delegate to the International Industrial Conference in San Francisco.

Cuban documents obtained from a Cuban defector in Buenos Aires reveal the details of the country-by-country plan for the infiltration and ultimate take-over of the Latin American press by the Reds. Every newspaper and magazine would have a "union section" of employees with pro-Castro leanings who would inculcate a "mystique" of the "inevitability" of the Cuban revolution and throw an "aura of heroism" around Fidel. This union section "must insist that capitalism has reached a critical point and it is imperative to put an end to the aggressions of Yanqui imperialism against the underdeveloped and semicolonial peoples. This must be," the plan continues, "a well coordinated and well disciplined action in which each militant member must zealously defend the interests of the socialist revolution."

The document calls for measures by the "union section" to bankrupt newspapers and other publications by extreme demands, reduced productivity, sabotage and defamation, and urges that each such union contain workers of all skills needed "to take over the press at the opportune moment."[10]

The manager of a Brazilian branch of a United States bank told me "The communists send large numbers of selected left-wing Brazilians to Russia, paying them well before and during their sojourn and after their return. There they give them thorough training in communist dogma and techniques, and then return them to Brazil to push the Red cause in their original environment whether press, radio, education, or labor union."

Communist penetration of faculties and student bodies of national universities, as well as secondary and primary schools, is widespread everywhere and the granting of United States foreign aid to the education ministries of most Latin American countries can be considered in most situations as tantamount to our financing of more communist indoctrination.

"The teen-ager entering Montevideo University is politically uninformed," says Eduardo Skidelsky, secretary-general of the Movimiento Estudiantil Democratico, one of the rare anticommunist student societies. "But by the time he is through freshman year, he has been initiated, and he has learned one lesson well—that the way to get along, the road to acceptance, is to be anti-United States."[20]

San Marcos University in Peru always has communists elected to its student council. In Venezuela, the dean of the school of Journalism has long been an avowed communist. It is not hard to understand how it came about that professional Red students and Red-inspired student catspaws rioted and spat upon Vice President Nixon in those two places in 1958, nor why it was that the governments were powerless to prevent it.

The Soviet embassy force in Mexico City includes 35 cultural attaches who attend the university as students. Equipped with adequate bankrolls, these adult subversives help form high school communist cadres and supplement the incomes of communist-oriented students. They finance riots and promote disruption. It was recently disclosed that a previous chancellor of the university had embezzled large sums of university funds which he used to counter-bribe the students in an effort to prop up his sagging regime by inducing them not to join in communist-inspired riots and sabotage.

One of the areas where the communists are most active is the farm. They are behind most of the agitation for agrarian reform. One of Lenin's fundamental theories was that cutting the land up into small parcels was a first step in communism. Reducing productive large-scale farm enterprises to a multitude of small one-man units quickly reduces output and in most cases ends in the organization of the communal farm. This is especially true where costly modern farm equipment is beyond the reach of the small farmer.

In Colombia's sugar cane fields, the communists control most labor unions. When the United States cut Colombia in for a share of Cuba's former sugar allotment, the communists inspired strikes against the mills to prevent Colombian farmers from taking advantage of the new export market. Through strikes, riots, agitation and the burning of private mills they hope to deepen the poverty and dissatisfaction of the workers, and pull off an agrarian revolution along Chinese lines.

In northeast Brazil, a rocky, thin-soiled property has been taken over by 144 peasant families from a debt-ridden owner squeezing his tenants. The seizure of this property has become a rallying cry for "peasant leagues" springing up in the name of land reform. The name of the property, Galilea, has generated a song associated with the movement, which is led by a fanatic pro-Castro Brazilian, Julião.

More than a decade ago in 1948, the Little Central American democracy of Costa Rica, with a population of 1 million people, was seized by the communists. The people took arms and threw off the yoke, but with a loss of 2,000 lives—six times more in proportion to our respective populations than we lost in the entire Korean War.[21]

Today, Jose Figueres, a former President of that small but brave country, has this to say: "There is a chance that not only Cuba but the twenty republics will join the Soviet Union. This is an awful thing to say. But you ought to know how scared and worried I am, traveling from one country to another in South America and listening to what the young people are being told, what they are saying, what erroneous conceptions are being infiltrated by an international organization which is very efficient, the international communist party."[22]

*   *   *   *   *

Karl Marx propounded the economic doctrine that capitalism will inevitably fail, and the refinement that its failure will always occur in a moment of crisis grave enough to produce actual or potential civil war.[23]

He also believed that as capitalism evolves out of post-feudal conditions, tumultuous class struggle occurs and, hence, it is at that precise point in time when the possibility of a communist alternative best presents itself.[24]

Marx felt the collapse of capitalism so inevitable that planning for its fall was hardly necessary, but he did think it desirable to work for nationalization of industry and expropriation of private property.[25]

To these precepts, Lenin added one more ominous footnote, so pertinent to the Latin American scene today that it might well have been written about Cuba. He wrote that "the victory of socialism may come originally in a single capitalist country. The victorious proletariat of that country, having expropriated the capitalists and having organized socialist production at home, would rise against the remaining capitalist world, drawing to itself in the process the oppressed classes of other countries."[26]

In the United States, under our form of modern, widely shared capitalism, these doctrines of Marx have been dispelled as myths and exposed as cloaks for cynical and materialistic dictatorship.

Yet Latin America has not succeeded in establishing, and we have not succeeded in exporting to her, our kind of private enterprise economy that works for all—offering optimum individual human choice and freedom while summoning up maximum individual effort, initiative and innovation.

As we face the deepening crisis in Latin America—the kind of situation which Marx predicted communism would feed on—we must above all things believe that the hour is not too late for our brand of capitalism in Latin America since it will take many decades to build a modern capitalistic society with strength and justice adequate to displace the threat of communism. Obviously, this will never occur if the right beginning is never made. Accordingly, belief in the availability of the time needed so to build is an absolute necessity.

Unfortunately, the painful realization that capitalism—our kind of system if you please—is failing in Latin America, coupled with the reality of communism fully established on our very hemispheric doorstep have led us into the hasty adoption of a set of policies, involving chiefly expanded United States foreign aid, of questionable character under the circumstances.

Thereby, we fashion our contribution to Latin America upon measures ill-suited for the struggle.

From the oft-repeated Marxist theory that capitalism is basically bad and its eventual fall therefore inevitable, one derives his corollary maxim that this is a long-term struggle. Thus, fortunately, it is Marx's own doctrine that gives us time—if we will but look beyond immediate crises and display a firm belief in the fundamentals of our own society. Through the quality of our contribution we can help to establish a just and successful system of modern capitalism in this now uncommitted and unstable world of Latin America.

CHAPTER I

REFERENCES

[1] James Morris, *San Francisco Chronicle,* July 16, 1961.

[2] *New York Times,* Mar. 1, 1962; *San Francisco Examiner,* Apr. 4, 1962.

[3] *New York Times,* Aug. 15, 1961.

[4] *San Francisco Examiner,* Dec. 5, 1961.

[5] *New York Times,* Feb. 2, 1962.

[6] *New York Times,* Oct. 3, 1961.

[7] "Is Uncle Sam Being Misunderstood?"—the American Chamber of Commerce for Brazil of Rio de Janeiro and Sao Paulo.

[8] *San Francisco Examiner,* June 19, 1961.

[9] *Time* Magazine, Nov. 3, 1961.

[10] *New York Times,* Oct. 1, 1961.

[11] Alexander Weyl, *Red Star Over Cuba,* Devon-Adair, 1961, p. 111.

[12] *New York Times,* Oct. 28, 1961.

[13] *San Francisco Examiner,* Nov. 28, 1961.

[14] *New York Times,* Sept. 11, 1961.

[15] "U.S.-Latin American Relations" Senate Doc. 125, 86th Cong., 2nd sess., Aug. 31, 1960, p. 715.

[16] *Ibid.,* p. 692.

[17] *San Francisco Chronicle,* Aug. 6, 1961.

[13] *New York Times,* Oct. 17, 1961.

[19] *New York Times,* Oct. 13, 1961.

[20] *San Francisco Chronicle,* Aug. 8, 1961.

21 "The Latin Americas," Canadian Institute on Public Affairs, University of Toronto Press, 1960, p. 5; Information Please Almanac, 1961, p. 618.

22 *Ibid,* p. 5.

23 *Capital, the Communist Manifesto and Other Writings by Karl Marx,* The Modern Library, Inc., N.Y. 1932, p. XXV.

24 *Ibid.*

25 George F. Kennan, *American Diplomacy,* University of Chicago Press, p. 109.

26 *Ibid.,* p. 108.

The Postfeudal Remnants

The differences between Latin American society today and the true feudalism of the middle ages in Europe are certainly more than trifling. There is little vassalism, bondage or serfdom as such, and knighthood clearly never flowered there. Business, industry and the trades have largely been divorced from the farm. Land is more or less freely bought and sold, rather than passed from generation to generation through restraints on alienation typical of our early common law. Every technology known to man is at work somewhere in Latin America, including head shrinking in its original style in some parts of the remote eastern slope of the Andes.

Nevertheless, the persistent usage of the term "feudalism" to describe the agrarian setting within these cultures, while somewhat inaccurate and certainly hyperbolic, characterizes a set of conditions in Latin America that work to retard development and farm and factory productivity. They also curtail the accumulation of savings, restrict the emergence of a middle class, and hold down the creation of new jobs to match the huge number of new entrants to the working force.

Paradoxically, in many respects it is the very departures from, rather than the adherences to, the agrarian feudalism of a century ago that are creating the red-hot social frictions cropping up in many countries today. In Latin America we are dealing, in a sense, with the same sort of postfeudalism with which Marx was already treating in mid-nineteenth century Western Europe, a corrupted and perverted society in

which the old disrupted social order had not yet been replaced by a satisfactory alternative. It was this unstable society
that Marx described as capitalism, and doubtless it deserved
a good measure of his derision. But it is a far cry from the
socially responsible private capitalism prevailing in the industrialized nations of the western world today.

In the Latin America of a century ago, the economic
structure was 90 per cent agrarian. In every nation, huge
land holdings were concentrated in the hands of a few elite
descendants of the conquistadores. By and large the revolutions that set Latin America free from colonial control were
not coupled with internal social upheavals at all—they merely
freed the indigenous wealthy, ruling class from foreign interference.

In this traditional society, wealth, social position, and
political control were vested in a rural-oriented landed aristocracy. This rigid agrarian system persisted in the main from
the early 19th century until World War II, although industrialization had its first widespread beginnings after World
War I, which had interrupted the accustomed flow of finished
manufacturers' products from Western Europe and the United
States to Latin America.

The great mass of the people were agrarian workers attached economically if not physically to one of the great
haciendas, i.e., the large plantations. Son followed father in
the performance of a specific task in the whole-world of the
farm economy. Cash wages were next to unknown, the accumulation of savings virtually impossible. Property for most
consisted of a hut-site allotted by grace, the clothes on the
back, a few tools and utensils, family and religious mementos.

Lacking communication and transportation, the hacienda
not only produced the food needed by the local society, but
also most of the articles needed for daily living and for conducting the farming operation. In miniature, each hacienda

was a manufacturer or producer of shoes, clothing, hats, leather, plows, flour, rope, lumber, adobe bricks and a hundred other articles. Internally, trade and commerce in these legal societies were conducted by barter. Little cash changed hands.

The mass of the people revolved in the orbit of the hacienda Church parish. Many clung to their ancient beliefs but added the Catholic faith "por las dudas sucias"—"for those dirty doubts," as the Indians of Mexico will say even today.

The Church educated the children, cared for the sick, the aged, the orphans, offered beauty, quiet, solace in the grim hour of loss or deprivation, and the promise of ultimate salvation and respite from grinding poverty. Generally the Church authorities depended on the support of the landed elite who represented the only source of wealth for the maintenance of the Church and its people. This gentry-Church relationship is the chief reason why, even today, private charitable activity in Latin America is virtually non-existent, except as it may be conducted by the Church.

While parish schools for limited lower grades were frequently available, more advanced education for any except the rural aristocracy—usually in Europe but more recently in the United States as well—was not ordinarily considered necessary or desirable. Illiteracy often hovered in the high 90's.

The first thing of importance to note in our definition of "feudalism" is that the way of life of the mass of agrarian peasantry, no matter how dreary, severe and unproductive, represented a culture in balance, "an old, physically satisfactory, primitive existence."[1] A simple life of hard labor was exchanged for cradle-to-grave security, with the pleasures of childhood and love and the solace of religion thrown in for good measure.

For the most part, the Indians of Latin America were not fierce and warlike and therefore not as liable to being killed off as were so many tribes in North America. The Spanish and Portuguese conquerors used rather than exterminated the placid and intelligent natives, building a near-slave society around them. Thus they sowed the seeds of the friction to come in a subsequent era.

Except in our own South where roughly analogous seeds of friction burst forth in bloody civil war, and social strife that still persists, there is no northern counterpart to the semi-serfdom of many regions of agrarian Latin America. In fact, except for our South, nearly everyone in pioneer United States had to be an entrepreneur just to get by.

In Latin America only the very few were thought capable of passing the test, the test of "needle's eye" capitalism, which still persists in industrializing Latin America and which is, as we shall see, one of the prime causes of the poverty and destitution prevailing there.

In contrast to this picture of the agrarian feudalism of a century ago, let us go now to a farm community of today and a city of today, to learn what changes have been wrought by the Age of Technology. First let us visit a small farm village in northern Brazil, not even typical of Brazil in many respects, but having some universal earmarks of the agrarian picture throughout Brazil, Latin America, and indeed the entire less-developed world of today.

This is cane country. The village is surrounded by a few large plantations. As contrasted with earlier times, today only a small core of workers are attached to a particular hacienda. Today, the "hacendado," or owner of the estate, in many instances no longer lives on the farm, no longer maintains personal contact with the lives and problems of the local peons. The city has become more convenient, whereas in former times the farm afforded a life of purpose and culture. Top management, one might say, is no longer on the spot to look after farm productivity and take part in community welfare.

The hacienda is no longer a factory for most things such as clothing and farm equipment. The items it needs for farming can be imported or sent from the larger industrial centers, so there is no industry in the village—only a few dispensaries of bare essentials. The inhabitants of the village are paid a wage—in cash—when they work, which is usually confined to about four months in harvest time.

The old rural culture has been destroyed. The simple, severe life of yesterday has been supplanted by an existence that is ugly and unsatisfactory. Accelerated population growth and farm mechanization have combined to create multitudes of rural unemployed and underemployed. Everyone who can has left and gone to town, to add another row of filthy cardboard huts, but the word has filtered back that there are no jobs in town and conditions are worse and such is the case.

Those who remain are for Castro. Why? Because Castroism offers the peasant villager the only way out of his dilemma of poverty: a piece of the land for himself. Translated into reality, for obviously no small plot of cane can be economically owned and operated as a unit, this means that the villagers will own the land collectively and reap its fruits in common.

Here and there, all over Latin America, the villagers have just moved in and taken over the land. They do not increase its productivity. Rather they reduce it. But the communists tell them it is theirs by original right and that Castro has made it stick in Cuba. Castro is their hero.

In Peru, Cerro de Pasco, the United States copper producing firm, owns a large amount of farm land purchased in payment of smelter gas claims. Cerro over the years stocked and improved these lands and made them more valuable and more productive, a matter of great importance in a country already importing far more basic foodstuffs than is economical or necessary. But then the communists told the Indians the land is their natural inheritance and induced them to re-enter. At first the government threw them off, but later did nothing as political pressures mounted. Cerro now tries to sell the improved land to the Indians at reduced costs, but the prospect is that it will sink back into reduced productivity again.

In Ecuador, in March 1962, the workers simply walked in and took over United Fruit's big Tenguel farm.[2] In the same month, the Indians of Peru seized four cattle ranches high in the Andes, exercising their "ancient rights."[3]

In Mexico, Jacinto Lopez, left-wing director of the Marxist-oriented General Union of Workers and Peasant Farmers, has developed a unique style of farm seizure. If the government fails to respond to his threats, his followers—known as "parachuters"—swarm out of nowhere and, within hours, hundreds have settled as squatters and erected prefabricated huts on the land.[4] A pattern emerges.

PITFALLS OF LAND REFORM

In this angry atmosphere, with a Chinese-type revolution virtually on the march, we have injected a vague and ill-defined requirement of "land reform" into our Alliance for Progress, always referring to it among those items deemed to constitute necessary "self-help" by the recipients of our aid. While there is no very clear evidence to indicate we plan to withhold aid in any case in which "land reform" is not carried out,* it is nonetheless a fact that to most Latin Americans, and to the authors of the Alliance, so far as appears, "land reform" actually means agrarian revolution à la Castro, seizure and redistribution of private farms in smaller plots to individual owners, and is commonly regarded as a step toward collective farming along the line of Red China's agrarian policy.

One Latin American authority, Federico Pinedo of Argentina ("The Agrarian Reform, Necessity or Prejudice," La Nación, May 27, 28, 29, 1961) has literally demolished the concept of land reform as applied to his country by showing

---

*For example, Chile's land reform bill—even prior to enactment—appears to have passed muster with our aid team even though it permits expropriation only of "abandoned and obviously poorly used" lands and only if substantial payment is made at the time of expropriation. (New York Times, March 6, 1962)

that small subsistence farming holds no solution for Argentina. He characterizes as "absurd" certain "advice emanating from abroad concerning what should be done to increase our wealth and improve our social structure."[5]

The phrase "land reform" is reminiscent of the thirties in the United States when some of our highest government officials went around the country alleging that too few people owned our farms and advocating that they be cut up into small parcels by withholding water allocations and other measures. Time has proven the falsity of this thesis because our farm population is now only one half what it was in 1939 but produces two to three times the 1939 crop from about the same acreage.

Yet the day of the politician is never over and the "farm problem" is a steady vote-getter if properly handled. Thus, in the latest Presidential inaugural address it was alleged with alarm that in recent years several million people "have been driven off the farms," despite the fact that this horrid process of "driving" people off the farms has been going on for two centuries in the United States, and has reduced our farm population from 90 per cent to 10 per cent of our total. Since 1939 alone our industrial, urban economy has gainfully absorbed one half of the 1939 farm population, and also the children of both halves. The farms have increased in size and, partly under the spur of subsidy, have become two to three times as productive.

Of course, the size of a farm does not limit farm ownership; millions of shareholders now own a part of America's corporate farming enterprises, just as they do of its industrial firms. At one time, our picture of mining was a bearded old man with a pick and a burro and a hole in the ground, or a fellow kneeling in a stream with a pan full of gravel in his hand, but now it is Anaconda, A S & R, Kennecott, United States Steel and Utah Construction and Mining Company.

The same is true of the farm, although in far lesser degree

since the majority of our farm production still comes from well equipped and highly capitalized family farms of 160 to 1,200 acres.

However, you have merely to glance at the New York Stock Exchange to find familiar farming and semifarming and farmer-processing firms with millions of shareholders: American Sugar (sugar), American Tobacco (tobacco), Borden and Foremost (dairy), Campbell Soup and Hunt Foods (multiple farm products), Weyerhaeuser and Crown Zellerbach (tree farming), Kern County Land (cattle, cotton and other crops), Pillsbury Mills (grains), United Fruit (bananas) and numerous others—not to mention incorporated farms whose shares are traded on other exchanges and in over-the-counter markets, and farms operated as partnerships, joint ventures and cotenancies. Then, too, the individual, unincorporated farmer has found another modern vehicle to increase productivity and efficiency, without sacrificing his property on the altar of Land Reform: the commodity cooperative engages in processing, marketing and a wide variety of activities on his behalf. Our current farm economy gives the lie to those who, only 25 years ago, would have led us to peasantry and subsistence farming.

There is a lesson in this for Latin America and for our land reform advocates. Today's farm is a business and it is high time we drained some of the emotion out of our attitude toward the soil. It must be mechanized, capitalized, incorporated, listed on the stock exchange, surrounded with modern attributes such as pension plans and stock employee programs. If we will abandon the wishing-well concept of farming held by our urban liberals who get carried away by a secret longing to have their own cow, we may be able to increase farm productivity in Latin America without courting communism.

A striking example of productive, privately capitalized farming is found in Fresno County, California, said to be the world's foremost agricultural county, with an annual production of nearly $400 million. The total value of the county's agricultural products has increased nine times in the past 20 years, and the population has only doubled. The number of farms has declined more than 10 per cent in that same period. But the number of those who have interests in farms or derive their livelihood from them, either through direct employment or indirectly, has increased enormously. Agriculture is the county's largest employer—37 per cent—while the next is manufacturing, chiefly processing of farm products.[6] The president of the Fresno Agricultural College refers to the economy of the county as "Agri-Business."

The New Frontiers in agriculture do not lie in chopping up acreage, but rather in the fields of modern farm management, applied chemistry, genetics, electronics and nuclear power. In the "factories without roofs" in the United States today the capital investment per worker is greater than it is in manufacturing.

Agricultural production per capita throughout most of the communist bloc—including East Germany, Hungary, Rumania, Czechoslovakia, North Korea and North Vietnam—has not even regained pre-World War II levels.[7]

It is a tragic fact that in Latin America today we are urging a communist rather than a capitalist solution to the farm problem. If nothing else, you would think we would be impressed by the consistent failure of communist farm phases. Red China is heading into another famine. Communist Outer Mongolia, a communist state recently given a full vote in the United Nations with our help, saw her livestock production plunge to 1929 levels following collectivization.

Professor Karl Brandt of Stanford University recently said to a gathering of the Commonwealth Club of San Francisco, "I have fought for 40 years for land reform, but I will not take the average farm from one man and give it in little chunks to peons with no knowledge of how to farm it . . . particularly where the government owns 60 per cent of the land and you

merely destroy the only land that is producing something
and prepare the way for the Soviets."[8]

The Chilean farm organization remains very indignant
over some of our government's published statistics, calculated
to show that land ownership was concentrated in the hands of
the few. The statistics, for example, counted as "one-farm,
one-ownership" an incorporated 30,000-acre sheep farm in
Tierra del Fuego that is listed on the Santiago stock exchange
and owned by thousands of small shareholders.

By and large, the farm in Latin America has been penalized
rather than subsidized or encouraged. A relatively high percentage of taxes are levied against land as compared to incomes
or chattels, and farm commodities are squeezed by export
levies—for example, coffee in Brazil, cattle and grain in Argentina and Uruguay. This has reduced the profitability and
hence the productivity of the farm and has driven the villagers
to the city at an artificially stimulated rate. In turn, the government paradoxically has subsized the industrial sector, thereby further accelerating the rural-to-urban movement to a pace
that cannot be absorbed.

"It may seem paradoxical," writes Dr. Brandt, "that in the
industrially advanced countries with excess agricultural capacity, either in the aggregate or for certain major commodities,
the farm policy typically involves heavy subsidization of farm
income and farm exports, while in the forcefully and coercive-
ly industrializing countries with their notorious shortage of
farm products the opposite is true; namely, the state subsidizes
industries at the expense of the farmers by a variety of measures which squeeze capital out of agriculture."[9]

Considering Latin America as a whole, an economy basically agrarian prior to World War I had become both industrial
and agrarian by World War II, and by 1960 the percentage of
the population placing their reliance upon farm activity was
reduced below 50 per cent.

More and more Latin American leaders are recognizing

that the introduction of modern farm techniques in mechanization, irrigation, and fertilization rather than fragmentation or
"land reform," and industrialization at the rural community
level rather than accelerated migration to the swollen urban
centers, must simultaneously become the twin targets of this
age. The one will increase farm productivity and reduce or
eliminate the costly importation of food, and the other will
diversify industry and hold back new hordes from migrating
to a few metropolitan centers already incapable of providing
jobs and ordinary community services, such as water, streets,
lights, and transportation to previous migrants.

Land reform in the sense of fragmentation is not a new concept in Latin America. It has been tried in several places and
has always failed to improve productivity. In the Arbenz revolution in Guatemala, the communists converted "land reform"
into a device for their own benefit, and Arbenz himself came
into possession of large expropriated coffee and cotton acreages.

Under Uruguay's "land reform" program, the government
has the right of first refusal to upset any private land sale,
to step in and buy it for the state with a view to splitting it up
and selling it to the landless over a period of 30-45 years and
thereby increasing farm productivity, supposedly. The government has exercised this right on numerous occasions and
now holds vast acreages, well over one half million acres. However, because of inflation and government red tape, the program is a failure and a farce. As the currency constantly de-
preciates, the nominal value of the land has risen above the
state's purchase price, but one faction, backed by the communists, prevents sale at the higher unit price, on the specious
theory that such a course would involve the state in "profiting
from the national inheritance." Equally powerful forces prevent the sale of the land at the original unit price because
that would be a windfall to the buyer and would depress the
current price of privately owned farm land. In consequence,
most of the land is leased—at rentals far below private rents—

for political considerations. Many "colonists" have sublet their land and are living on the proceeds. Not unnaturally, there are over 12,000 unfulfilled applications, and it is estimated that the Institute of Colonization would have to have a billion pesos to fill these demands for land. As it is, however, they have no funds, and all of the proceeds from rents and instalments is spent for salaries and administrative expenses of the bureaucracy (more than 200 employees) that operates the Institute.[10]

Peron confiscated large amounts of the big estates in Argentina and the result was complete control of farming and livestock raising by government decree, and a consequent decline in output. Brazil under Vargas had a "land reform" (seizure) program aimed at those who, in the opinion of some government bureaucrat, undercultivated their land. Even Trujillo had a "land reform" (redistribution) program which permitted individuals to scout out land not being cultivated, so the government could go and get it for them.[11]

None of these schemes have succeeded and all of them, of course, have had full communist endorsement. Even in Mexico the increase in food production has *not* been the result of the land allotted to the peasants under the "ejido" system. Rather it has been the bringing in of new, large, privately owned farms (often owned by syndicates of several co-owners, or incorporated with many shareholders), resulting from new irrigation works.

Under the Mexican land reform, involving a communal property arrangement known as the "ejido" system, the government takes over privately owned land by purchase or expropriation and distributes it in small units to nearby villagers, with ownership continuing only during the person's lifetime. Under the regime of President Lopez Mateos, over 9,000,000 acres have been so distributed by the government, the latest to be expropriated being some 266,760 acres of property in southern Mexico owned by private United States interests. The highest implementation of the ejido agrarian reform law took place in the period 1934-1940 under the regime of Red-sympathizing Gen. Lazaro Cárdenas. During the presidency of this "hero of the peasants" nearly 45,000,000 acres of land were placed under the ejido system. Doubtless through pure coincidence, Gen. Cárdenas is now one of the largest landowners in Mexico.

As may be expected when private land is given to persons without capital or know-how, the ejidral system has not been a success. Because of poor crop and land management, and in some cases indifference, the ejido lands yield 20 to 25 per cent less per acre than that obtained on private farms.[12]

On the other hand, the Mexican government itself owns large amounts of land in more remote areas, such as the state of Yucatan and the territory of Quintana Roo which could be colonized under policies similar to those followed by our government on our open western lands in the last century. A colonization program does exist under which the colonizer gets a fee title, but it has gained little favor due to the availability of more accessible ejidral lands. Furthermore, the government has power to expropriate land for colonization and is tempted, instead of opening new land to production, to go into the remote areas and expropriate and offer for colonization, land already fully developed by private interests. This was done in the case of the great Cananea ranch, expropriated from private United States interests in 1958.[13]

One can prophesy how Castro's "land reform" program will work out since it is so similar to those Latin America has experimented with over past years. Meanwhile, however, it has widespread appeal to the masses, based on a skillful identification of Fidelismo with simple human aspirations for land and enough to eat. The communists know that without technical knowledge, roads, fertilizer, capital, financing, and a host of other things, breaking up farms could leave the peasants worse off than they were as wage-workers or share-croppers.

But Red cynicism shines forth in the remarks of Cuba's "Che" Guevera on this subject. "The way to make agrarian reform," he says, "is to take land from the man who has a lot and give it to the man who has none. Talk about it being more complicated is a siren song."[14]

Most low farm productivity in Latin America—and it is often very low indeed—can be laid at the door of government. Owners' fears of seisure stifle new capital expenditure needed to modernize and expand, and heavy taxes on exports of farm commodities reduce incentives to grow for this purpose.

Corrective measures in these areas would, of course, greatly improve farm production, and release foreign exchange for the importation of heavy plant and equipment needed to expand the industrial base. Such measures would also pour additional farm workers into the industrial scene, making necessary the adoption of some such plan for the inflow of foreign private capital as that presented in subsequent chapters.

Those who appreciate that you are not "gonna keep 'em down on the farm" by splitting up private holdings into non-economic units, or communizing them, are on the right track in seeking, wherever possible, a *local* solution to unemployment rather than in encouraging more people to migrate to the hub of the wheel.

A number of Latin American countries are intensifying their study of this problem. For example, in Colombia the Technological Institute, a private scientific organization financed by private industry, the Colombian government and a grant from the U.N. Technical Fund, is trying to induce more capital to flow into these backward areas by searching out illustrations of new products and processes that might be developed with local materials and skills. But the difficulties of generating effective action at the local community level in Latin America cannot be overestimated. Due to the colonial system which brooked no local power, Latin Americans in early days acquired little experience in local self-government.

Ordinarily, even now, they lack local taxing power for schools and other community services. Hence everything must wait upon action by a remote central government, motivated by political considerations equally remote from and unfamiliar with local needs and conditions. There is a somber lesson in Latin America's plight for those in *our* society who advocate more and more assumption by our federal government of rights and responsibilities once held and exercised by our own local authorities. No better way can be found to atrophy local talent.

One thing Latin American governments can do to alleviate the over-rapid urbanization of their populations is to open up remote government-owned lands by building access roads and financing other basic facilities and making land grants to settlers on nominal first-come-first-served terms. Programs of this character have recently been adopted in Peru and Brazil, and the opportunities for constructive action along this line are present in nearly every Latin American nation. Our own Export-Import Bank recently made a $20 million loan to Peru for part of the cost of an access road into the lush valleys of the eastern Peruvian Andes.

If land reform in its accepted meaning is no solution to Latin America's predominance of large agricultural estates, and if revised government policies toward the farm are long overdue, still it remains imperative that the landowners themselves contribute to the alleviation of the grim conditions prevailing in the farm community. Housing, schooling, hospital facilities, water, sewage disposal and other fundamental services at the community level cannot await the attention of the remote central government, already preoccupied with huge urban needs. It is not enough to say that community service ended when the comprehensive role of the rural hacienda came to a close and industrialization began. The farm enterprise as well as the factory needs to prove the social conscience of capitalism and private enterprise.

But whether it will do so remains a moot question.

We listened as a speaker, in earnest friendliness, asked a Chilean "hacendado," owner of a large irrigated farm near Santiago, "Aren't you afraid the inquilinos* will march up the hill to the great house and put a knife in you, unless measures are taken to improve their lot?"

"Thirty days before that happens, my family and I will take what we can and fly to Europe," was the reply.

This of course is not a typical response and many rural leaders are now taking an interest in health and housing and education, trying to find ways to move into the vacuum left by the absence of local authority and the remoteness of national government. Unless such steps are multiplied a thousand times all over rural Latin America, the inquilinos, agitated and pushed by the Red propagandists, will indeed march up the hill to the great house. In view of the Castro success and our own advocacy of land "reform," some violent land seizures by the peasants and some crash government programs to like effect appear almost inevitable. This does not mean it is too late for us or Latin America to get behind more rational approaches to the problem, however.

A major answer to Latin America's agrarian problem lies in the development of food and farm product processing and manufacturing, coupled with diversification of farm output itself. In the past, Latin American nations have been over-dependent on a few commodities or even a single commodity, such as coffee, oil, grain, meat, or metals. They have peddled their large export surpluses abroad, hoping to acquire enough foreign exchange to allow the importation of needed food-stuffs and finished products. Frequently their foreign markets have been inadequate for this purpose, sometimes because of third-country competition, price declines, and their own punitive tax policies toward their major exports. In recent dec-

---

*"Inquilinos" is a term used to describe tenant farmers in Chile.

ades, the concentration of Latin American exports into a few commodities has been tightening, and prices declining, while the cost of imported foods and other finished products has increased. As pointed out more fully in subsequent pages, the answer to this squeeze cannot be found in international price fixing, but rather in diversification and local processing.

The contribution of United States capital to this solution is beginning to become significant. Almost every major American producer of food products has joined the parade to Latin America. Corn Products Company is putting new facilities in Brazil, Chile, and Venezuela as part of a $15 million overseas expansion in 1961, and is introducing its mayonnaise and peanut butter to Mexico, using local ingredients. General Foods Corporation of New York is making its "Tang" soft drink in Venezuela, calling it "Manani." Foremost Dairies Corporation of San Francisco is making powdered milk in Latin America. Standard Brands Corporation, in a joint Brazilian venture with General Mills Company, has started to manufacture powdered whole milk. Kellogg Company, the big breakfast cereal producer, has installations at 21 locations in 17 countries, the most recent being Brazil and Venezuela. General Mills has recently expanded the output of its flour milling plants in Guatemala and Venezuela. In 1960 California Packing Corporation established a chili products plant in Mexico, and a fruit nectar packing unit in Venezuela.[15]

While most Latin American countries encourage these operations, since they create jobs and stimulate the growth of new farm products, we will see that because of the political risks faced by our firms in Latin America, and the inadequate policies of our government, the private capital flow to Latin America, while substantial, is a mere trickle as compared to present needs, and particularly to what it could be if the Cold War risks could be erased.

*   *   *   *   *

Let us go now from this impoverished Brazilian village to a sobering view of poverty in the industrial center. Here the destruction of the "satisfactory culture" of the 19th century rural community is often absolute. Bereft of the last vestiges of the paternalism of the soil, such as semifarming, chicken raising, intrafamily dependence, the new entrant to the urban work force is just another unskilled person in a sea of surplus unskilled workers. He has come to town because the farm has nought to offer, because the lure of the bright lights is like a magic rainbow luring him and his family to an urban pot of gold.

When he gets there, only industry can feed him and his family of eight children—by giving him a job. In the long pull, Food for Peace and the Care Package may only create more like him because items given away by one country to citizens of another can only postpone the day when the latter might have jobs producing the same products locally. But too often industry cannot use the newcomer driven by poverty to come in from the village. Typically, he cannot read or write. If he knows a simple trade, it has been rendered obsolete by time and technology. So he becomes a jackal. He preys upon the town and its garbage dump. He markets the wares of his family—from beggary to prostitution. Some of his kind never do get a job, but in either case they are easy bait for the ever-present communist because they hate the status quo with a dark and angry passion.

Yet the penchant for climbing the ladder under capitalism is there, even among Peru's 10 million Indians. The man who has proven that these people want to be capitalists is a hand-picked Maryknoll monk, a Denver boy named Dan McLellan.

Whereas Peruvian bankers have not made loans to Indians and they, in turn, have had an aboriginal distrust of banks, they have literally poured their dusty, mudcaked bills into Father McLellan's credit unions, whence it is loaned to Indians for everything from sewing machines to community water systems and, now, housing. In five years the loss ratio has been less than 1/10th of 1 per cent of loan volume.* The communists in Peru are so concerned they tried to engineer a run on one of Father's banks last year, but he had been forewarned and was able to rush the resources of other unions to pay off all the depositors and thus restore confidence in the credit unions.

The big-city pool offers a lot of fishing, it is true, and the Indians of Peru are bright and resourceful. A Peruvian businessman told me of loaning Peruvian "soles," the currency of Peru, to an Indian, which he used to buy a TV set on instalments. "The man now has a flourishing movie business at one 'sole' per viewer," he said, "powering his set with improvised generating equipment that displays true electronic genius."

Some will allege that the uneducated and illiterate of Latin America are unprepared for the Age of Technology. Of course, when it comes to advanced technical and managerial skills, this is true. As for lesser talents, however, the Otavalos of Ecuador are masters of every art except missilry and the Jivaros can shrink heads, clearly a more exacting discipline than the laying of brick or the fitting of pipe.

Edmund Littlefield, president of Utah Construction Company, will tell you that the Peruvian Indian quickly learns, and carefully performs, the work of maintaining the complicated equipment used in his company's Peruvian iron ore operations.

At the great Toquepala copper mine of American Smelting & Refining Corporation, a village of modern homes in the sky has been created by the company, and 4,000 Indians have been taught advanced mechanical skills.

Why, then, have these urbanizing, industrializing nations been unable to create new jobs fast enough to absorb these

---

*One thing inflation insures is the maintenance of a good credit rating. In societies where inflation is 20, 40, 60 or 100 per cent per year and wage raises lag behind, the man who has to pay cash is a dead duck.

people? The causes are complex, but a lot of the blame must be charged to the remnants of a perverted pseudo-feudalism. The engrafting of the concepts of "needle's eye" capitalism upon the industrial economy seriously retards the generation of new, internal, long-term, job-producing capital development in most, if not all, Latin American nations.

A relative handful of able and well-to-do entrepreneurs, usually revolving around the axis of leading banks, hire a large proportion of the available savings at rates of interest that we would consider fantastically high, but which are merely discounting the risk of currency depreciation in a highly inflationary society. Interest rates of 8 per cent and higher on ordinary savings accounts are the rule. These funds are invested in enterprises within the orbit of this limited entrepreneurial group, or loaned on a short-range basis to finance imports, working capital, inventory and the like. Since the rates of interest on these loans run anywhere from 15 per cent to 30 per cent per year, an extremely high return of profit has to be foreseen before new long-term equity investments will be undertaken by the owners and managers of money.

Savings not loaned to the banks and financiers tend to go into tangible personal property and especially into land, and thereby the attempt to protect against inflation creates more inflation.

In Mexico since 1932, the "financieras," or finance companies, have been the chief source of new money for the creation or expansion of private enterprises. Yet today 58 per cent of their outstanding funds are loaned for less than one year at a time, and most of the rest for less than two years. The real annual cost of "financiera" money is approximately 14 per cent a year, estimates Sr. Luis Latapi, investment banker of Mexico. "This means," he adds, "that a new firm financed with such funds has to figure on being worth up to 50 per cent more after just three years of life, and then has to be able to pay a 20 per cent dividend, before it can attract long-term investors into its common stock."[16]

Thus do the various attributes of "needle's eye" capitalism, taken together, keep to a trickle the new job-creating capital formations. They foster inflation and channel money into land and other non-productive investments. The amount of idle capital in Latin America, in the sense of not contributing to economic growth and development, is undoubtedly very great, probably the largest source of new internal capital we shall be able to unearth.

But the failure to use internal capital in a job-creating way is not the whole story. A Mexican economist has estimated that Latin Americans, chiefly the wealthy landowners and industrialists, have between $6 and $8 billion (U.S.) invested in the United States and Europe—sent there to avoid inflation and to protect against confiscation.* The head of the Central Bank of Venezuela told me wealthy Venezuelans alone have an estimated $400 million "resting" in United States bank accounts alone, not including investments in stocks or any funds in Europe or elsewhere.

As things are now, the few can and do ride hard upon the flank of inflation, whereas the ordinary consumer and worker on salary and wage suffer from a built-in lag which stifles their capacity to save, consume, and invest. The long-term lender, the institutional financier as we think of such in the United States, hardly exists in Latin America and cannot exist until the "needle's eye" is broken and there is a freer flow of capital internally and a checking of inflation.

The inflation can be cured, by known measures—chiefly by holding down new money in circulation—but the cure is accomplished by severe withdrawal symptoms, especially vis-a-vis the lower income groups, because prices continue to rise,

*This is four years of Alliance for Progress at $2 billion per year.

due to inflationary momentum while money supply stands still. Bidding up and hoarding of commodities enters the picture.

In Argentina last year the cost of living was six times what it was in 1953; in Bolivia 33 times; in Chile 12 times; in Brazil more than four times. Living costs have risen by about 50 per cent in the last three years in Chile, despite a determined government stabilization program.[17] Living costs in Brazil in 1961 went up 42 per cent, and money in circulation was increased 54 per cent in that year.[18]

In countries like Peru and especially Venezuela, where recent inflation has not been so rampant, the cost of living and other factors have already priced all but a handful of the people out of the consumer market.

The problem of inflation is the responsibility of the Latin American governments, and they are coming to recognize it. Inflation's debilitating effects are numerous, but emphasized here is its capacity to destroy the red corpuscles of a capitalistic society—the incentive to make long-term risk investments in new plant.

Then, too, the mass of people who do get jobs do not thereby enter some kind of a modern paradise. An executive of Sears Roebuck in Latin America estimates that less than 10 per cent of the people in areas served by Sears stores are inside the "money economy" in the sense of being able to buy at Sears stores.

Subsistence pay and inflation combine to limit savers to the very few. Even strong depreciation accounts are eaten into inadequacy by inflation. Company training programs are limited, despite the spirited bidding for anyone who is trained. Competition is suspect and considered destructive. Hence cartelism is prevalent. Leading industrialists in nearly all Latin American countries commonly advocate that competition be held down by government action, such as tariff barriers against competing imports.

"We do not believe in your antitrust laws," said one prominent Chilean industrialist. "We prefer to see just one firm in a given business and if it gets out of line on prices or anything, the government can step in and allow some cheaper imports to teach the firm a lesson."

This "industrial feudalism," this protection of a social and economic status quo in Latin America chokes off money, men and markets and works against the jobless and—by the stagnation it creates—for the communists. It also drives the more moderate politician into socialism, neutrality or professional indifference toward the Reds—attitudes that are the forerunners of communism.

Our business community, too, as subsequent chapters will unfold, contributes to this "needle's eye" philosophy by going into these environments through the 100 per cent subsidiary route, by secrecy of profits and, in general, by failing to carry to Latin America a modern personalized message for modern private enterprise. By this mode of commercial penetration we have handed the communists one of their most effective weapons in the Cold War against our kind of capitalism in these unsettled regions.

CHAPTER II

REFERENCES

1 Oscar Lewis, *Five Families,* Basic Books, Inc., New York, 1959, p. x.

2 *San Francisco Examiner,* Mar. 31, 1962.

3 *New York Times,* Mar. 4, 1962.

4 *New York Times,* Mar. 30, 1962.

5 Federico Pinedo, "The Agrarian Reform, Necessity or Prejudice," *La Nación,* Buenos Aires, May 27, 28, 29, 1961.

6 "The Growth and Economic Stature of Fresno County, Etc.," Security First National Bank, 1961.

7 Igor Igonesoff, "Red Farm Woes," *Wall Street Journal,* Oct. 25, 1961.

8 Dr. Karl Brandt, address at the Commonwealth Club, San Francisco, December 1961.

9 Dr. Karl Brandt, "Agricultural Productivity, Economic Growth, and the Farm Policy Motivation of Urban Electorates," Food Research Institute Studies, Stanford University, May 1961, p. 83.

10 "National Institute of Colonization," U.S. Embassy, Desp. No. 356, of Montevideo, 1960.

11 Edward Tomlinson, *Look Southward, Uncle,* Devin-Adair, New York, 1959, pp. 39-44.

12 *New York Times,* July 26, 1961.

13 *Ibid.*

14 *Wall Street Journal,* Aug. 11, 1961.

15 *Ibid,* Aug. 10, 1961.

16 Seminar, International Industrial Conference, San Francisco, September 1961.

17 *New York Times,* July 30, 1961.

18 *Wall Street Journal,* Apr. 3, 1962.

CHAPTER THREE

Socialism Superimposed

It would be nice and neat if one could simply ascribe Latin America's ills to an archaic system described as feudalism and close up with a few curative cliches such as "land reform" and "social progress."

Unfortunately there is another menace, to be called socialism herein, that works just as hard to prevent development in Latin America as does our feudalist and, at the present time, may have the upper hand in helping the communists.

We have already seen some of the dangers inherent in the socialists' desire for "land reform" à la Castro, and will later touch upon his unquenchable thirst for total master-planning of development. All of these appetites are far more compatible with Sino-Soviet tendencies than with our own.

The case against Latin America's indiscriminate state ownership of private-type facilities and the case against her productivity-hampering social security and labor laws also need to be documented.

It is a fact that state ownership of producing and service facilities, and state intervention in some areas of the private sector, have always been a characteristic of Latin American society. When Guanajuato's mines produced 85 per cent of the world's silver, every ounce belonged to the Queen of Spain. Even today, oil and minerals under Spanish practice do not pass with the grant of land. Instead, they remain in the state as a temptation for governmental proprietorship. Exports and imports and, somewhat more recently, rents have been typical subjects for licensing and regulation in Latin America.

Hence the question arises: Why are we concerned about socialism in Latin America and what makes us think it is any of our business? The answer is that it is our business—not, to be sure, just to be shooting down someone else's way of life— but because we are deeply and adversely affected by the establishment or perpetuation in Latin America of any economic system that is a stepping-stone to communism. Also, we certainly should have more than a passing national interest in the use of our foreign aid to finance the seizure of American private property by Latin American governments.

"We no longer distinguish between socialism and communism in Chile," a prominent Chilean told me recently. "Socialism," he added, "has turned out to be more of a cloak for communism than a shield against it."

In this, as well as in the Marxist belief that nationalization is a first requirement for communism's success, there is a clear message for those who would sponsor or accept socialism in the less developed countries as an agreeable alternative to capitalism.

"On the surface," a Voice of America official said to me in Brazil, "their lines are the same—business and industry are exploiting the people."

Latin America is probably the most fecund area in the world when it comes to giving birth to state-owner enterprises, just as she clearly is number one in human population growth in all the world. Every known method of state acquisition is thoroughly tried and tested. This includes such amateurish methods as plain expropriation without just compensation, as in the case of oil in Mexico in the thirties, tin in Bolivia in 1952, and the recent total takeover in Cuba.

It also embraces, however, the "squeeze-out" technique, usually employed against privately owned utilities whose rates are frozen by the very same politicians who cause the inflation that makes necessary the increase in rates they will not grant.

When the property loses consistently enough to become virtually worthless, in the sense that no private capital would buy it without fresh rate increases being guaranteed, the government opens "negotiations" for its "sale" to the government. Later, after the purchase, the government often finds out that it cannot raise its own rates because of political objections and public clamor and is, so to speak, hoist on its own petard. But then, of course, one can always fall back on the general tax revenues. On one 70 kilometre stretch of electric railway in Argentina, the passenger fare is equivalent to 3¢ in United States currency.

Many of the fine utilities—railroads especially—built by the British fit this category. No finer systems existed in the world than some of these, completed at and before the turn of the century, but now national governments own every single major common carrier railroad system in Latin America. In Argentina, the government's annual railway deficit is over $250 million, more than one half of that country's total budgetary deficit. Due to massive feather-bedding and the maintenance of uneconomic routes, nearly three-quarters of all rail operating expenses are in the form of government wages and salaries.[1]

This "squeeze-out" technique culminated in 1960 in the nationalization of two Mexican privately owned power and light companies.

As recently as February 1962, bitterly anti-United States, left-wing Governor Brizola of Rio Grande do Sul in Brazil, confiscated the properties of Companhía Telefónica Nacional, a local telephone company owned by the American firm, International Telephone and Telegraph Corporation of New York.

The Governor offered to "pay" only approximately 5 per cent of the value of the seized properties, even that amount in rapidly deflating Brazilian currency instead of U.S. dollars. The mild protest issued by the United States Department of State may well be taken in Latin America as expressing a policy of tolerance for the seizure of American properties.

Brizola's expropriation order was viewed as another move in his campaign to build his reputation as a Nationalist leader. Since taking office he has confiscated an American & Foreign Power Company subsidiary and a Swift & Company packing plant in his state, and last year he took over several big Brazilian-owned ranches "to give to the poor."

Hard on the heels of this seizure, President Goulart of Brazil, who happens to be Governor Brizola's brother-in-law, came to Washington on a state visit to President Kennedy. President Goulart succeeded in "thawing" any reservations our government might have harbored on the subject of nearly three-fourths of $1 billion in new aid to Brazil. Even more remarkable, he succeeded in getting President Kennedy, in a joint communique of April 4, 1962, to express "great interest" in a Goulart plan to "transfer" all American-owned public utility enterprises into Brazilian government ownership and to force the American owners to reinvest the purchase price in other "sectors important to Brazilian economic development."[1a]

This Goulart visit may turn out to be one of the boldest diplomatic coups d'etat in history particularly in view of the fact that Brazil is suffering from persistent budgetary deficits; therefore any compensation paid by Brazil to the owners of confiscated American private enterprises there would inescapably be traceable to our foreign aid.

In the wake of this Brazilian episode, several members of the Congress introduced or supported legislation to authorize the President to withhold aid from aid-recipient nations engaging in such practices. As this work goes to print, the fate and efficacy of such legislation remain uncertain.*

Then there is the "retroactive tax" methodology. A re-

---

* See Congressional Record, June 5, 1962, p. 8957; June 7, 1962, pp. 9204-9207.

cent illustration of this is afforded by an American-owned oil concern in one South American nation. The technique involved an assertion that the company's titles are no good. The decree or law granting the oil concession has turned out to be "imperfect," but this can be "cured" by the payment of large amounts of back taxes.

Some nations have resorted to the "import license checkmate," a subtle form of competition-killer. Most Latin American nations control imports on a decree basis, commodity by commodity and often case by case. Through this and other pressures, Mexico is now engaged in "Mexicanizing" mining firms owned by United States and other foreign citizens. This can be avoided by selling 51 per cent to Mexican citizens, but the implied threat is "sell or be expropriated." Now, when a vital import license is denied to an existing United States non-mining firm, the owner suspects that the principle of the new mining law is going to be applied to him by executive fiat.

Nowadays, most state ownership results from what we shall call expropriation "going in." Two illustrations occurred last year: the Venezuelan government's deal to acquire one half of the stock of the new local aluminum plant, and Mexico's governmental decision to own and operate a truck plant.

The last mentioned transaction qualifies under a subhead to be known as "Going Into Business With United States Aid" since the plant is being financed by a loan of funds borrowed from the United States Treasury via the Export-Import Bank of Washington. This type of government-to-government aid* has been going on for a long time on the theory that (a) it helps our exports by financing the original equipment and replacement parts and, sometimes, continuing units, and (b) if we don't do it somebody else will.

In Brazil our Export-Import Bank has financed state-owned iron ore development in the amount of about $250 million. The latest bite, $17 million, was contemporaneous with Brazil's refusal—still in effect as this book goes to print—to permit

---

* Export-Import rates are frequently one-third or less of local charges, hence to be classed as a form of foreign aid.

a private firm in which United States citizens have a substantial interest, Companhía de Mineracao Novalimense, to
ship anything more than token shipments of ore from its
fabulous deposits there. Political opposition from the communists and the left-wing fringe is thus buttressed by United
States government loans.

Our Export-Import Bank has loaned over $100 million to
finance the largest state-owned steel mill in Latin America,
the Volta Redonda plant situated between Sao Paulo and Rio.
The steel plants in Peru and, until recently, in Chile are also
state-owned and were financed by United States government
loans. The Venezuelan government owns a majority of the
stock in the new steel mill there. The Mexican government
financed and has a large share of control over the big steel mill
at Monterrey, Compañía Fundadora de Fierro y Acero de
Monterrey, S.A., and the Altos Hornos mill as well. Our
Export-Import Bank has been involved in the financing of
both mills all along the line, and has now put $26 million
more into a recent expansion at Monterrey.

A very large proportion of the steel industry in Latin
America has been nationalized, with the indispensable aid of
the United States government.

The chief tragedy is the degree of power over private industry this gives to government officials, usually unskilled in
business and frequently basing their personal decisions on
patronage factors.

It is a tragic by-product that most of these mills were at
time of installation, and some still remain, uneconomic on
any basis of calculation and they have simply swallowed government funds that could have gone into schools or hospitals.
A high government banking official of Venezuela estimated,
for me, the annual loss from state-owned enterprises at $125
million dollars (U.S.). When governments of the poorer
nations put money into this kind of business instead of non-

earning basic requirements such as roads and port facilities, it is no wonder that the international breadline grows.

The Colombian mill tells a graphic story of economic waste. After several years of losing operations, Colombia is forcing the taxpayers to buy the common stock of their government-owned steel enterprise by imposing a 4 per cent special income tax which can be used by the taxpayers to buy steel stock at about 10 pesos per share. The fact that the stock is selling on the local stock exchange in Bogotá for less than 2 pesos per share is a pretty good clue to the economics of the mill. The citizens are being forced to pay five times the true worth of the stock in order to bail out the government's original investment. However, even that does not tell the whole story because the 10 peso price takes no account of state-incurred costs in the way of previous operating losses, nor of inflation since the date of construction.

The spectacle of a government forcing the citizenry to buy a patently "watered" stock out of the proceeds of their own income tax payments is novel in the annals of government ingenuity. Nevertheless, the Colombian move must be classed as a constructive one, since income tax payments are not ordinarily productive of any traceable quid pro quo from government. Also, the tax will ultimately return the activity to potentially productive private hands, at a value reduced to real worth. Through this special tax, approximately 65 per cent of the ownership has already been placed in private hands. The realistic citizen shareholder will now, in effect, paper his wall with four-fifths of the shares acquired with his tax payments, and go about trying to make a profit on the other one-fifth.

Our government Export-Import Bank also, of course, makes loans to private enterprise in various countries of Latin America, and its requirement that every loan have the guarantee of the host government has tended to deliver the private borrower into the hands of the government officials. This has given Latin American governments a ready mode of entry into the business of economic planning through intervention, regulation and total veto.

Private international bankers have, from time to time, also expressed the view that the Export-Import Bank and the International Finance Corporation, the multinational affiliate of the World Bank with power to loan to private firms, compete unfairly with private banking and thereby retard the availability of private funds for development purposes. In an address to the American Management Association in 1960, Victor E. Rockhill, president of Chase International Investment Corporation, charged that Export-Import and International Finance Corporation "compete with private capital unfairly in contravention of their charter powers" and, in consequence, private developmental capital firms "may become discouraged by the slow pace of growth caused in part by this competition."[2]

It has always been difficult for a private firm to compete with one that does not have to make a profit or pay dividends, pays no taxes and is backed by the Treasury. No amount of experience seems to teach us to confine government lending to situations like roads and dams and other non-revenue producing or special cases. After the war and before the U.S. government's Reconstruction Finance Corporation was dismantled, a borrower quite commonly had a choice between taking either a private or a government loan on roughly equivalent terms despite the fact that RFC was prohibited by law from competing with private lenders. The same, it is feared, will be true of the new Inter-American Development Bank set up by the Organization of American States to make development loans to governments and industries in Latin America since human nature is much the same abroad as at home. While it would take an audit to prove it, the suspicion lurks that some of the very first loans by the Inter-American Development Bank were made to private firms with plenty of credit in the private market. Also, one is not reassured by the description of socialism, by the chairman of the Bank's 1961 meeting in Rio de Janeiro, as a doctrine "to which we are by no means hostile."[3]

There is much contrary opinion in Latin America, a fact which reinforces the critical importance of the choice we make in our policies toward our southern neighbors. As stated last year by Dr. Pedro G. Beltran, Prime Minister and Minister of Finance of Peru, "I must say that it seems to me frankly foolish for governments to use up their always insufficient resources in trying to take the place of private enterprise in economic activities which private individuals can carry out for the benefit of themselves and the community."[4]

In fairness, too, it must be said that the Export-Import Bank has been under heavy domestic pressures to make their loans; for example, a real need to create the United States exports such loans have generated, the urgent pleas of the export community and, oftentimes, of their representatives in Congress, the threat that foreign suppliers would otherwise "get the business." And, of course, the Bank's policies have ordinarily been made or approved at the highest executive branch levels. Also, private industry, including the investment banking industry, has not come forward with resourceful solutions to these domestic pressures, nor found a modern capitalistic solution for many real and justifiable capital needs in Latin America. The effect is to hasten the march to Marx in Latin America.

The attitude of helplessness on the part of business is exemplified by a recent incident in Tito's Yugoslavia where the U.S. Government is lending the funds for the creation of a $23 million state-owned chemical complex to be furnished by U.S. suppliers and builders. The manager of one of the U.S. firms employed to design the plant says: "I approve of American industries and labor making a living, but I can't say I approve of all the aid going to Yugoslavia. However, I assume the people in Washington who set the policies know what they are doing."⁵

In nearly every nation of Latin America the government sits on a huge heap of state operated industries, some acquired by expropriation, some financed by government in the first instance, and some indeed financed by the United States government.

The ardor of the hardiest capitalist is daunted when, in administration after administration, new industries are added to the list of those in state proprietorship. Free of many ordinary restraints with regard to pricing policies, free of the usual penalties for inefficiency, frequently manned on the basis of patronage rather than merit, these governmental industries hover over the capitalistic horizon like a huge cloud. They work for communism because state ownership of industries is the first plank in the communist platform.

Our Left unfailingly rises to the defense of any and all degree of state ownership, usually pointing to Uruguay in Latin America as a living example of a socialistic paradise and often referring to Germany under Hitler or Argentina under Peron as dictatorships of the right.

But the orthodoxy inspired by our so-called liberals—that tyranny always comes from the right side—is plainly fallacious. The chief problem in Germany was too much government intervention in the private sector, not too little. It was under socialism that Hitler, with his National Socialist party, took control of every aspect of German economic and social life. In this sense Hitler was a dictator of the far left. The trouble with our so-called liberals is that they will applaud any given degree of state management of society so long as the *forms* of democracy are observed. As soon as these forms are swallowed up, as they often are, they uniformly describe the affair as a rightist movement. Peron, always described as a dictator of the right, nevertheless had and still has the support of the communist dominated labor unions in Argentina. The communists cheered as he took over plants and farms by the dozens like a true blue socialist. In due course he suppressed the press and the students and perverted the electoral process, and that makes him a rightist.

The point is that excessive intervention by government, whether right or left, whether by a single tyrant or a committee of benign college professors, always destroys man's freedom and always, in the end, winds up in an attempt to exercise absolute power.

Probably the most dangerous of all dictators in our time is the unconscious hypocrite of the far left who can sell to himself and the public a package of super-ideals to be achieved by more government intervention with such charm as to make the abrogation of the forms of civil liberty unnecessary. Prior to 1952 we had had at least two of these in this century.

A few illustrations of the state of socialism in Uruguay will suffice to reduce it to something short of Utopia.

Uruguay is a unique little* country in many respects. She has remained far more pastoral than the other Latin American countries, chiefly because she alone of all Latin American nations has a low rate of population growth.

Her landed aristocracy drift along in 19th century placidity, paying no income taxes and sending their sons to law school for the prestige of it.

Most of her taxes are levied on exports because, as one government official says, "they are painless, easy to collect and not opposed by the wealthy and influential."

The country is governed by a board of directors chiefly made up from elements of the two major parties, the Reds and the Whites. The Reds dominated the situation from the latter part of the last century until 1958 when the Whites, of a somewhat more conservative bent, gained control. The socialist fabric was solidified before the communists came along,

---

*Size of Missouri, however.

and so it was impossible for the communists to ride in on it—
a tactic they are using successfully elsewhere in Latin America.

Swift & Company went into Uruguay in the early days and
was taken over. However, a series of strikes, backed by government forced the company to give the plants to the employees
because it could not pay the huge amounts of severance pay
that would have been required by law if it closed down the
plants. Ironically, the government then established a government meat monopoly in Montevideo, Uruguay's largest and
most concentrated market, to protect its own meat business
against the employee-owned meat plants located outside of
Montevideo. This did not work either. The people went outside the town to buy their meat because it was cheaper and
better and now most of the places formerly owned by the
government are closed and the government has reopened the
city to private entrepreneurs.

The following picture of Uruguay in 1958, painted in
Tomlinson's *Look Southward, Uncle,* portrays the depths to
which government ownership and intervention have carried
her:

> In its attempts to set up a welfare state, Uruguay economi-
> cally has become one of the sickest of all the southern republics.
> The prospects for an early recovery are not very promising.
> The railroads and the electrical industry in Uruguay are
> run by the government, as are the domestic airlines, several
> of the big hotels, all the gambling casinos, and some of the big
> night clubs. It operates the seaports, the principal oil refinery,
> and the fishing industry. The government meat packing plant
> has a monopoly on *the sale of fresh meats* for Montevideo.
> These and many other enterprises are set up as autonomous
> corporations, with their own boards of directors and general
> managers. But all the officials are political appointees *who
> change with every administration,* which means every four
> years. Few are specialists in the businesses they operate. Most
> are politicians first. The law requires that three of the five
> directors of the oil refinery, the railroads or the electric

company be chosen from the majority political party and two from the opposition.

The railroads were nationalized, or bought from the British, back in the thirties. The experienced technicians and managers resigned, of course, and were replaced by political appointees. Today's roadbeds are seriously depleted. Schedules are no longer regular, and the annual deficit is almost as large as the income. By 1957, they had accumulated a deficit of 300,000,000 pesos.

The oil refinery has had to give up its retail business and let private companies supply gasoline and motor oil. Although it charged exorbitant prices for its products, it still managed to lose money. Practically all the government corporations have to be sustained by large subsidies.

The government is the largest employer in the country, and once a man is on the government payroll, he no longer has much incentive to produce or to give efficient service. And the labor laws are such that practically nobody is ever fired.[6]

Fortunately, the more conservative Blanco party regained power from the Colorado party in 1958 and new policies are beginning to pull Uruguay out of stagnation. Most foreign trade has been freed from government restriction and a new personal and corporate income tax has been adopted.

To attract new private enterprise, firms which manufacture products not previously made there in appreciable quantity are exempt from tax for 10 years. In 1961 Uruguay ratified the Treaty for a Latin American Free Trade Area composed of Argentina, Brazil, Chile, Mexico, Paraguay, Peru and Uruguay, a development that may offer the greatest benefit to Uruguay, on account of the present small size of her internal market.

These measures and firmer attempts at internal budget stability have assisted in attracting important new enterprise to Uruguay. In 1960 alone, Corn Products of New York completed a new industrial starch plant, Philips of Holland expanded its light bulb plant, a group of Uruguayan and foreign business concerns formed a corporation to develop Uruguay's substantial iron ore reserves, partly for local use and partly for export to Argentina. Aluminia del Uruguay S. A., 70 per cent owned by Aluminum, Ltd. of Canada, embarked on an expansion program to double its present capacity of sheet, foil, and extrusions. IBM of South America moved its headquarters to Montevideo in 1960.

Private job-creating developments such as these will be the ultimate solution to Uruguay's chief problem, its rural slums, recently described by Blanco party leader Luis Alberto Herrera as "a public calamity, a den of malignancy and thievery, the center of diseases of all kinds, without hygiene, without schools."[7] Yet the road out will be long since one in every three citizens of Montevideo has a government job and three fourths or more of the national budget goes for salaries of government employees. The cost of living has risen 20-30 per cent per year in each of the past three years.

Fortunately, a number of modern political leaders in Latin America are keenly aware that the state ownership habit seriously retards new internal private capital formulations, drives domestic savings into foreign investments, and discourages United States and other needed external private capital from coming in to create development, growth and— the ultimate need—more jobs for people.

For example, President Frondizi of Argentina was, until his ouster, moving strongly in the direction of unloading the state enterprises acquired during past regimes—companies seized or purchased from British owners long ago, industries taken from the Germans in World War II, properties nationalized during the regime of Peron.

Argentina can only be classified as an "underdeveloped" country because of the regression that has marked her recent decades. Early in this century she was a model of progress for the time, illustrated by such things as an efficiently nationwide rail network, a rapid urban subway system, a highly developed stock exchange and a sparkling cultural life.

Until the recent political upheaval, Argentina appeared to be emerging from her long intervening sleep of decline, most recently evidenced by the regime of Peron and the enervating financial policies which, to cite only one consequence, have multiplied her cost of living eight times since 1951.

Government budget deficits were being reduced to more manageable proportions, and the cost of living stood still in January 1961 for the first time in a decade.

Argentina is somewhat unique in that, whereas most Latin American governments are muscling more and more into the private business sector, the Frondizi government was actually trying to get rid of the array of private firms acquired or developed over the years.

"The trouble is that these firms have been run at a loss by the government, and they are not easy to sell," says Jose Mazzaferri, tall, dynamic executive vice president of Dinie, the government holding company. "Whenever we can sell a part to private interests," he adds, "we put them in charge, hoping that when they get the business back on its feet we can make a public sale of the rest of the stock."

New foreign investments were being offered attractive incentives, generally consisting of income tax freedom for a period of years, and immunity from import tax levies on the importation of the original plant and equipment.

As a result of these policies, the amount of new United States and other private foreign investment in Argentina had been shooting upward: $316 million in approved projects (exclusive of oil) from September 1958 to the end of 1960, compared to only $20 million in 1957 under Peron. And much more is projected. This is big money, dwarfing foreseeable United States government aid funds.

Since mid-1958 the way has been opened for foreign private investment in oil exploitation under contracts with YPF, the state oil monopoly, and the results have been dramatic. In 1960, oil production reached double the 1958 figure. Foreign oil companies produced 26.1 per cent of the national total in 1960, up $2\frac{1}{2}$ times over 1959, and it is estimated that a majority of all oil will be produced by private concerns by 1964.

Through government's unleashing of private initiative, Argentina had been approaching self-sufficiency in petroleum, and the money heretofore spent for imports and state petroleum activities had been freed for schools and highways.

These recent investments have been large and dramatic, covering significant areas of modern development—oil, chemicals, synthetic rubber, carbon black, autos, exotic fibers, and dozens of others. They were creating economic growth, private jobs and national wealth for Argentina at the very moment when Red-sponsored exiled Peron lent his exiled prestige to far lefters—then private enterprise became the pawn of the communists in Argentina. Now Argentina teeters giddily between military government and popular communist-tainted domination, and the future of modern capitalism remains in doubt.

Chile, too, under President Alessandri is striving to attract private capital and to lessen the burdens of government intervention, but the practical and political factors are formidable. Corfo, the state industrial combine, is virtually confined to petroleum, sugar and mining. It has sold its stock in Cap, the steel company, and the Cap is now making a "profit" on the basis of paying no taxes and getting its ore at cost from Bethlehem Iron Mines of Chile as an accommodation.

Under ideal circumstances in a small country like Chile, finding private Chilean capital adequate to lift the government enterprises off the back of the economy would be difficult enough, but it is rendered virtually impossible by the fact that a strong socialist-communist alliance not only opposes private ownership but advocates more and more nationalization of industry, especially industry owned by United States firms.

The large American copper producers in Chile, involving over one-half billion dollars of investment, are being subjected to increasing government pressure. Last year the Chilean government commenced a drive to force the copper companies to increase output 15 per cent every three years and to increase the percentage refined in Chile from about 60 per cent to 100 per cent using, if necessary, state-owned refineries now under construction. Two Chilean senators, one a member of the Conservative party and the other of the Christian Democrat, have urged that the copper firms be expropriated and paid for with United States aid funds. Under a bill introduced by Senator Salvador Allende, who was the close runner-up to President Alessandri in the 1958 Presidential race, the government would nationalize the copper firms, paying only $209 million, and even that only in 30-year 3 per cent promissory notes.[8]

In Colombia, strong forces resist state ownership, including a dedicated group of modern capitalists known as CEAS, but the squeeze play has been on against a private power firm. The company cannot expand without assurances of needed rate increases to match inflation, and assurances against expropriation. Government properly insists on expansion, but political factors prevent it from offering either assurance. And, so, the buy-out squeeze is taking shape.

An American secondary recovery oil company was in trouble when I was last in Colombia. Allegations that its concession had turned out very profitably had led to a public and political outcry of such intensity that the company and government felt impelled to enter negotiations for the sale of the firm to the government.

Icollantas, a Colombian tire concern, with the majority of its stock owned by Goodrich, must buy all of its rubber from the government of Colombia, although the rubber cannot be used for making tires. The prices go up and up, fixed by executive decree, and Icollantas keeps finding boulders in the center of the bales. They have to throw away all the Colombian rubber and import quality rubber, but still they cannot increase tire prices because they are fixed by the government.

In some Latin American nations, far from seeking to reverse the trend, government officials are cheerfully anticipating more state acquisitions.

Thus in Mexico, José Hernandez Delgado, the quiet, soft-spoken Director General of Nacional Financiera de Mexico, sits on top of Mexico's biggest industrial heap—scores of state-owned enterprises ranging from ore to movies, steel to chemicals. Sr. Hernandez looks for Nacional Financiera's public ownership activities to grow, even if more capital might be attracted to Mexico through other measures. As of June 30, 1961, the director stated, Nafin had a total of nearly $1.3 billion (U.S.) invested in 533 business activities and of these, 73.5 per cent were in basic industries and public works.[9]

Yet another of Mexico's great men, Luis Legorreta, head of Banco Nacional de Mexico, says that business opposition to this trend has brought it to an end and there is substantial opinion that this is the case. The future of private versus state ownership in Mexico does not seem clear at this writing.

In Venezuela, the head of the Central Bank, Sr. Alfredo Machado Gomez said to me, "Our losses from government operations in steel, power, petroleum and the like are more than $125 million per year."

"In effect," he added sadly, "these operations were chosen in lieu of schools."

Unlike steel, which is now preponderantly in government hands in Latin America, the overall story of petroleum remains to be written, but the trend against private enterprise is plainly evident. Brazil clings doggedly to the proposition that oil shall be a state monopoly despite the fact that the last eight years of government activity in the interior vastness of Brazil and the expenditure in those years of $300 million have not produced enough indigenous fuel to run a motorbike.[9a] In Mexico all oil is government, all refining. In Venezuela, the government has newly entered the arena, completed its first well in mid-1961. Its intrusion began when it upped the government's share of proceeds from 50 per cent to 70 per cent a few years ago. The private companies were forced to turn back large parts of their unexplored concessions in 1960. While government officials deny it, qualified observers believe that the bulk of future expansion of the oil industry in Venezuela will be in the state sector.

Argentina, under former President Frondizi, broke away from the state aid monopoly established under Peron to the extent of granting contractual exploration rights to private firms. The results, as noted, had been striking up to the Peronista victory at the polls in March 1962 and the resulting military takeover. Argentina had also encouraged private firms to enter chemical production fields that would utilize in Argentina the refined products that might be produced from the state-owned refineries.

Not long ago Bolivia let United States and other private firms in on a limited concession basis, to compete with the state-owned oil firm. In the last four years, private oil companies spent an estimated $70 million in Bolivia. Our Gulf Oil of Bolivia alone spent $33 million in this period, constructed some 3,000 miles of road, several bridges and eight airports in the Bolivian tropics. Beginning in September 1960 the private firms began to hit and now it is clear that Bolivia is rich in oil and will, through taxes and royalties, share in the abundant revenue with private investors, both foreign and domestic.

In June 1961, a meeting of the state-owned petroleum companies of Latin America, called by the Venezuelan Minister of Mines and Hydrocarbons, was held in Maracay, Venezuela. They created a formal organization called the "Conference of State Oil Enterprises of America" (Conferencia de Empresas Estatales Petroleras de America—CEEPA). The new organization adopted recommendations providing that state oil companies be financially self-supporting, with a maximum of autonomy, and that they should be the "controlling factor in domestic markets and contribute to normal development of overseas markets." It also recommended that state-owned companies should aim at becoming self-sufficient, with their own facilities for exploration, production, transport and marketing. According to this conference, the title of the new organization was purposely adopted, especially the inclusion of the embracing word "America," to *"provide for subsequent entry of any future state-owned petroleum company of the United States or Canada."*[10]

Clearly the conference was a communist triumph, but news of it reached no United States newspaper. At the same time, the Venezuelan Finance Minister announced that the following foreign aid from the United States and multinational agencies was either agreed upon or in the process of negotiation: Export-Import Bank, $100 million; Inter-American Development Bank, $88.4 million; World Bank $105-120 million; U. S. Development Loan Fund, $10 million; and Bank of Paris and the Low Countries, $20 million.

This conference of government-owned oil enterprises doubtless derived even greater encouragement from the fact that, shortly before, our own government formally renounced its previous ironclad policy of refusing foreign aid to state-owned oil enterprises.

This little-noticed action on the part of the Kennedy Administration marks a major change in the United States' economic philosophy toward the underdeveloped countries, particularly in Latin America. The previous policy was based upon the idea that aid should be withheld whenever private investment could do the job and, more fundamentally, upon the premise that our national interests are not served by encouraging state socialism in Latin America. The reversal of this policy constitutes a resignation to state ownership as a fact of life in Latin America and a succumbing to the debasing idea that if we refuse to aid these state-owned business firms the Soviets will.[11]

Said the *New York Times:* "The Kennedy Administration's change of policy was a result of recognition that the Latin American oil monopolies are a fact of life, and that Soviet bloc suppliers are eager to conquer the Latin American market through barter deals and financing plans."

In a letter to far-left* President Paz Estenssoro of Bolivia released May 14, 1961, President Kennedy promised U. S. loans and grants for the state tin and oil enterprises among others, possibly a mortal blow to those who hoped to see the reemergence of a capitalist society in Bolivia.

Ironically, in that same week the *London Economist* released a study of "Creeping Capitalism" in the USSR, showing among other things that half of Russia still buys its farm produce from the individual peasant who has refused to yield to communism, and that unlicensed workshops and even private home builders abound.

Last year, the Soviets finally had to decree the death penalty for private enterprisers who commit serious "economic crimes." This followed a like decree adopted in 1954 in Bulgaria, in 1958 in Hungary and Rumania and 1960 in Poland.[12] While men are dying behind the iron curtain to keep the spark of capitalism alive, are we to finance "creeping socialism" in Bolivia and elsewhere in Latin America?

"Bolivia has literally millions of acres of underdeveloped land which studies have proved to be suitable for agricultural, pastoral and extractive enterprises," finds Professor Wm. S. Stokes.[13] But instead it has adopted an official program for the expropriation and distribution of lands already in use, to be valued on the basis of current tax assessment and "compensated" in the form of 2 per cent 25-year "agrarian bonds."[14]

---

*A marxist revisionist, according to Dr. William S. Stokes of Claremont Men's College.

What about the record of tin in Bolivia since nationalization? In 1952 the government seized the three great tin interests—Patino, Aramayo and Hochschild. In the next two years, 1600 smaller privately owned tin mines went out of business, chiefly due to extreme taxation, which was often 100 per cent of profits.

The management of these mines by the government has been a colossal failure, as shown by figures collected by Dr. Stokes. During the period 1952 to 1958, tin produced declined from 27 million to 17 million kilos, tin exported from 25 million to 14 million kilos, and tin value from $65 million (U.S.) to $28 million. "Almost every pound of tin taken from the Bolivian mines since 1952 has been at a loss," said the Bolivian ambassador to Washington in 1957.[15]*

The rising trend toward state ownership in Latin America is a deadly curve that can only end in communism unless arrested. Yet this is not to say that all is lost. Australia is an illustration of a now advancing nation that began its era of industrialization with a heavy dose of state ownership of basic industries and later sold them into private ownership. The nationalization of industry in England under the socialists after the war is being eroded back to normality, and in Germany, Volkswagen, long government-owned, is being sold to the citizens and employees. Of course none of these can be compared, either to England with her highly developed industrial base and settled institutions, or to Germany with her

---

*For the information on the Bolivian tin mines I am indebted to William S. Stokes, whose brilliant study "The Contraproducente Consequences of the Foreign Aid Program in Bolivia," should be required reading for all who may be tempted to flirt with the state ownership concept. Furthermore, his revelations concerning the black market in United States Food for Peace in Bolivia—so successful a cornering of the market that black marketeers from neighboring countries were able to gear up an export program of similar United States granted commodities at lower prices—are without parallel in the shocking annals of United States foreign aid.

prodigious individual productivity, or to Australia with her pioneer spirit, to a Latin America characterized by unsettled institutions and low productivity.

Yet these illustrations do establish that such trends can be changed, and the change in this trend in Latin America must become a cardinal principle of our foreign economic policy toward Latin America.

While the will to escape the tightening coils of communism must chiefly come from Latin America herself, policies of ours—if shaped to further modern capitalism in Latin America—can have a critical impact. Furthermore, our pursuit of socialist principles abroad must ultimately have a decisive effect on our own domestic policies.

We cannot long pursue a double standard of capitalism, fostering state ownership abroad while renouncing it at home. Our three-mile limit is just a line on a map, not a seawall that can prevent the backwash of socialism. An illustration of the kind of schizophrenia that cannot long endure is found in the railroad situation. Last year the United States government refused* to loan a mere $5.5 *million* to keep the New Haven Railroad out of bankruptcy, and yet since 1946 our government has loaned and given to the railroads of foreign countries, most of them already government-owned, the enormous sum of $1.4 *billion,* more than 250 times the New Haven request.[16]

Welfare statism in the fields of labor legislation and social security, excessive or misguided and sometimes both, is another aspect of Latin American socialism that works to retard her development in most places and to engender the distress upon which communism thrives.

Oftentimes these laws are at one and the same time oppressive to the worker, punitive to the employer, unfair and il-

---

*Properly so, under existing law and, indeed, under existing economic concepts.

lusory vis-a-vis the lower income groups. Taken overall, they help stagnate Latin American society by destroying incentives for increased productivity or new technology. While some are highly regressive in character, they are classed herein as socialism. Broadly speaking, they fall within the class of measures by which government super-planners hope to guide and manage the economy.

Consider the elements of labor legislation in Colombia. They have a *maximum* wage law on most brackets of work, not a minimum, whereby any excess is not deductible for tax purposes by the employer. This is supposed to "spread the work" but obviously it chills both productivity and the employer's incentive to raise wages. They recently decreed a profit-sharing scheme, but it will only apply to a handful of top-salaried employees because it requires the employee to save before the employer can match, and only a few can save on the maximum wage applicable to their category of work.

Under this decree Sears Roebuck of Colombia will not be able as a practical matter to put in their usual, highly beneficial profit-sharing plan in Colombia.

In Peru and elsewhere in Latin America, the labor laws manifest a tendency to engraft the near serfdom of colonial days onto the structure of the modern corporation. About 40 per cent of direct salary is paid in mandatory indirect deferred benefits in Peru.

Terminal pay and vacation rights are high and they both accelerate with each year of employment until after 35 years the terminal pay, for example, becomes 100 per cent of total salary each year until the employee's death. As on the hacienda of yore, this retards the payment of cash salaries adequate to permit savings. Any raise requires a retroactive increase in reserves for severance pay and retirement.

Argentina's broad social welfare laws have been described as "quite a burden to carry" by a top executive of one United States concern there, which has experienced a high rate of absenteeism because of the loose definition of fully paid sick leaves under the law.[17]

The manager of Sears Roebuck of Brazil, who had spent years in Peru, informed me that in his experience, "the social security laws of Brazil and Peru and other Latin American countries actually retard the standard of living because they immobilize the work force.

"They involve so many deferred compensations based on the latest take-home salary," he added, "that they tend to lock the employee into a job rigidity and to forestall raises, due to the effect these would have on pensions and terminal pay. At the same time the deferred compensation is whittled into nothingness by inflation."

Informed Latin Americans realize that only through increased per capita productivity will Latin America produce the earnings and savings needed to make development match population growth. Chilean Felipe Herrera, in his opening address to the Second Annual meeting of the Inter-American Development Bank, held in Rio in April 1961, said this:

Social progress is not a substitute for economic development. It is absurd to think that our countries can raise their people's living standards without first developing their capacity to produce. Such is, moreover, the historic experience in any system of economic organization. Every country that has tried to bring off the trick of raising living standards without improving the foundations of its national financial structure has only managed to create greater needs which, in the end, could not be met. Essentially, social progress results from greater production and better distribution.[18]

Yet on the very heels of these observations the Peruvian legislature, by the action of both houses, enacted a new law which grants to all "obreros"—the blue collar workers—a mandatory 30-day vacation with full pay each year.[19] Thus is low productivity pushed even lower by misguided social laws sponsored by the socialists and warmly endorsed by the communists. This trend gains impetus from the fact that "social reform" is a key phrase in our government's Alliance for Progress, apparently based on the idea that, since a moderate amount of share-the-wealth is not working out, an excess will do the trick.

Emil Rieve, a vice president of our own AFL-CIO, with whom I had several visits during a recent trip to Latin America, told me, "I think that the major problem retarding Latin American industrial growth is the remarkable labor rigidity that prevents sufficiently rapid technological development that would lead to new products, new plants and new jobs." He told me that as compared with the United States the rights of labor in the plant are unbelievably strong. The established right of a worker to continue to operate a given machine is frequently so firmly secured that the owner cannot replace the machine with another that might produce more, make the employee more productive, or produce a product at a lower price that more people could buy. I asked him for a suggestion, since we both recognized that the political leaders would not ordinarily be able to abrogate these rigid social laws without fear of retaliation at the polls. He suggested that freedom on the part of management to deal with plant technology should be "traded," to use his term, for a promise to the employees that they would not be discharged.

These findings seem all the more pertinent, coming as they do from one who has spent his life in support of the labor position, and who was making an intensive study of labor conditions in Latin America.

It seems foolish that capital and labor should be like the chicken and the egg, the one clinging to a bygone feudalism and the other, perhaps in retaliation, clinging to the pitiful protection of outmoded social welfare statutes; practices that combine to prevent increased productivity and stifle economic growth and new jobs.

Bear in mind: reduced to simplest terms, Latin America's

problem is 30-50 per cent unemployed, a far shout from the 6 per cent "insured" unemployment which concerns us.

THE MAJOR COMMODITY PROBLEM:
SOCIALISM AT THE INTERNATIONAL LEVEL

It has become almost a political necessity for public figures in Latin America to take the line that many of her woes are traceable to the fact that she does not have a stable world market at stable world prices for her major agricultural and mineral commodities. If the "rich" countries would only buy a predicted quantity at a predicted price, the thesis goes, Latin America would get the foreign exchange needed to develop itself industrially. Instead, the picture is one of feast and high prices in time of short supply, and famine when world market prices fall in times of glut.

It is fashionable to describe our continued insistence upon free world market prices and our unwillingness, as the major consuming nation, to enter into worldwide quantity and price maintenance agreements, as a kind of commodity imperialism tantamount to exploitation. These allegations are embellished by the further charge that not only do we buy their raw products as cheaply as we can, we then process them into finished goods and sell them back to Latin America at 5, 10 or 20 times as much. This is especially vicious, it is claimed, since much of the original profit from the growth or extraction of the raw product was garnered in Latin America by foreign branches of United States firms, and remitted to the home office in the form of dividends or other remittances.

The remedy for all this injustice, they say, is to have all of the major producing nations of each given commodity get together in one room with all of the major consuming nations of the same and then and there assign quotas and fix prices. After all, this is nothing new for the United States in principle, they correctly say, since we have allocated our sugar requirements for years and paid a special price to Cuba, and we have import quotas on lead and zinc and petroleum and various products; and, above all, we have fixed the price of our own agricultural commodities, such as wheat and cotton, on the international market by restricting imports and paying subsidies.

So why not go the whole distance, control production and prices on all major world commodities? they ask. Why not adopt the entire socialist credo at the international level and abandon, as to major commodities in which Latin America is interested, the principles of free enterprise, competition, free trade and free markets which, despite the blatant exceptions noted above, we have always considered a vital part of our concept of capitalism?

Recently a new refrain has been added: The higher prices we will pay for Latin American commodities can be in lieu of foreign aid we intend to give them anyway, and so they would really cost us nothing. Recently the manager of the Colombian coffee association in Bogotá said to me: "If you people in the States would raise the price you pay us for our coffee every year, say a few cents a pound or a cent a cup, this would finance Colombian development."

In April, 1962, in Buenos Aires, at the third annual meeting of the Inter-American Development Bank, Finance Minister Jorge Mejia Palacio of Colombia complained that "the losses suffered in the markets and prices of coffee" in the previous year had been "two or three times" the amount of Alliance for Progress aid to Colombia.[19a]

Still more recently, at the gathering of top business leaders from around the world in San Francisco in September 1961, under the sponsorship of the Stanford Research Institute and the National Industrial Conference Board, the Latin American delegation (not without dissent) took the rostrum to formally endorse this remedy: fixed, higher prices for commodities, potentially an alternative to foreign aid.

Surely, the idea of a group of hard-headed free enterprisers entertaining a proposal for supranational price and production controls would be little short of hilarious were it not for the serious extent to which the idea has already infiltrated government and private economic circles.

The notion received an important booster in the Act of Bogotá in which the United States government joined in recommending that "urgent attention be given to the search for effective and practical ways, *appropriate to each commodity,* to deal with the problem of the instability of exchange earnings of countries heavily dependent upon the exportation of primary products."

In our government's presentation of our foreign aid program to the Congress in June 1961, the subject is cautiously broached as follows: ". . . we must try to afford the less-developed countries with protection against rapid fluctuations in export earnings on products which comprise their main exports."

These words are widely interpreted in Latin America as an endorsement of the regulatory remedy and this interpretation gained further justification from the fact that at the Punta del Este Conference in Uruguay in 1961, assembled to put flesh and blood into the Alliance for Progress aid program, the Secretary of the Treasury explicitly committed us to join the international coffee control group.

Even our own private sector seems to be walking up to the idea with a friendly attitude. The Committee for Economic Development (CED), composed of 200 leading businessmen and educators, in "Cooperation for Progress in Latin America," published in April 1961, stated, not without dissent: ". . . the United States should seriously consider participation in an international coffee agreement, accepting a responsibility to impose import quotas if necessary. . . ."[20]

There is no doubt that the problem is a very severe one

for most Latin American countries. The chaotic condition in
coffee, which is Latin America's largest export after petroleum,
illustrates this. Exports of coffee are 50 to 75 per cent of the
total exports of Brazil, Colombia, Costa Rica, El Salvador,
Guatemala and Haiti and they range between 15 and 30 per
cent of the exports of Ecuador, Honduras, the Dominican Republic and Nicaragua. Prices in 1959 fell to 50 per cent of
the 1954 level. Since 1960, 95 per cent of all coffee exports
are accounted for by members of a new agreement of coffee
producers capable of withholding coffee from the market to
prevent a price collapse. But confidence in its efficacy is
evidently lacking. Greater production appears to be the goal
of the African and Indian coffee growers today, despite the
fact that their current quotas under the international agreement have been reduced.[21]

World production of coffee exceeded consumption by 50
per cent in 1959-60. Despite greatly increased world consumption, exports of coffee from all of Latin America in 1959 just
about equaled 1950—$1.5 billion (U.S.).

To a lesser but significant extent, these tribulations apply
to a number of other Latin American commodities: lead and
zinc, copper, sugar, cotton, petroleum, but the market action
of all of these—unlike coffee—is influenced by recent United
States government action such as quotas limiting imports in
the case of lead, zinc, sugar and petroleum, a new level of
tariff in the case of copper, subsidy in the case of cotton.

Latin American export of bananas, cacao, sugar, wheat,
meat, wool, lead and zinc, nitrate and tin, have declined or
barely held their own in the last 12 years in absolute terms,
and their poor showing is even poorer as a percentage of the
expanded world market over those years. On the other hand,
petroleum exports increased 120 per cent; copper 25 per cent;
cotton 20 per cent. Even coffee exports increased 70 per cent,
1948 to 1959, but the element of fluctuation is seen in the
fact that coffee exports climbed rapidly from 1948 to 1954

and then fell 50 per cent in the next six years.* This mixed picture is alleviated somewhat by the longer term showing: Latin American exports, in the 11 years 1948-1959, rose from $6.5 billion (U.S.) to $8.5 billion.

The adverse overall Latin American trade situation, compared to other areas of the free world, is shown by the fact that while between 1947 and 1960 the Middle East increased the value of its exports by 70 per cent, Asia by 109 per cent, Western Europe by 184 per cent, the total of Latin American exports grew only 27 per cent.[22]

Despite these unhappy figures, the plain fact nevertheless is that most international commodity problems are the result of too much, rather than too little, government intervention. The remedy the Latin Americans propose would not succeed and would only make their "one commodity plight" worse. It is this very kind of remedy that has gotten them into the fix they are in. The reason there is too much coffee around is because the price is too high. In many areas of the world, with present costs, it will continue to be profitable to produce coffee considerably below present prices.

The reason the price is so high is illustrated by the government's action in Brazil. In 1935 Brazil had 65-70 per cent of the world market for coffee. Now she has less than 40 per cent. She lost her position, first, by trying to raise her prices in the thirties and, more recently, through the practice of soaking her exporters by giving them an artificially low number of Brazilian cruzeiros for the United States dollars their exports produce. In this way Brazil has jacked up the world price of coffee, dried up her own coffee production, and made it possible for other areas of the world to get into the coffee business. These other areas have other advantages too, such as the preference given existing and former French colonies that lets coffee from those areas enter France—and ultimately the Com-

*All of these figures are in United States dollars, not quantities.

mon Market—duty-free. Similar disadvantage, for Brazil, prevails in relation to coffee going to England from the Commonwealth.

Now Brazilians are seeking to have us subsidize the coffee price handicap they themselves helped to create. Perhaps if the subsidy would succeed, our sympathies would dictate compliance, but history teaches otherwise.

In an illuminating study, Professor Yale Brozen of the Graduate School of Business, University of Chicago,[23] has demonstrated the thesis that the policy pursued by less-developed countries such as Brazil, in the way of taxing, restricting, "stabilizing" and placing umbrellas over their major raw material exports, has been and is now a major factor in retarding their industrial development. The contracting parties to the GATT* measured, he found, the relative changes in the production of food and agricultural raw materials in the industrial and non-industrial areas between 1938 and 1952. These compilations show a 38 per cent rise in food production in the industrial areas in contrast to only a 10 per cent rise in non-industrial areas such as Latin America. They reveal that the non-industrial areas imported 138 per cent more food from the industrial areas than was the case at the beginning of the selected period, and the industrial areas imported less than they previously had. Thus the less developed countries like Brazil consumed (or failed to get) valuable foreign exchange which would have been available to import equipment and materials for manufacturing and processing.

As the figures show [writes Dr. Brozen], the industrial sector of the world increased agricultural production in the face of the attempts of the non-industrial sectors to reduce the supply of these commodities. Also, synthetic production, sub-

---

*General Agreement on Tariffs & Trade, which is the international organization through which multi-country negotiations on tariffs and quotas is conducted.

stitutes and extenders can be and were developed, partly in response to restriction efforts. Silk has been replaced by nylon, wool has suffered the competition of orlon and dacron, natural rubber has been partly replaced by man-made rubbers, cocoa supplies have been extended by the addition and mixture of various fats with cocoa butter. Coffee has been made into "instant" compounds which double the number of cups obtainable from a given supply.[24]

Dr. Brozen sees the loss of these profitable markets, as a consequence of specific governmental interventions on the part of the less developed nations. Brazil, he shows, has underpaid its exporters of coffee, cotton, cocoa and iron for the foreign exchange earned—in the case of coffee, the Brazilian exporter gets only 45¢ of the 65¢ New York price, say, and the Brazilian government gets the balance. Malaya restricted the increase in rubber planting and thus started synthetics on their way. Argentina penalized its growers of cereals, meat, oil seeds and wool. City folks in our country took up ranching in the United States when Argentina's meat exports dwindled and prices went up. Others rushed into wheat farming when restrictive schemes in the non-industrial world offered new chance for profit in that commodity.

When the United States started price supports on cotton, the Mexican cotton industry came into being; and later the United States had to subsidize the export price of United States cotton to make it salable on the world market. Certainly if we had Cuba to do over again there would be no sugar subsidy which held Cuba back from healthy diversification. Clearly, if we had it to do all over again we would never have taught the world the folly of agricultural price supports. Surely it should be our policy to gradually eliminate them, as well as the quotas in lead and zinc, sugar and petroleum, and the tariff in the case of copper. If we ourselves will move more faithfully in the direction of our traditional concepts of free trade and free private capital flow, we will offer the best opportunity for a non-communist kind of development in Latin America.

If we really mean to be the world's exponent of modern free market capitalism, we had better stop protecting inefficiency and start increasing productivity. When compared to the restrictive practices of our own and other governments on the international scene, not to mention the international cartelism embodied in the New Frontier proposals, the antitrust violations by some of our domestic concerns are the merest peccadilloes. As a matter of moral consistency, we should start by rebating their fines.

Apart from principle, there is not the slightest chance that a price-fixing quota scheme would bring the results its advocates predict. It would spur research into synthetic coffee, which already appears to lurk around the corner. The fate of other commodities teaches us that demand for none of them is permanent and inelastic. Much of our own trouble in the distressed areas of our eastern coal fields is due to the fact that some simply refuse to accept the obvious, that coal has been priced out of large sectors of the market and displaced by other fuels. Didn't Father say coal would reign for a thousand years?

Venezuela has the same attitude toward its oil: a storehouse of riches to be counted on forever. But the existence in the Middle East of vast reservoirs of less costly, high quality oil is a fact. And the dawn of the age of atomic fuel is surely here. Venezuela, instead of taking 70 per cent of its own oil in taxes, should be finding ways to be more competitive with it, and also to diversify against the possible day when all the oil still left in the ground will, like most of our anthracite, remain there forever.

The cheaper coffee of Africa is a fact that will not go away. Europe will not join a pact to prop up Brazilian coffee. If the United States were to do so alone, Brazil's facing of life's realities would be postponed by a delusion.

The real tragedy of Latin America's commodity past is

that her truly fabled wealth has slipped through her fingers and left her underdeveloped and poor. Now in the very moment when the strength of the world position of her commodities is fading, she has nothing in the bank in the sense of an adequate industrial base. Had she not protected manufacturing at the expense of agriculture, in her impatience to fulfill a narrow concept of industrialization; had she instead maintained the primacy of her major products from field to kitchen, she could have gained the foreign exchange with which to build the processing facilities that were built abroad. Instead, she used her precious international earnings to build steel mills and other monumental facilities, with a high capital-labor ratio, and to import food stuffs in which she had long been self-sufficient.

Now she has up to 50 per cent unemployed and desperately needs assistance. But of what kind? That is the question.

It is the twin fetters of advanced socialism and feudalism's remnants that predispose Latin America to communism. It is against those environmental conditions that we must shape our own foreign economic policy. Before coming to that, however, we must gain an insight into two aspects of Latin America's social structure so different from ours as to almost lie beyond the reach of our understanding: her education and her population.

CHAPTER III

REFERENCES

[1] *New York Times,* May 31, 1961.

[1a] Kennedy-Goulart Communique, Apr. 4, 1962, *New York Times,* Apr. 5, 1962.

[2] Victor E. Rockwell, president of Chase International Investment Corp., "The Role of 'Edge Act' Companies in International Financing," addressing American Management Association, New York City, Oct. 5, 1960, p. 15.

[3] Clemente Mariani, Governor for Brazil, Minister of Finance and chairman of the meeting, proceedings of the second meeting of

the Board of Governors, Inter-American Development Bank, Rio de Janeiro, Brazil, Apr. 10, 1961, p. 11.

4 Dr. Pedro G. Beltran, Prime Minister and Minister of Finance of Peru, an address in Rio de Janeiro, Brazil, Apr. 14, 1961.

5 *San Francisco Examiner,* Oct. 29, 1961.

6 Edward Tomlinson, *Look Southward, Uncle,* Devin-Adair, New York, 1959, pp. 119-120.

7 Lewis Hanke, *South America,* Van Nostrand, Princeton, N.J., pp. 47-48.

8 *Wall Street Journal,* Aug. 10, 1961.

9 *Foreign Commerce Weekly,* U. S. Department of Commerce, Sept. 25, 1961.

9a "Brazil's $300 Million 'Dry Hole' Oil Try," Frank C. Adams, *World,* May 1, 1962.

10 *Foreign Commerce Weekly,* U. S. Department of Commerce, Sept. 11, 1961.

11 *New York Times,* May 10, 1961.

12 *London Economist,* May 13, 1961.

13 William S. Stokes, "The Contraproducente Consequences of the Foreign Aid Program in Bolivia," Claremont Men's College, 1961. (Note: In pre-publication status.)

14 *Ibid.*

15 *Ibid.*

16 *New York Times,* July 13, 1961.

17 *New York Times,* Aug. 17, 1961.

18 Felipe Herrera, president of Inter-American Development Bank, address in Rio de Janeiro, Brazil, Apr. 11, 1961.

19 *La Prensa,* Lima, Peru, July 6, 1961.

19a Washington D. C. *Evening Star,* Apr. 25, 1962.

20 "Cooperation for Progress in Latin America," Committee for Economic Development (CED), New York, Apr., 1961.

21 *New York Times,* Jan. 1, 1961.

22 *Time Magazine,* July 21, 1961.

23 Yale Brozen, "The Path to Industrialization," Livraria Agir, Editora, Rio de Janeiro, Brazil, 1957, pp. 92-97.

24 *Ibid.,* pp. 93-94.

Education: A Blighted Crop ?

There is more than one way of looking at the problem of education in Latin America. One is through the eyes of a North American completely accustomed to our notions of mass public education—although this, as we shall see, bears little relation to the realities of education in Latin America in the foreseeable future.

We invest perhaps $25 billion in the operation and expansion of our educational plant every year at all levels of effort, excluding adult education and vocational training. We pass laws and hire truant officers to make certain, as far as seems reasonably possible in a free society, that everyone goes to school through the 12th grade, and our literacy rate is 98 per cent. To be against universal education in the United States would be something like being against Mother, and we are rapidly acquiring, by transference, the same attitude toward education in Latin America.

Regardless of its validity as an abstraction, we are entirely predisposed to the idea that there is an almost divine relationship between education and economic progress, between education and democracy.

We therefore find it easy to believe that standards of education along the United States pattern are a necessary prerequisite to Latin America's achieving adequate economic development, i.e. getting people jobs, and supporting democratic rather than communist institutions. For example, in his pamphlet, "Voice of Latin America," former United States Senator

William Benton says, "In my judgment, the present yawning gap between the universality—and the intensity—of the Soviet system (of education) and the Latin system must be narrowed—and dramatically—and soon."

This line of thought has led our citizenry, with our characteristic capacity for seizing upon an oversimplified idea, to the dangerous assumption that not much can be done about poverty or communism in Latin America until mass education becomes a reality.

The first difficulty with this thesis is that it is impossible to prove, with any degree of certainty, that mass education has very much at all to do with our own economic welfare or growth or, for that matter, with our adherence to democratic capitalism instead of communism. On the contrary, as stated by Richard La Piere of Stanford University,[1] "Over and over it has been demonstrated that the majority of high school graduates are barely literate, that they are hardly aware of the natural or political geography of the world in which they live, and that their knowledge of history begins with Washington—who founded our country—and ends with Lincoln—who freed the slaves."

Certainly we cannot claim that mass education in the United States, especially since it became dominated by the progressive school, has done anything to reduce juvenile delinquency, or the crime rate in general, or to prepare our youth for the mental and physical rigors of military service. It may even be true that mass education produces inherently poor results. As La Piere states: " . . . it may very well be that the current low level of academic standards in our public schools is an inevitable consequence of the attempt to educate forcibly, and at public expense, every child born into our society. For that attempt is based upon the assumption that all men are or can be made equal by education and that equality is socially desirable."[2]

Nor can we assert that education and freedom have very

much in common. The literacy rate in Soviet Russia is slightly better than ours, perhaps by a percentile, yet they all live under the yoke of tyranny. People, unfortunately, can be trained or forced to be drones, serfs or free men. Boys and girls who receive a communist education are likely to turn out to be communists. This is our real challenge in Latin America since the existing educational system, from primary school to university, is pervaded by communist instruction and indoctrination.

While conceding that the idea of mass education is deeply imbedded in our culture, has had something to do in the way of providing a ladder for individual status changes in our society, and would be a fine thing for Latin America, it is quite apparent that no combination of local effort and United States "federal aid-to-Latin-American-education" could possibly have much effect on popular education in Latin America for many generations to come. In the United States our annual expenditures for education exceed $100 for every man, woman, and child, or $20-$25 billion per year. In Latin America, on the other hand, where annual per capita income ranges from a low of $70 to a high of $700, such a per capita contribution to education is entirely unthinkable.[3] It is undoubtedly less than $5 per capita.

In Venezuela, the richest of Latin American countries per capita (average), at least 70 per cent of the children who enter school at all drop out before the third grade, I was told by a well-informed and public-spirited citizen of that country. In Mexico, I was similarly advised, only about 40 per cent of all boys and 30 per cent of all girls attend grade school at all, and a large but unknown number drop out after a year or two.

Since most literacy based on a few years of grade school is temporary at best, the number of people who are illiterate in the practical sense probably exceeds the admitted 70 or 80 million out of a total population of 200 million people.

In most of rural Latin America there is no public school system in the sense we know it. There are no local municipalities with local taxing power adequate to build schools and hire teachers. In the more remote areas, most of the natives speak only a dialect for which there is no written counterpart. While change is coming, education in Latin America has been church and gentry orientated, private and reserved for the economically elite. School statistics are unreliable in Latin America, but it is probably a safe assumption that in most places less than 50 per cent of the children of school age are attending school, many of these for too short a time to become literate.

But this is not the whole story. In the United States, we are operating from a highly developed educational base. For two centuries we have added every year to the little red schoolhouse and the corps of skilled teachers who operate it. The present value of our physical school plant alone is probably more than $200 billion. Surely Latin America's is no more than 5 per cent of that. To predicate our foreign policy upon the proposition that adequate economic development in Latin America must await the coming of popular education, or that mass education there can become a reality within time allowed by Cold War considerations, is to be indifferent not only to fiscal realities but also to the horrible urgency of the facts now facing that part of our hemisphere: 25-50 per cent of the workers now unemployed and communism on the rampage. Certainly a father with four hungry babies will trade any claim to popular education for a communist promise of a job that will fill their swollen bellies.

From the students now in secondary (high) schools and universities in Latin America, a bare 3-5 per cent of school-aged boys and girls, will come the majority of Latin America's leaders. This emerging generation of potential leaders has been and is being subjected to a massive dose of communist indoctrination.

The pertinent question for our time is this: has the current crop been destroyed? Can catalytic methods save it for our side, build a leadership opposed to communism and dedicated to western ideals? Must we wait another entire generation, at least, to get a crop sturdy enough to wrest Latin America free from the coils of communism?

This is the first field of education into which the full force of our foreign economic policy should be directed. The second is vocational, job-related training, through United States and local industry, on a massive scale.

Instead of being overly fascinated with illiteracy statistics and preoccupied with the quantity of education, we should ask ourselves how we can change its *quality* to rid it of its deep Red bias.

Starting at the top with the universities, never minding for a moment how few students reach this level, what is happening to those who do?

The Latin American university lies completely outside our own experience. As almost nowhere else in the world today, they still embrace some but not all of the idea that a university is a group of students who get together and hire some professors. This is known as the Bologna plan, and in this day and age that description just about fits. The results are far-reaching.

No one is ever flunked out. Recently a new and separate school of mines and geology was started up in northern Brazil, with the aid of United States foundation and public money. It seemed a good idea because of the limited petroleum discoveries that have been made in the vastness of Brazil. It was separately organized because of the communist infiltration of the existing universities. Top professors were attracted but when they failed to pass a few, all the students quit, went on strike and insisted that the offending professor be discharged. It almost destroyed the effort, but the faculty stood their ground and ultimately enough students came back to resume operations on a limited basis.

The University Movement, as backed by the majority of the university people in Buenos Aires, now stands, among other things, for "No tuition payments, academic freedom largely in the sense of freedom of speech in the classroom, no permanent tenure for professors, cheap lunches, dormitories, and a voice and vote for students and alumni in running the universities."[4]

Of course, the impact on the faculty is disastrous. The head of our government aid mission in Argentina, Albion W. Patterson, an imaginative and creative civil servant, told me that for this reason a high percentage of that country's educated elite are now teaching in foreign universities. "The first thing to do," he told me, "is to find a way to establish new regional universities free of student domination and communist influence, and then pay these men enough to get them back into the cultural stream."

"There are innumerable cases," says H. K. Silvert, a long-time student of Latin American universities, "of students ousting individual professors by strike or simple hectoring; they are now neck-deep in the fight to maintain the colleges as integrally and academically autonomous cells as against the proposed establishment of departments plus colleges as in the United States; they have hamstrung research projects, rumored classes out of existence, and stopped the normal functioning of the university on many occasions, serious as well as frivolous."[5]

Professorship as a career, then, has little to offer in Latin America. This may be illustrated by the University of Mexico, housed in one of the most dramatic campuses of the entire world, where the School of Economics has about 5,000 students and 400 professors, all but a half dozen of the latter being part-time professors. The few full-time professors—presumably qualified to hand out doctorates in economics—are paid less than a beginning civil service employee in the Mexican Ministry of Finance, and most of them are communists.

The situation is similar throughout Latin America. Referring to Buenos Aires, one authority on Latin American education has said, "The professor in charge of a course will normally be paid fifty or sixty United States dollars per month for teaching it; his assistant will be fortunate to receive half that amount."[6]

An American university, possessed of Ford Foundation money to train Latin American teachers in the disciplines of graduate schools of business administration—virtually unheard of in Latin America—could not up to the time of this writing find two potentially qualified professors in all of Peru who were able or willing to leave their full-time non-teaching job to receive the necessary free, full-time training in the United States.

It has been a Latin American tradition that its young aristocrats take down a degree in one of the "prestige" callings —chiefly law or medicine—entirely without regard to their intention to practice the calling. A degree in either entitles the holder to decorate his name with the word "Doctor" for the rest of his natural life.

This philosophy persists and completely unbalances the educational picture. For example, in 1961 there were 3,000 law students attending the public university in Montevideo. This is perhaps four times the number of law students attending, at any given time, all the law schools of Northern California, a fairly well developed area with a larger population than the whole of Uruguay.

It goes without saying that the overwhelming majority of these students have no intention of practicing law. This, plus the fact that they cannot be flunked, seems calculated to reduce scholastic zeal to the minimum and to leave them the maximum time to participate in campus politics, which in Latin

America are a far cry from the mild popularity contests conducted in our universities. "Every contest without the cloisters
is fought out within them as well," says Silvert.[7]

Politics is serious business in Latin American universities,
usually regarded as important as well as influential by the
non-university community. The campus candidates are identified with, supported and oftentimes financed by the actual
political parties whose leading figures frequently appear on
campus to reinforce their boys' campaigns.

This is an ideal environment for the communists—right
down their alley. For one thing they set up a corps of permanent "students" who quickly become pros in swinging student
sentiment their way.

In Mexico City, the Russian Ambassador has 35 "cultural
attaches" attending the University as "students." Through
them, the salaries and stipends of left-leaning professors and
students are supplemented, thus virtually assuring their ultimate orientation to communism.

There are three student parties in Mexico—left-wing,
liberal and just anticommunist, the last named being the
smallest of the three. The mothers of sons of known conservative bent fear for the very life of their progeny.

The School of Engineering in the University of Venezuela
was having its elections of the student council when we were
there. The non-communist student coalition squeaked through
with a majority victory but their leaders worked night and
day to do it and even enlisted the non-communist graduates to
return to campus to help them out with speeches and personal
persuasion.

Veir, Inc., in a 1960 study for a Senate subcommittee,
found the following:

Where the communist parties are outlawed, communist
student organizations develop under other names. Indeed,
such disguises are common throughout these countries. As in

the case of labor organizations, penetration of student groups is widespread. This is especially serious in Brazil, Cuba (sic),* Venezuela, Peru, Chile, Ecuador, Argentina and Uruguay. Close observers believe that communists dominate some student organizations in the leading universities of perhaps half the countries of Latin America.

Brazil is an example of the more successful efforts of the communists. Both the national union of university students and the national union of secondary school students are extensively penetrated. The top officers of the university student union always include communists.[9]

Communist student leaders often mean communist professors since, under the Bologna system, the student council has an important voice in the selection of the university authorities and professors and in the conduct of university affairs. The case of a recent president of the University of Mexico shows the amazing degree of student influence. The communists as a matter of standard practice are wont to inspire riots, car overturnings, attacks on prominent visitors and the like, using their special cadre of paid "pigeons" and followers as a nucleus. The president, in a desperate effort to quell this sort of thing, began a system of counter-bribing of the miscreants, secretly supplementing their income even more. This put his accounts out of order and enabled the communists to blackmail him, which they did. Student decorum was entirely out of hand when the "embezzlement" was finally discovered and a new president installed, who took the courageous stand that, while there would be no reprisals, these fiscal practices would not be tolerated.

---

*Our State Department's white paper on communism in Cuba released in April 1961 states: "In characteristic communist manner the regime has seized control of the nation's educational system, introduced communist propaganda into the schools, destroyed academic freedom and ended the traditional autonomy of the universities."[8]

Under these circumstances, the indiscriminate or unsupervised giving of United States government aid to Latin American governments or education ministries for use in these universities seems foolish.

Essentially the same is true of the secondary and primary schools. In Venezuela, for example, a recent survey, we were advised, had disclosed that the percentage of communist teachers in the grade schools ranges from a high of 86 to a low of 33 per cent. In April 1961 when Venezuelan public secondary schools — which correspond most closely to our high schools — held their student elections, also an out-and-out political dry-run under the Latin American school system, the communist student ticket won out in every school except two.

Our course of action vis-a-vis education in Latin America now seems clear:

First, we should join with leading private citizens in Latin America in establishing regional universities of outstanding quality, divorced from state influence and student management. The faculty of each would be of the highest caliber, drawn from the region and elsewhere in the western world and well paid. They and the appointed administrators would run the show, not the students or the politicians.

It will be imperative that the initiative and funds come from private Latin American sources, supplemented by United States foundation and private support. Otherwise our government-to-government aid-givers will necessarily have to let socialist and communist influences into the act.

The students should be drawn, by scholarship where necessary, from the public and private secondary schools of the region. Admission would be limited — as it is in many of our top privately endowed universities today — to boys and girls of Latin America who have demonstrated records of achievement, scholarship and decency. By decency, I mean a family and personal record of adherence to the ideals of Western, Christian, capitalistic civilization.

Thus we might save some leaders of today from the blighted crop and give them the best possible weapons with which to fight the struggle in the dark days of tomorrow.

At the present time, in at least two Latin American nations, new high-quality private universities are being organized free from the communist influences now found in all Latin American state institutions. A group of Mexican leaders are raising funds from businessmen and other private sources for a new private university in Mexico City, to be called Universidad Ibero-Americana. This university has been founded on Western Christian principles to get away from the leftism of the state-run university. Students and faculty will be chosen on the basis of intellectual capacity plus adherence to these principles.

In Venezuela, also, Eugenio Mendoza, a private businessman, and his family have donated a prize tract of land in Caracas for the development of a new university there which will be privately operated and equipped to offer high quality instruction free of communist infiltration.

Thus Latin America is already taking action to implement the idea that the first requirement is to establish centers which will not only provide high quality instruction at the university level to selected students with leadership potential but which also can operate as a counter-force to the heavily infiltrated public institutions.

Second, we should expand greatly and systematize the training which business firms are now providing to employees and their families in Latin America. This is discussed in detail in a later chapter. The educational opportunities afforded by these company schools and training programs are very great and, again, are almost unique in that instruction is not coupled with communist indoctrination.

These schools often teach, for example: reading, writing and arithmetic to the entire family; cooking and sewing to the girls; trades to the boys; advanced skills to the employee himself.

Our firms should form teams of personnel technicians prepared to teach indigenous business firms to set up similar company schools.

After all, neither a Ph.D. from Harvard nor a course of instruction from a Peace Corpsman is needed to operate a drill press or a transit. These jobs can be taught in conventional company training schools.

The profound responsibility of United States business for educational progress in Latin America has been repeatedly recognized by our business leaders. In a recent address to a group of leading business executives in Chicago, Harry H. Jarvis, president of Creole Petroleum Corporation, Venezuelan operating company of Standard Oil Company of New Jersey, said:

One of the most discouraging and baffling forces at work against us at this time is the anti-Americanism which pervades so much of the secondary and higher education levels in the countries in which we operate. If we want to survive, I do not think we can afford to let this generation of students grow up hating the United States and despising the free enterprise system of economy. Many individual companies, as well as our own government, have been nibbling at the edges of the education problem, but the system has to be systematized and coordinated.[10]

Under this second heading falls the fine work which United States Chambers of Commerce and other associations of United States businessmen in Latin America, as well as private United States institutes, are doing at the present time. The scope of this work is very wide, but three illustrations will suffice to illustrate.

In Peru, United States business firms are providing transmitters and one-frequency radios to the Catholic fathers who use them to set up "school-by-radio" in the remote villages. These "schools," we were advised by James Freeborn of Grace Line of Peru — an executive of the American Society in Peru — teach reading, writing and arithmetic by radio. They are also used to counter the massive communist propaganda being disseminated in rural areas.

In Venezuela some of the outstanding projects carried out by our North American Association there during the past two years were: a four-year scholarship in the United States for the winner of the annual Venezuelan Soapbox Derby; a two-week seminar at Columbia University for 12 Venezuelan newsmen, to be followed by a second seminar; assistance in arranging a visit to Venezuela by 16 United States newspaper editors; an invitation to William Faulkner, American author and Nobel Prize winner, to visit Venezuela in April. Others were: the establishment of a Student Counseling Service for Venezuelans going to the United States to study; a round-table discussion at the Experiment in International Living in Putney, Vermont, for Venezuelans attending colleges and universities in New England; employment of an American coach to assist in the training of Venezuelan athletes. The association's activities also include collaboration with the American Friends Service Committee in a work and study project; the construction of a swimming pool on YMCA land in El Retiro; financial assistance to a trade school in Maracaibo; support of two professorships (for two years) at Universidad Católica "Andres Bello"; and textbooks for youngsters attending the poorer primary schools in Maracaibo.[11]

In Cordoba, Argentina, local and United States business and professional people established and financed a private institute called Iicana. For $2.38 per month, thousands of citizens of Cordoba, from kindergartners to 70-year-olds, are learning English and after that are studying American history, geography, the arts and literature. Enrollment has more than doubled in the past five years. At present 3,500 students are registered for the thrice-weekly classes, and total enrollment, including regular and occasional students, is about 6,000.[12]

Third, our government activity in the field of education should be confined to two activities:

1. Helping finance students of promise who seek specific educational opportunities in the United States, and helping send carefully selected United States students to the regional universities referred to earlier. This former activity should be undertaken only after the most careful planning to make certain that, unlike many instances in the past, the foreign scholar does not return to his home thoroughly disillusioned by the social ostracism and racial prejudice to which he was subjected while attending one of our colleges.

2. Using all our diplomatic resources to persuade the Latin American governments to throw the communists out of school and off the faculties, and generally to clean up and strengthen their own educational institutions. Our own educators can and are offering much technical assistance here. This should be expanded, preferably through initiative from the universities and foundations, rather than federal grants.

A point of view often expressed by American observers of the Latin American scene, including some distinguished educators, is that mass education and literacy on something like the United States scale are a prerequisite to economic growth, institutional democracy and higher standards of living in Latin America.

The difficulty lies in the fact that, starting from the present base, the accomplishment of this elevated condition precedent does not seem to be feasible within the time allowed—extended as that time may be—within which the Cold War will probably be fought to a point of resolution. Accordingly we should bring our help in the field of education into the areas of capitalistically oriented leadership and private-job skills.

CHAPTER IV

REFERENCES

1 Richard LaPiere, *The Freudian Ethic*, Duell, Sloan & Pearce, New York, 1959, p. 112.

2 *Ibid.,* p. 113.

3 "United States-Latin American Relations," 86th Congress, 2nd sess., Senate Doc. No. 125, p. 568.

4 H. K. Silvert, "Other People's Classrooms," letter, Buenos Aires, Jan. 10, 1958, p. 3. (American Universities Field Staff, 522 Fifth Ave., New York 36, N. Y.)

5 *Ibid.,* p. 5.

6 *Ibid.,* p. 6.

7 *Ibid.,* p. 3.

8 "Cuba," Department of State, White Paper, Department Publication No. 7171, Apr. 1961, p. 15.

9 "United States-Latin American Relations," 86th Congress, 2nd sess., Senate Doc. No. 125, Aug. 31, 1960, p. 741.

10 Harry A. Jarvis, "The Changing Role of the American Businessman in Latin America," Proceedings, 1961, Inter-American Industries Conference, Chicago Association of Commerce and Industry.

11 Gerald Maxfield, North American Association of Venezuela, president's report, 1961.

12 *New York Times,* July 13, 1961.

CHAPTER FIVE

Population: A Surplus Crop ?

It is a sad commentary that Latin America's greatest potential resource, her people, now represent in a sense her greatest economic liability.

Fifteen of the twenty republics of Latin America have registered or estimated birth rates ranging between 40 and 50 per 1,000 per year, nearly twice that of the United States. This probably reflects a reproductive performance close to the limits of human capacity.[1]

These high birth rates, coupled with death rates that have declined very rapidly since the war, thanks to the use of such miracles as DDT and modern antibiotics, give Latin America the fastest growing population in the world. This growth is 30 per cent more rapid than that of Africa and Asia. It is at least 60 per cent faster than our own, approximately 2.5 per cent per year as against our 1.6 per cent.

In some areas of Latin America, the difference is even more striking. In Mexico, for example, the statistics bureau says Mexico's population is growing yearly by 3.4 per cent; it is now 36,000,000. This is more than twice our rate of growth.[2]

The astonishing, unequaled population splurge of Latin America can be illustrated by the fact that Venezuela during the last ten years has shown an increase of two and a half million persons, the same figure by which Great Britain increased its own population during the same period. Yet Venezuela's population today is just over 7 million, while Great Britain's is almost 50 million. This comparison indi-

cates a population growth in certain regions of Latin America
approaching ten times that of some areas of industrialized
Western Europe![3]

Because of the high death rate, Africa's population growth
of 1.9 per cent a year is not as great as that of Central America (2.7 per cent), South America (2.3 per cent) or Oceania
(2.4 per cent) which includes Australia and New Zealand.
Asia, where the overall growth rate is 1.8 per cent a year, is
increasing in population about twice as fast as Europe and
Japan, where the increase is a mere 0.8 per cent. Asia's overall
growth rate parallels our own at present, but both her death
and birth rates are far higher than ours.[4]

Yet Latin America tops them all. By the year 2,000, less
than forty years from now, Latin America's population is
likely to be twice ours, according to current projections. She
is expected to sprint from her present 200,000,000 to nearly
600,000,000, while we go from our current 180,000,000 to a
figure slightly in excess of 300,000,000, according to informed
demographers.[5]

Equally if not more significant are the characteristics of her
population. More than 80 million of Latin America's 200 million people are in the economic dependent group, under 15
years of age. More than 40 per cent of the people of all of the
Latin American countries except Argentina and Uruguay are
under 15 years of age, compared with 30 per cent in the United
States.

As recently as a generation ago, the Indian women of the
Andes had to bear ten children to keep four, but that loss is
now virtually cut in half and will be further reduced, rapidly.

As one authority puts it, "Better health and greater
longevity are strongly held goals everywhere, and the means
now available for achieving major improvements (in the
death rate) involve little or no conflict with other values or
the general way of life."[6]

For example, since 1945 the death rate in Chile has declined 50 per cent, over 40 per cent in both Venezuela and Mexico, and one-third in both Argentina and El Salvador. During this same period it declined only 13 per cent in the United States.[7]

These two major characteristics of the Latin American population—its rapid rate of growth and its very young composition—have a profound bearing upon her chances of achieving higher popular standards of living.

They mean, for example, that Latin America's annual economic development, just to maintain the present wholly inadequate per capita relationship with ours, has to progress more than 60 per cent faster than ours. They mean that a far higher percentage of wages and salaries must go into supporting dependent children, instead of into savings, which would in turn be invested in development. This high dependent-earning ratio greatly reduces Latin America's per capita output and her per capita savings. They mean that the annual cost of "social overhead" in the way of schools, water systems, housing, and other essentials would be astronomically higher than ours—even if they now had a satisfactory plant in being which, by and large, they do not.

Insufficient capital investment in new plants is the inevitable handmaiden of these population characteristics, and its continuance will make impossible the achieving of adequate per capita economic growth in Latin America.

The overwhelming difficulty of envisioning a rate of economic growth that will match these population factors in Latin America is ample justification for the arguments of birth control advocates—even for mandatory control. But the prospects are not such as to lead one to be euphoric. Rather, the chances are that before we see any relief in Latin America, Asia and Africa will have caught up with Latin America in the area of death decline; then, their rates of growth will have become similarly increased.

No Latin American government has adopted any population policy for action and none of any significance is foreseen. Not the slightest mention of the problem, as bearing upon our foreign aid policies, is contained in the Act of Bogotá or the Alliance for Progress, despite our alleged insistence upon Latin American "self help" as a condition attached to our aid. While the Catholic Church has given its blessing to the regulation of births by methods to be contrasted with the usual concepts of birth control, medical science has not yet succeeded in developing a sufficiently simple and safe methodology falling within the framework of the papal permission. Furthermore it it is probably a long step from the discovery of such a method to its widespread use by illiterate peoples often lacking such rudiments of modern life as electric lights.

"With a Latin culture at the top of the socio-economic 'totem-pole' and an Indian culture at the bottom, the barriers to education in demographic fundamentals are numerous. Moreover, religious opposition can be expected to be relentless, as it has been in Puerto Rico," says the Population Bulletin.[8]

We are dealing with an incontinent continent and birth control is not going to be much of a weapon in the Cold War. Yet it would probably be a fair guess that within a decade or two we might see some modest amelioration of Latin America's population growth, since the human growth rate appears to bear some rough relationship to the degree of urbanization and industrialization found in a given society.

In an agrarian society, children are less of an economic liability. They are easier to feed and clothe, and education is not an imperative. Furthermore, the practice of requiring young boys and girls to assume full-time duties is widespread even today in rural Latin America; working in the fields, tending animals and gathering firewood from afar are commonplace for boys as young as eight, and for the girls it is the making of clothes, cooking for the men and tending to farmyard and household chores.

In urban life this situation is somewhat reversed. The paternalism of the soil is gone and the children must be educated to gain economic advantage. Girls frequently take jobs, marry later, have fewer children. Men find it more difficult in the city to acquire the minimum economic position required for marriage and, therefore, tend to undertake its responsibilities later in life.

Latin America is rapidly urbanizing, even if the industrial base to justify it is often lacking. Mexico City has over 5 million people and Buenos Aires, Argentina, is larger than either Chicago or London, as also is Sao Paulo, Brazil.[9]

A recent survey found that in every Latin American nation except Brazil and Colombia, the largest city had more inhabitants than all the other cities of 100,000 and more combined. In 13 of the 20 countries, at least 10 per cent live in the single largest city. In six of these the largest city contained one fifth or more of the national population—in Montevideo, Uruguay, 33 per cent; in Buenos Aires, Argentina, 29 per cent; in Santiago, Chile and Panama City, 23 per cent; and in the capitals of Cuba and Costa Rica, 21 per cent. One out of every six Venezuelans lives in Caracas, the capital of Venezuela. By analogy, 36 million people would be living in Washington D.C. today.[10]

These forces may ultimately help retard the birth rate, perhaps aided to some extent by a realization on the part of our southern neighbors that it works to perpetuate poverty.

Another thing to remember is that nothing is more uncertain than estimates of population growth. The experts have misguessed in the past and they will misguess in the future. For example, ten years ago a population explosion was predicted for Japan. Instead, during the past five years her total growth has been only .08 per cent per year, one of the lowest in the world, about equal to that of Western Europe.

Nevertheless, a realistic approach on our own part clearly requires that we base our Latin American economic policies upon an assumed continuance of the factors presently operating. So viewed, we should realize that when we inaugurate a policy of government-to-government aid, premised upon the idea that we will rid Latin America of poverty and illiteracy in a "Decade of Development," we may be creating more "rising expectations" than we can ever satisfy.

Latin America's great need is an individual per capita productivity high enough to overcome these formidable population handicaps. This productivity cannot be achieved by "social reform," "redistribution of wealth," and "land reform." If by "social reform" we mean shorter hours for the same or more pay, more prohibitions against child labor, more vacations and other such attributes of the welfare state—and this is the meaning those words ordinarily convey—these will simply reduce Latin American productivity. If by "land reform" we mean cutting up the large farm units and distributing them to new entrants to the farm community lacking both technical skill and capital—we shall further reduce productivity. And "redistribution of wealth"—presumably from the rich to the poor—may satisfy socialist ambitions, but it will do little to close the lag between the rate of productive capital formation—i.e., economic growth—and the population curve. If we undertake to close this gap by government grants and loans, especially when coupled with these productivity-reducing features, we may find ourselves with a drain that rises somewhat proportionately to Latin America's population growth and somewhat indefinitely.

The central test of every aspect of our foreign economic policy vis-a-vis Latin America, therefore, must be its effect on per capita productivity. This is the lesson of the population facts. Yet when our policy rests on giving government-to-government aid, we necessarily espouse the policies of the recipient government. In Latin America few politicians can hope to win votes by advocating austerity, hard work or the sacrifice of benefits enjoyed for many years. In Lima and in

Montevideo, people do not work on summer afternoons. Recently, as mentioned earlier, Peru decreed a full month with pay for all laborers.

While there is no intention herein of opposing all forms of government-to-government aid to Latin America, it seems apparent that ways should be found to induce new *private* investments to take the place of most of such aid. Unlike government aid, the repetitive job-creating capacity of private investment is tested for productivity in the market place and need not—indeed cannot—endorse the non-productive views of a government of the moment.

THE MARSHALL PLAN FALLACY

In defense of massive government aid to Latin America, our Alliance for Progress is often described by its proponents in the United States and Latin America as a "Marshall Plan for Latin America."

This phrase appears intended to convey the idea that nearly everyone in the world except Latin America has enjoyed a United States-originated Marshall Plan, and it is high time she received one, as well as the further idea that since the Marshall Plan succeeded in restoring Europe, a like effort will succeed in developing Latin America. However, upon analysis, these implications seem peculiarly unjustified. In fact, the entire concept seems to be one of the most illusory ever to grip the American mind.

In the first place, Latin America has never been devastated by war, as was Europe. Quite the contrary, Latin America received a "Marshall Plan" in our immense war purchases that made her wealthy, practically built industrial cities like Sao Paulo. Then, too, in one of the major areas of the Marshall Plan operation, Germany, we *were* the government—actually conducting the restoration in collaboration with our victorious allies. Nothing even vaguely analogous exists in Latin America, since Latin America vigorously resists our annexing of "conditions" or "strings" of any kind upon our aid, let alone our assuming management of her affairs.

Elsewhere in Europe, in the main, we were dealing with stable governments and economies that had fathered the Industrial Revolution more than a century earlier. In England, we were dealing with the most highly industrialized nation in the entire world, as well as the most highly educated, if we leave the idea of mass education to one side. All of the needed skills and technology and the entire industrial base were there—intact except for the destructions of war.

Without dealing with the limitations inherent in the Marshall Plan as against using private capital in the postwar situation—and there were significant limitations*—the Marshall Plan was simply a short-term booster to an already fully developed society. In areas involving less stability such as Greece and Turkey, we engrafted the Truman Doctrine on the Marshall Plan, and actually ran the economic programs ourselves. No Latin American government today, regardless of its instability, is willing to accept this degree of control in return for a "Marshall Plan."

On the other hand, it is the very absence of an industrial

---

*It is interesting to note that the governments of Europe cheerfully declined to follow much of the economic advice which economists now high in the Kennedy administration handed out at the time of the Marshall Plan. Dr. Walter Heller, now chairman of President Kennedy's Council of Economic Advisers took part in the 1951 Economic Report on Germany which recommended that she pursue an inflationary policy, avoid encouragement to business, forget "nostalgic hopes" of a private capital market, establish low interest rates and cheap money and denounce "conservatism and free enterprise." In a concurrent essay Dr. Heller decried the fact that in West Germany "the great bulk of investment is directed—one might say misdirected—privately rather than publicly."[11] Erhard and Adenauer, in effect, threw this advice into the wastebasket. While West Germany has become the most prosperous nation in Europe, the philosophies she rejected have become the New Frontier's orthodoxy both here at home and in Latin America.

base adequate to employ its people that besets Latin America. The creation of such a base will require decades since the need is not remotely similar to the mere short-term restoration involved in most of the Marshall Plan effort.

Comparison of the postwar effort in Europe with the development needs of Latin America is impossible. This is nowhere more evident than in the case of the people. In Europe, we had a highly educated, literate, technically skilled reservoir of homogeneous peoples, with a population growth less than ours and highly mature. In Latin America we have, for the most part, a highly mixed and volatile population, with widespread illiteracy and communist infiltration, growing so fast and so composed as to make satisfactory per capita development a truly long-range project.

*　*　*　*　*

The population facts of Latin America should not be used to discourage our will to aid her. Nor would it be realistic to condition our assistance upon her adoption of measures to curtail population growth, as some have contended. What we need to grasp is that these population facts are going to be with us and they mean "foreign aid forever"—*if* foreign aid be the instrument of assistance we choose to use.

Yet, says Reston of the Times, "Nothing is surer than that there will be a decisive revolt against foreign aid one day if the population problem is not faced."[12] Since "facing it" will not make it go away, the revolt he predicts is inevitable. Therefore in the long game ahead we are likely to last best if we start building now with the bricks and mortar of people's capitalism—a method, it also happens, better conceived to displace the communists.

In sum, it is a dangerous departure from realities to predicate an attack upon Latin America's plight upon the notion that mass education and reduced population growth must come to Latin America in our time.

CHAPTER

REFERENCES

1 Population Bulletin, Population Reference Bureau, Inc., Washington, D. C., Apr. 1961.

2 *San Francisco Examiner* (AP), Aug. 26, 1961.

3 Dr. Manuel Perez Guerrero, chief of Planning Office of Government of Venezuela, "Venezuela Today," Proceedings, 1961, p. 122, Inter-American Industrial Conference, Chicago Association of Commerce and Industry.

4 United Nations Demographic Yearbook, United Nations, New York, 1961.

5 *Ibid.*

6 George J. Stolnitz, "The Revolution in Death Controls in Non-Industrial Countries," Annals of American Academy of Political and Social Science, 316: 94-101, Mar. 1958.

7 Population Bulletin, *supra,* Note 1.

8 *Ibid.*

9 *Ibid.*

10 *Ibid.,* p. 34.

11 Lawrence Fertig, "Economic Orthodoxy: Heller's Pet Aversion," *World Telegram and Sun,* July 3, 1961.

12 James Reston, "Race Between Production and Reproduction," *New York Times,* July 20, 1962.

CHAPTER SIX

Pavlov, Washington and Latin America

For the better part of 30 years, ending in 1936, the Russian psychologist Pavlov engaged in research in the building up and tearing down beliefs and behavior patterns in dogs and in applying the results of this research experimentally to human beings.

He found, as had Hippocrates long ago in the case of human beings, that there are four basic categories of dogs, described—to reduce them to easily recognizable terms—as excitable, lively, calm and melancholy. A simple illustration of the building up of a conditioned reflex or induced pattern would be his use of a metronome sound to create an association between the rapidity of the sound and the giving of food. If the metronome were to be sounded for a period of time at 500 strokes per minute and food then produced, exactly the same quantum of saliva would be produced by such number of strokes even without food being present, but none at all if the rate were reduced to even 490 strokes.[1]

An example of Pavlov's way of producing a breakdown in the dog's capacity to maintain its habitual response to things would be the constant lengthening or erratic altering of the time between the 500-stroke beat and the actual giving of the food.

These and other techniques of Pavlov to throw the animal mentally off balance and disrupt normal nervous stability, such as long periods of arduous work, undernourishment, threat of death coupled with sudden reprieve, are now found repeated in chronicles about the Korean prisoners of war, the Chinese communist converts and the Soviet purge trial confessors.

Pavlov found that breakdown occurs far sooner in lively or calm dogs than in the excited or melancholy extremes. These and later experiments with battle fatigue, war neurosis and war prisoners suggest, too, that the normal, cooperative human being succumbs more easily to these brainwashing techniques.

Parenthetically, these findings seem to have a curious application to our feverish ambition to be admired or loved at all cost by other nations and other peoples. This national characteristic is evidenced in many ways. Our "prestige" becomes a major issue in the presidential campaign, and new pen-pal, care-package and other such people-to-people schemes are advanced nearly every day by both government and private individuals and groups. While some of these efforts do have a constructive aspect, they are a lot like looking at one's self in the mirror. All the "good will" and "friendly feelings" in the world cannot create a job—the main thing needed in Latin America.

Pavlov and his findings received scant attention outside of Soviet Russia and were not translated into English until the early forties. On the other hand, though he remained to his death an outspoken critic of the Red regime, he was encouraged by Lenin after the revolution, and from then on he received generous support from the government, including a psychiatric clinic for the study of the application of his findings to human beings. In the field of political indoctrination, Pavlov's work came to be a major instrument of Soviet policy, as witness the fact that in 1950 an official Russian directive was issued, calling for a reorientation of all Soviet medical doctrine along Pavlovian lines.[2]

Today the communists apply these techniques on a global basis to condition the world, but especially the people of the

United States and its leaders to accept the idea that capitalism is an inefficient and wicked system that works for only a few while impoverishing the mass, that capitalism, colonialism and imperialism are one and the same thing.

In developing their grand strategy to undermine us, the Russians are quite aware that psychological techniques can win wars before they are started. Hitler was a master of this methodology and openly announced its proposed use in the text of *Mein Kampf*. He expressed his philosophy by saying that "our real wars will in fact be fought before military operations begin."

"How to achieve the moral breakdown of the enemy before the war has started," he declared, "that is the problem that interests me."[3]

Hitler, by threats of force, followed by peaceful manifestations and then, swiftly, by overpowering strikes at weak points such as the reoccupation of the Ruhr, created an image of invincibility that undermined all Europe. Britain was not unaffected and was finally spared only because she was an insular nation and had a superior fighter plane. Russia was virtually conquered and was able to redeem herself, principally, because of inherent conflicts between Hitler and his general staff over actual military operations, i.e. how to deliver the coups de grace.

Even before Hitler, however, it was Lenin who enunciated the principle: "The soundest strategy in war is to postpone operations until the moral disintegration of the enemy renders the delivery of the mortal blow both possible and easy."[4]

B. H. Liddell Hart, the noted military strategist, has documented with numerous illustrations, from the time of Alexander to the present day, this "immemorial lesson that the true aim in war is in the mind of the hostile rulers, not the bodies of their troops; that the balance between victory and defeat turns on mental impressions and only indirectly on physical blows."[5]

Now Russia in the Cold War is softening us up by measures as old as the history of war itself, aided by a full understanding of the techniques of Lenin and Hitler and the modern scientific procedures of Pavlov.

First they utilize intensive propaganda measures to convince us that, as a people, they are the bravest of the brave. They play "Russian roulette" with each other just to prove their courage. Blindly obedient troops march through mine fields to act as human detonators. Rumors fly that they have burned up a few spacemen by callous experimentation. We become convinced, to an exaggerated degree, that the Russians will throw away human life, in Shakespeare's words, "as 'twere a careless trifle."

Meanwhile we continue to nourish a converse picture of ourselves: We are nature's noblemen, gentle as kittens, unwilling to hurt a sparrow.

We desperately want to be liked, whereas we are led to believe that the Russians do not care how they are regarded. They may be gracious one minute and, in the next, are willing to take off their shoes and bang the table, get loaded at official gatherings and engage in all sorts of shocking and ungentlemanly conduct. They will fly directly in the face of what we describe as "world opinion" and detonate the 50-megaton bomb.

We have an openly avowed policy against a preventive war, having made it clear that under no conceivable circumstances would we toss the bomb first. Russia's announced national policy is just exactly the opposite: if they suspect we may be preparing to attack them, they will not hesitate to strike.

These concepts that Russia is ruthless and aggressive, while we are reticent and deeply humanistic, erode our confidence in our ability to prevail over communism and our foreign policy comes to be based on one word: fear. It assumes a hurried and eclectic aspect in which we seem to be simply reacting, in move after move, to the communist plays as they unfold.

There comes Sputnik I or any other Russian act of triumph or aggression—for example, the closing of the Brandenburg Gate, or the renewal of nuclear bomb testing in the atmosphere—and the cries in favor of summitry (Chamberlainism) mount wildly in the Western World. The Russians generously accede and we sigh with relief and happiness as doves circle Moscow and Washington. Then with a crash, the U-2 incident is revealed, the Soviets blow the Paris Meeting sky high, or the prospects of accord on some important issue such as Laos or bomb testing are worn away by months of fruitless negotiation, accompanied by gradually mounting disillusionment. Our national nervous system, hopefully if falsely predisposed to doves, now undergoes a severe shock.

President Eisenhower goes on one triumphant tour after another until the confidence of the nation in our popularity and prestige reaches a dizzying pinnacle. Then the nadir approaches and the Soviet pulls the rug in Japan, Khrushchev "kicks the President in the shins" in Paris, devastates the Paris Meeting, demands apologies for our U-2, cancels the invitation for Ike to visit Russia, and prevents our President from completing a visit to our strongest ally in the Far East.

Our conscience-stricken national panic over the revelation of U-2, the greatest intelligence weapon since Mata Hari, is a sorry measure of the extent to which the Soviets have gained mastery of our national mentality.

The spectacle of an alien Red influence being strong enough to induce the government of once-conquered Japan to deny access to our head of state is pure Pavlov, creating almost unbearable anxieties and conflicts in our psyche and further reducing our capacity to endure the tensions of the Cold War.

Our fear of being disliked in Latin America, of being thought of as "imperialists" and "interventionists," leads us to view the seizure of more than $1 billion worth of our private property in Cuba with scarcely a murmur and causes us to "throw" a military invasion of the little island. At the same time, Castro's presence in our midst, not to mention his constant insults and the adherence of much of Latin America to his cause, further adds to our tensions.

Then along comes Berlin and the seeming abandonment of the posture, long held, that we just *might* toss the bomb in a situation short of an all-out nuclear holocaust. Instead we are going to be prepared to fight any and all localized wars with localized weaponry, so that we can have a handy alternative to either all-out surrender or all-out war. Now what was once unjustified fear on our part can be realistically entertained. In view of the huge Sino-Soviet perimeter, at almost any point of which the Reds can mass large numbers of conventional troops on short order, an announced policy placing new emphasis on our nuclear reticence and our in-lieu willingness to skirmish wherever and whenever Khrushchev chooses, is truly alarming.

All of us are familiar with the effects of brainwashing in specific situations. The man who will not smoke anything but Brand X cannot, when blindfolded, tell it from any of five others. If the margarine is colored yellow and the butter is white (freshly churned) 95 per cent of the ladies present will unwittingly transfer an optical sensation to their taste buds and call the margarine "butter," describe it as "pure" and "fresh" and the butter as "greasy" and "oily."[6]

We have read of the husky, healthy pilot who, after a few days of indoctrination, suddenly goes communist and pleads for a chance to go on the air and atone for his adherence to "capitalistic imperialism."

We have often marvelled at the intensity achieved in some religious ceremonies when, at the height of chant-induced ecstasy and the moment of conversion, poisonous reptiles are fondled without injury.

We have heard tales of the gentle Chinese father who kills himself because his militant Red son has told him one too many times that he is inconvertible to the new society and not worth preserving.

We are taught that even in our own society some police interrogation methods can lead an innocent captive into a false confession, can convince both the interrogator and the victim that the confession is true.[7] The Chinese, we are told, are past masters of this technique.*

The snake and the bird, the Hitler and Quisling, are nothing new to us. But we are not prepared to believe that these very things could be happening to us in the Cold War struggle. We are losing confidence in our system and our chief motivation is fear, but we do not know why.

Our most popular economic and political writers, as the poet said, "feed hard on our discontent." *The Affluent Society* attempts to shatter our most cherished belief by telling us that the idea of individual freedom under limited government is passé—the individual has come to exercise his freedom unwisely and the only solution is for him to turn more of his personal resources over to the "public sector" for channeling into constructive purposes by the government master- planner.[9]

The Ugly American is calculated to convince us that we are a venal and incapable lot, blundering around the world making enemies at an incredible rate. This really hurts because we are always watching that old image in the mirror.[10]

And so the best-sellers go. And every time they take another libelous punch at our now-shattered ego, the foreign aid bill goes up. Every time the Bear growls or a Gagarin goes sailing around, the defense budget goes up a few billions and Khrushchev comes out with a new prediction that capitalism

---

*The Chinese communists use this method in such mundane affairs as getting a man to voluntarily turn over his business to the State.[8]

will drown itself. Thus do we substitute defense funds for courage and foreign aid for capitalism.

This fear of the Reds and loss of confidence in our system of free enterprise has a profound relationship to the problem of the economically retarded world, including the old countries of Latin America. Unlike the Soviets, we are not carrying to these uncommitted areas a militant purpose to recreate and strengthen *our* system of modern capitalism. Quite the contrary, we have adopted as our national policy the entirely negative proposition that we will support the revolutions of these nations *"regardless of which political or economic route they should choose to freedom."*[11] (Inaugural Address of the President, Jan. 20, 1961.)

In other words, we are attempting to meet the explicit anti-capitalist, pro-communist offensive of the Soviets with an announced policy that we shall have no policy; or, as in the case of the President's ad-libs with the Izvestia reporter mentioned earlier, with the pronouncement that communists are agreeable to us so long as they come to power through the polling place.

In embracing the concept that all sorts of different political and economic systems can lead to "freedom," we encourage revolution, regardless of whether it will lead to communism or any other system of government alien to our own. We implicitly reiterate the very distrust of our way of life inculcated into us by the Russian brainwashing.

Stung last fall by the Belgrade "neutrals' " tolerant attitude toward the Soviet resumption of testing above ground, coupled with their charges of imperialism against us, President Kennedy was prompted to suggest that, in administering our aid programs, "we should give particular attention to the needs of those countries which share our view of the world crisis." Subsequently, as the *New York Times* editorial put it, he "amplified his formula" by saying that he did not maintain

that governments receiving our loans and grants "must agree
with us."

"This is common sense," soliloquized the *Times*. "The
last thing we could wisely plan to do would be to make other
peoples over in our own image."[12]

This curious notion—that impatience with intransigence is
per se dictatorial and should be promptly repressed—was not
entirely original with the *Times*. It had already been laid
down as a basic plank in our foreign aid program. Said
Secretary of State Rusk in a preface to the "New Act for International Development," "We do not wish to make the world
over in our image."[13]

Is our image so bad that we may not even try? The whole
thing sounds as if the problem were to avoid "feuding" between two large and powerful nations, to seek some happy
compromise, and meanwhile to prevent third parties from
"choosing up sides," rather than what it is: A struggle between
two systems, one of which is built on the principle of freedom
and the other of slavery.

Little wonder that our ambassador to a Latin American
country could say to me, "I wish you wouldn't use that word
'capitalism' down here. The people don't like it because it
smacks of imperialism and has overtones of colonialism." Unwittingly, the speaker disclosed to me that he, too, had been
successfully brainwashed by the communist propaganda, which
always pictures "capitalism" as a fat tyrant with dollar-signs
on his vest, chewing on a big cigar and wringing the neck of
some poor peasant.

Another United States ambassador in Latin America said
to me, "In my opinion, the objectives of our private enterprises down here are inconsistent with America's goals in the
Cold War."

This point of view was not new to me. About a year
earlier I had experienced a briefing on Latin America by a
State Department official the burden of which was that the

future of private capital development south of our borders is dead.

One of our economic officers in another Latin American nation recently told me, "Anti-Americanism increases in proportion to our private investments in these countries."

No wonder, when the head of our Voice of America contingent in another Latin American country could say, "We do not consider it politic to openly defend our firms doing business here."

In a non-classified communique from our embassy in one newly emerged nation of Africa to our State Department, the official advocated the open espousal of socialism, collective farming and the like, saying this is the only way we could "compete" with Russian aid programs there. This is an endorsement of the views of the socialist Swedish anthropologist, Dr. Gunnar Myrdal, who writes: "Apparently nobody in the advanced countries sees any other way out of the difficulties which are mounting in the underdeveloped countries other than the socialistic one, however different one's attitudes may be toward the economic problems at home."[14]

The net effect of these attitudes and practices is summed up in a statement from a recent study obtained by our Senate Foreign Relations Committee: "The United States must accept, *and in some instances even encourage,* the neutrality or non-alignment of underdeveloped nations in the Cold War. The existence of a sizeable uncommitted group of nations can serve as a powerful force in reducing international tensions."[15] (Emphasis added.)

Here is the ultimate delusion—actual advocacy of a system other than ours. The meaning of "non-alignment" is transparent enough and certainly it does not mean communism or feudalism or absolute monarchy or dictatorship. What it encourages in practice is socialism—heavy governmental proprietorship and intervention in the economy and lives of the citizenry—the very opposite of the revolutionary choice we made in 1776, and the quickest known road to communism. Naturally, our own extreme liberals are ecstatic at the prospect of ringing us with socialist states. Armed with new mountains of foreign aid, free from the daily scrutiny of domestic press and a sometimes balky Congress, they can cheerfully push forward the frontiers of socialism.

The proponents of large United States foreign aid use the threat of massive Soviet aid to lobby the Congress into granting ever-larger aid appropriations. In the official State Department presentation of the $26 billion Kennedy aid program to the Congress, which embraces the Latin American Alliance for Progress, profound concern is expressed over the communist bloc aid to less-developed non-communist countries.

The phrases employed in this document are deeply revealing of the way in which our aid planners regard competitive Russian aid. "There seems to be," they say with more than a hint of professional concern, "a growing receptivity to aid from the communist bloc even among countries close to the United States which desire the benefits of aid and at the same time wish to reduce what they regard as drawbacks of an exclusive tie with the United States."[16]

Our aid experts can nevertheless write about Russian aid with a curious detachment and even a hint of envy. "On the whole," they say, "it would appear that the aid of the communist bloc countries has been negotiated and administered with skill, speed and sensitivity."

Presumably, it is said, the communist aid-givers "encounter some of the same nationalistic, neutralist and bureaucratic sentiments and difficulties the United States has met." To give the devil his due, however, the document does admit that "most bloc personnel have confined themselves to their proper fields of activity," by which the authors presumably mean to convey the idea that our Soviet aid adversaries have a separate crew of specialists for things like, say, murder and sabotage.

Not for one minute, however, are we going to let the Bloc

get away with claiming they originated this business. They may have invented electricity and the cotton gin, and have the biggest missile booster, but their aid efforts "followed those of the United States." Indeed, to get one more twist, their copying of our aid tactics is a "recognition that the United States has used good political judgment in attaching such importance over the past decade and more to economic and technical aid to the less-developed countries."

To show our deep dedication to aid and our consequent objectivity, we are quick to point out that we should by no means "seek to prevent countries from accepting aid" from the Bloc, for that would "open us to the charge of not being sympathetic to the economic development of other countries except on our own political terms."

All in all, to close on a reassuring and comforting note, we should not be "alarmed" or become "frantic." We should treat the Bloc aid as a "challenge and a reminder" that we cannot afford "less than a major effort" in meeting this competition.

These fear tactics employed upon the Congress and the American public are highly effective in unleashing the Treasury's purse strings. A balky Congress in 1961 came through with pretty much what the Administration asked for, after being bombarded with allegations concerning large-scale Red attempts to woo the uncommitted peoples of the world through foreign aid. In the light of the known facts, however, this fear campaign is revealed as considerably exaggerated. As against our $104 billion of foreign aid since World War II, the Soviet Union has granted just $2 billion to non-communist nations, according to official Soviet figures recently released.[17]

It seems obvious that Russia's primary aid responsibilities are going to have to be directed toward Red China, the world's largest and most underdeveloped country, and to her satellites—especially those newly acquired, such as Cuba. The

Soviet study reveals that communist nations received $8 billion
in Red aid while the uncommitted ones received $2 billion.

If we were to say "go and get it" to every duplicitous neutral threatening to go to the Reds for aid, doubtless the latter
would soon be crying "Uncle" and the runaways would be
home for supper.

The point, however, is not that communist aid is trivial
or uninfluential. It would be foolish to so contend. For one
thing, it has been concentrated in a few important places.
India has been by far the largest recipient. Soviet operations
there, as of about a year ago, were concerned with thirty-two
plants and installations, with the credits totaling more than
$800 million.[18] Of course, all of these result in state-owned-
and-operated enterprises. In steel, India now has three state-
owned plants, one of them built on long-term credits by the
Russian government.

The Russian success can be measured from the fact that
the Indian government recently turned down a request by the
Tata Mill, which is a privately owned mill with 47,000 Indian
shareholders, for permission to put up a strip mill, upon the
ground that it is now government policy to reserve most steel
expansion for the government-owned sector of the steel
industry.[19]

As India goes so goes Ceylon, you might say. In April,
1962, the government of Ceylon, whose oil sources are the
Soviet Union, Rumania and Egypt, confiscated 108 private
service stations selling Shell, Esso and Caltex gasoline. According to news accounts, the United States Embassy protest
was limited to "advice . . . that the United States government
and public would not look with favor on American-owned
equipment being used to distribute Soviet oil."[19a]

Doubtless, too, the Russian and Chinese Soviets will make
every effort to make a Red showplace out of Cuba, and surely
they could succeed, at least for a time, since Cuba is tiny and
rich in confiscated U. S. property.

As soon as the communists established themselves in the tiny Caribbean nation of British Guiana, the Soviets pushed East Germany into the aid business. The latter has offered to establish ten state-owned factories in British Guiana on a barter basis, taking rice, bran, timber and diamonds in payment.[19b]

No, certainly, the point is not that Red government-to-government aid is insignificant. Rather it is that we have chosen to meet the challenge of underdevelopment and communism with precisely the same, ill-advised techniques.

The truly frightening thing about the treatment of Bloc aid in the presentation to Congress is what it does *not* say. In comparing and indeed praising the Russian aid outlays, the presentation fails to observe the fundamental fact that our major development instrument is the flow of our private capital, a weapon unknown to the Russian arsenal.

More than mere words are missing when United States government aid can be compared with communist government aid in an impersonal evaluation that omits even a single word of reference to the most vital and fundamental of all distinctions between capitalism and communism, between a free society and a totalitarian one.

The reason, to face the unpleasant truth, is that we have been brainwashed into an abandonment of capitalism as an instrument of foreign policy, and into a full-fledged adoption of communistic foreign economic methodology.

What is the difference in quality between a Peace Corps-man and a friendly Russian technician? Which is worse, a Russian barter deal of Brazilian coffee for Czech machinery, or a gift of surplus wheat from the United States that displaces a wheat sale Argentinians might have made in Brazil?

In fact, our preoccupation with government aid frequently takes place while "private" trade goes to the Soviets. In August 1961, our embassy in Bolivia reported to Washington that a modest business improvement was anticipated because of the expectation of greater United States aid to the state-owned mines. In the same report, they revealed that "Iron Curtain suppliers achieved several *commercial* successes in the Bolivian market during the quarter," chiefly in the automotive and hospital equipment field.[20] (Emphasis supplied.)

Russia invented the 5- and 10-year plan of state-dictated development, but now as a condition precedent to receiving our government aid, each Latin American government must submit a 10-year plan to us for the approval of our government officials.

Our foreign aid master-planners are opposed to the idea that development can be left to private growth aided by limited government nourishment, by way of creating a climate in which capital expansion can flourish. Instead they are dedicated to the proposition that long-range government planning, backed by long-range government aid expenditures, is the modern economic truth as applied to areas such as Latin America.

The government's "Highlights of President Kennedy's New Act for International Development" states: "The process of fostering the development process requires . . . the preparation of an overall integrated development plan for each country in order to avoid a piecemeal approach."

In a Department of State publication introduced by President Kennedy and entitled "A New Program for a Decade of Development," it is said: "Putting countries on a substantial development basis means fashioning an overall plan for each country, in order that *every* proposed project fits into a well-planned system of priorities. That is the *only* way to be sure of putting first things first."[21] (Emphasis supplied.)

"Foreign aid now," said the then director of our foreign aid establishment, Henry R. LaBouisse, in San Francisco on July 20, 1961, "is a most powerful and constructive element of the foreign policy of our country."

Foreign aid should no longer be thought of as an emergency

or "crisis" measure. "We want to move gradually away from this type of emergency assistance," he said. "We intend to devote increasing efforts to the encouragement and support of *long range planning* and development by aid recipients . . . We propose, therefore, to make a concentrated effort to have each recipient country identify its *total requirements* for a *given* period ahead . . . what are the *priorities,* what reforms are necessary, what can be drawn from its own resources and what external assistance is required." (Emphasis added.)

A major portion of our Alliance for Progress aid is to be allocated and administered by the new Inter-American Development Bank, whose chairman said at the opening of the Bank's annual meeting in Rio de Janeiro in April 1961: "We are by no means hostile to socialism."[22]

In response, Secretary of the Treasury Dillon said: "The phrase 'self-help' should *not be interpreted to mean conditions* imposed upon a country as the price of external assistance . . . As we see it, development planning does not imply regimentation of economies through governmental controls. It does mean *consistent programming* of public investment aimed at broad development targets—programming supplemented by economic and social policies designed to activate a nation's energies and resources, *including the indispensable private sector.*" (Emphasis supplied.)

In other words, the intervenor's dream—a state-planned, state-programmed society—coupled with the idea that there must be some kind of a private sector as a means, perhaps, of distinguishing the economy from what the communists mean when they advocate socialism.

Says Adolph A. Berle, Chairman, Task Force on Latin America, Department of State, "A mighty weapon is the modern instrument of social planning, to make sure that the surge of production does not merely make the rich richer, but directly advantages the poor."

It should be obvious to us that huge amounts of government-to-government aid can only result in the expansion of the centralized power of the recipient government officials and thus we sponsor the very ideals our Constitution rejects—that a few individuals should have absolute power over the rest.

"I believe that the adoption of comprehensive planning measures by these countries runs the risk of socializing if not communizing them," writes Peter T. Bauer, Cambridge University economist and author.[23]

Recently, the noted economist Milton Freedman of Chicago, in commenting upon the present fetish for over-all government-directed development plans, coupled the ultimate truth with an amusing touch: "the striking thing about those criteria," said he, "is that under them the United States of America would never have qualified."[23a]

Recently, a distinguished American, Robert L. Garner, retired from the presidency of the International Finance Corporation, a subsidiary of the World Bank. Mr. Garner served five years in this post of distinction and the previous nine years as vice president of the World Bank itself. No man in the world today is better qualified by experience and ability to speak of the development problems of the less developed areas of the world, including Latin America. In a speech in Vienna in September 1961, Mr. Garner, in summing up his long government banking experience, expressed two major conclusions. The first was that "the most assured method of getting development, barring outright totalitarianism, is to rely on private initiative and the private profit motive." The second conclusion was a conviction that "government-to-government financial aid cannot successfully be used to gain and hold political advantages for the country supplying the funds."[24]

In a recent article in *Fortune* Magazine, Max Ways says:

The truth is that for many years United States foreign policy has been unhinged from the American political character and interests. United States policy should be based not on some mirage of "world opinion" but on American belief in individual freedom under limited government. And limited government is no mean or negative concept to proclaim before the world; it is a prerequisite for the freedom of the individual citizen and for a minimum of international order.[25]

In Latin America my wife and I sat in a small, book-strewn apartment overlooking Rio's sparkling Copacabana beach and conversed with Albert Byington Jr., on the subject of brainwashing. A third-generation Brazilian of American extraction, this tall and reflective man is head of Conclap, the private Brazilian organization established to wage war on a dozen fronts against the heavy communist infiltration of Brazilian life.

The very day the Soviet trade group arrives in Brazil ready with loud promises of advantageous barter deals to be made over coffee, Conclap will have readied as a propaganda counter-measure an announcement of a Hungarian's defection, and accurate statistics regarding Russian previous "dumping" of bartered coffee on world markets.

Byington's study of Soviet methodology and the Western response has led him deep into the caverns of mental preconditioning at the global level.

"The only possible way to win the Cold War here now," he said to me, "is through a program of action that will prove that private enterprise is *in fact* a more efficient and more productive kind of society than communism and Castroism."

Khrushchev knows this, if we do not, and so does "Che" Guevara, whose clever maneuvers on the part of the Red Internationale in Latin America are frequently hidden behind the antics of its stage-struck front man, Fidel Castro. "Capitalism and communism," Khrushchev said in laying down a cornerstone of Soviet party policy last year, "are engaged in a critical competition for favor with the underdeveloped countries. Communism is bound to win because it has a more efficient, rapid, better planned system for lifting people out of darkness and poverty."[26]

→Sad to relate, we appear thus far to have chosen this system for ourselves, in every important aspect: long-term government-to-government credits, 10-year master plans, gifts of government wheat, government coffee quotas, government financing of state industries, pervasive government allocation of resources and dictation of development priorities. We seem to have elected to "out-run" communist aid with more of the same.

Our Secretary of the Treasury, at Punta del Este in Uruguay in August 1961, said, "future development loans made by our new aid agency will be on a long-term basis, running where appropriate up to 50 years. We also intend to make the bulk of these loans at very low or zero rates of interest."[27] Presumably, as in the past, these development "loans" to Latin American governments would be repayable in inflation-prone foreign currencies. Altogether they may be considered grants, described as "loans" to assuage United States public opinion and certain foreign attitudes.

While the course of foreign aid is never easy to predict or trace, public utterances by officials concerned indicate that our government aid bill for Latin America alone may amount to $1.7 billion per year or, for 10 years, $17 billion in toto,* in soft "loans," outright grants, grants to international welfare agencies for Latin American use, and Export-Import Bank loans.** This does not include United States "grants" of an untold amount of surplus food (sold for soft currency and 85 per cent "loaned" back), Food for Peace, nor the Peace Corps,

---

*The figure projects to about $50 billion worldwide in 10-year United States economic aid to the less developed, excluding our share of contributions to international funds and military aid. In this writer's opinion our current approach to the rest of the less-developed world is, for like reasons, as badly in need of redirection as it is in the case of Latin America.

**The figure was $902 million for the first 10 months of the Alliance for Progress ended April 30, 1962 (Congressional Record, June 6, 1962, p. 9114).

nor our share of World Bank, International Finance Corporation, and International Monetary Fund Loans, nor military aid.[28]

These funds will go to governments to be spent in accordance with "master plans" not yet developed; meanwhile they go into emergency projects.

These same sources have suggested that United States private industry will bring another $300 million per year to Latin America in new investment, and that the public and private sectors of other developed countries will add a like amount, bringing the total new capital to $2 billion per year.

Under present risky environmental conditions in Latin America, and in the absence of any new inducements to attract these projected private capital outflows, these private investment predictions seem extremely doubtful, to say the least. Taking these predictions at face value, however, it is apparent that we are placing our reliance, in overwhelming preponderance upon public funds. And the melancholy fact is that, absent a change of policy, this reliance on foreign aid as our chief instrument will grow rather than recede, as Latin American needs and pleas mount, despite the fact that Congress has technically retained the right of annual review of the program.

Yet even though amounts are being increased, perhaps doubled, there is nothing essentially new in the idea of United States government aid to the less developed countries. We have been at it for some time and the glimpses afforded by the past are most unrewarding.

In concluding a comprehensive study of the past course of our foreign aid program, conducted by Pulitzer Prize-winning Felix Morley, former editor of the *Washington Post,* and his daughter, the authors state: "The patchwork history of foreign aid is more complicated than inspiring. It has been a succession of improvisations for the most part stimulated by hostile communist initiatives."[29]

Guatemalan expert Edwin A. Lahey, who was one of those originally instrumental in bringing about the aid program for Guatemala after the communists were thrown out in 1954, said recently:

"What happened to that $115 million we sent to Guatemala?

"How can you spend that much money on 3 million persons without making a dent in their desolate way of life?

"It took some doing, but we did it.

"This is the big glossed-over question in the new . . . crash program called the 'Alliance for Progress' . . .

"Guatemala is only a small laboratory specimen."[30]

In *The Case of our Vanishing Aid Dollars in Haiti*, author Lester Velie points out that our current outlays in assistance and cash grants to Haiti are equivalent to about one-half of her entire national budget. Yet this aid takes on a "mad hatter quality," he says, since Haiti has no budget director or controller, and "our government is . . . in the curious position of giving millions of dollars to a bankrupt who conceals his assets."[31] No wonder conditions in Haiti in the last ten years have gotten worse instead of better despite $77 million in U.S. aid!

The communist conspiracy cannot be met by a divisive receptiveness toward socialism and other alien philosophies, by a fear of hurting the feelings of the uncommitted or incurring the wrath of the communists, by the adoption of instruments of foreign economic policy peculiar to communism. It can only be met by an international crusade in favor of our kind of modern private capitalism in which the United States, as its foremost exponent, provides militant leadership.

A reformation of United States foreign policy along these lines will necessitate the abandonment of some and the reorganization of all of our foreign aid programs so as to render them more pertinent and consistent with a rationale expressing confidence in, rather than distrust of, the values inherent in our own society. This will also require the adoption of new policies and programs, to be outlined herein, insuring the purposeful enlistment of our private sector in the struggle to recreate, through private development, the kind of modern widely-shared capitalism that alone can spell the demise of communism.

The fact that we may not succeed in every place at every turn, or all at once or in our time, the fact that we may not be "popular" with everyone, are not important at all. What is important is that we stand up for the ideals which, pursued at the time we were underdeveloped, have made us strong and free.

The mere adoption of clear national purposes to this effect would throw off the fear and doubts with which we have been indoctrinated.

CHAPTER VI

REFERENCES

1 William Sargant, *Battle for the Mind,* Doubleday, New York, 1957, p. 35.

2 *Ibid,* p. 30.

3 B. H. Liddell Hart, *Strategy,* Praeger, New York, 1954, p. 224.

4 *Ibid,* p. 164.

5 *Ibid,* p. 219.

6 Vance Packard, *The Hidden Persuaders,* Pocket Books, Inc., New York, 1957, pp. 125-126.

7 Sargant, *Battle for the Mind, supra,* pp. 185-218.

8 *Ibid,* p. 171.

9 John Galbraith, *The Affluent Society,* Houghton-Mifflin, New York, 1958.

10 William J. Lederer and Eugene Burdick, *The Ugly American,* Norton & Co., New York, 1958.

[11] President Kennedy, Inaugural Address, Jan. 20, 1961.

[12] *New York Times* (edit.), Oct. 14, 1961.

[13] State Department Pamphlet, "New Act For International Development," 1961.

[14] *The Underdeveloped Lands: A Dilemma of the International Economy,* compiled and edited by DeVere E. Petony, Chandler Publishing Co., San Francisco, 1960, pp. 69-95, esp. p. 92.

[15] "The Operational Aspects of U.S. Foreign Policy," Maxwell, Graduate School, Syracuse University, 1959. "Strategy for the Sixties," Foreign Policy Clearing Association, Washington, D. C., 1959, p. 84.

[16] "An Act for International Development," State Department, June 1961, pp. 185-189.

[17] F. P. Bystrov, "International Credit Relations of the Soviet Union," *Foreign Trade, U.S.S.R.,* September, 1961.

[18] Report of the Office of United Nations Secretary General, quoted in *New York Times,* Oct. 16, 1961.

[19] *New York Times,* Dec. 26, 1960.

[19a] *Wall Street Journal,* Apr. 30, 1962.

[19b] *New York Times,* Apr. 4, 1962.

[20] Foreign Commerce Weekly, United States Department of Commerce, Aug. 21, 1961, p. 13.

[21] "Highlights of President Kennedy's Act for International Development," State Department, 1961.

[22] Clemente Mariani, Proceedings of second meeting of Board of Governors, Inter-American Development Bank, Rio de Janeiro, Brazil, Apr. 10, 1961, p. 11.

[23] P. T. Bauer, "Economic Growth and the New Orthodoxy," *Fortune* Magazine, May, 1958.

[23a] Milton Freedman, "An Alternative to Aid," *Wall Street Journal,* Apr. 30, 1962.

[24] *New York Times,* Sept. 21, 1961.

[25] Max Ways, "The Illusions that Thwart U.S. Policy," *Fortune* Magazine, July, 1961.

[26] *New York Times,* Aug. 1, 1961.

[27] *Wall Street Journal,* Aug. 12, 1961.

[28] *San Francisco Examiner,* Aug. 8, 1961, Aug. 10, 1961, Aug. 16, 1961; *Wall Street Journal,* Aug. 8, 1961, Aug. 11, 1961; *New York Times,* Aug. 9, 1961.

[29] Felix and Lorna Morley, *The Patchwork History of Foreign Aid,* American Private Enterprise Association, Washington, D.C., 1961, p. 51.

[30] Edwin A. Lahey, "End of a Latin Love Affair," *San Francisco Chronicle,* June 30, 1961.

[31] Lester Velie, "The Case of Our Vanishing Dollars in Haiti," Latin American Report (Vol. IV, No. 8), International Trade Mart, New Orleans 16, La.

Private Investment: Neglected Weapon of the Cold War ?

It has long been an economic axiom that the rate of productive capital formation through new private investment is a key factor in economic growth.

"It hardly needs elaboration," wrote William B. Dale, until recently the senior international economist of Stanford Research Institute, "that capital formation at a high level has historically accompanied high rates of economic growth."[1]

One would suppose, therefore, that our principal method of accelerating the rate of capital formation would be to induce more United States private capital to flow to Latin America, for investment in job-producing plants and facilities that would speed Latin America's development. Not only would this create more private jobs, consumer expenditures, and savings, but it would automatically displace a given amount of government-to-government activity.

However, as we have seen, this hitherto axiomatic approach has been running into opposition on a variety of fronts. Distrust of business as a purveyor of the things Latin America needs is not confined to the echelons of government, either.

Recently a noted economist and author said to me: "Private enterprise—our business and industry—has had its way in Latin America for a long time. They have had their chance to contribute constructively to the solution of Latin America's problems. They have failed and now it is up to government."

Then, too, it must be admitted that the ability of our foreign industries to act as our primary development ambassadors is somewhat impaired by the intense propaganda which the communists level at them, with the socialists and nationalists chiming in when it suits their purpose.

"I will have to concede," said Carlos Trouyet, sometimes called the Economic Revolutionary of Mexico, "that United States business is a scapegoat for many of our ills."

Furthermore, in addition to communist propaganda and just plain anti-Yankeeism, United States business in Latin America has had tough sledding in other respects. The threat of confiscation is always there, exemplified in the thirties by Mexico's nationalization of our private oil interests, and more recently by the Cuban seizure of all of our property. As we shall see, our government offers practically no protection against this kind of risk and none can be purchased in private markets. For this reason, and because of Cuba and other recent communist manifestations, our investments in Latin America are on the decline.

Are the handicaps of the Cold War too much for private industry? Is my economist friend correct when he says the private sector has had its time at bat and struck out?

Certainly one would suppose that our capitalistic merchandise in Latin America itself would be the showcase sample by which we would inevitably be judged rather than by anything we might send in government aid or impart by advertising our wares through Voice of America propaganda or other media. Therefore it behooves us to take an intimate look at the quality of our private efforts in Latin America, to determine the nature of the part they are playing in the closely related struggle of development and Cold War.

Is American enterprise in these lands struggling purposefully for its life in the front lines of the Cold War, assuming huge non-commercial risks, selling free enterprise and creating capitalists, marketing its equity stock on the instalment plan, finding new products and teaching new skills, helping employees and people of small means to acquire a share in the future? Or, as the communists, socialists and nationalists claim—is it shipping home the wealth of the host peoples and leaving nothing but unsightly holes in the ground, draining the wealth of the country, living in luxury amidst poverty, practically manufacturing ingredients for the insatiable communist propaganda machine? And, as a corollary, is our government really doing anything to put a uniform on our major Cold War weapon? Is it offering any meaningful incentives, benefits or protections to help make our profit system work in these formidable environments?

The answer to these questions necessitates a closer look at our private trade with and our capital investment in the regions to the south, for it is upon these enormous, privately created economic foundations that any new foreign economic policies of ours will have to be erected.

The dollar volume of our private merchandise trade with Latin America over the past seven* years adds to a staggering total of nearly $54 billion, an amount exceeded only narrowly by our two-way trade with all of Western Europe over the same period of years. Our trade with Latin America is nearly 40 times as great as her trade with the entire Sino-Soviet bloc which has been running in the neighborhood of $200 million per year.[2]

Furthermore, this enormous volume of commerce between the United States and Latin America is characterized by a virtual balance between our exports to Latin America and our imports from that area, whereas, in the case of every other major area of the world, we are a net exporter. Our exports have exceeded our imports in dollar value over this period in

---

*1955 to 1961.

the case of Canada, Western Europe, Asia and Africa.[3] In the case of Western Europe alone, in 1961, we enjoyed a $2.7 billion export surplus.

This relatively balanced trade between the United States and Latin America as a whole does not apply universally to every part of Latin America, of course. In recent periods, the balance of trade between the United States and Argentina has been quite adverse to the latter, although this is now being remedied in the balance of payments sense by a large inflow of United States private capital investment into manufacturing in Argentina.

In the case of Mexico, too, our exports substantially exceed our imports, but this again is more than offset by the net volume of tourist and other private expenditures in her favor. Our trade balance is heavily in favor of Venezuela, due to her large exports of petroleum to United States buyers.[4]

The share our people currently purchase of Latin America's major commodities, as illustrated by the year 1957, is in most cases impressive: 40 per cent of her oil, nitrates, sugar and bananas; two thirds of her coffee, lead and zinc; a third of her cotton; half or more of her copper, iron ore, and cocoa; nearly 50 per cent of her tobacco; 92 per cent of her wool.[5]

This picture of the great size and importance of our two-way trade with Latin America, including the overall favorable balance between exports and imports, fails to take into account some of the less satisfactory aspects and trends of Latin America's trade with us, especially in recent years.

The first is that the amount we buy from Latin America, instead of growing, has just about held even since 1954—holding close to $3.5 billion.* Our imports from every other area

---

*i.e., $3.328 billion in 1955, $3.589 billion in 1958, $3.528 billion in 1960. Senate Studies, pp. 98, 155; Survey of Current Business, August 1961; President's Economic Report, January 1961, p. 212.

of the world except Africa have grown steadily and substantially during this same period: imports from Canada increased approximately 15 per cent; from Western Europe 75 per cent;
from Asia, 40 per cent. Most of the growth in Asia is traceable
to one developed country, Japan; Africa stood nearly as still as
Latin America. The fact that our purchases from the developed areas of the world have jumped ahead, while those from
the underdeveloped regions have stood virtually still, seems
to bear out United Nations' findings, referred to earlier, that
in recent periods the industrial nations have been in the
process of displacing raw material supplies from the non-industrial world by increasing their own domestic production,
by new processing technology and by the development of
synthetics.

Leaving out petroleum, Latin American exports to us have
even fared worse than is indicated by these findings since
petroleum, her largest export by far—accounting for about
25 per cent of all Latin American exports—has made both
volume and price gains over the period.

A second disappointing aspect of Latin American trade
in these same years is the overall decline in the prices United
States citizens pay for major Latin American commodity imports. Major agricultural products such as coffee, cotton and
wheat, and metals such as lead and zinc, have experienced
major price declines. While others such as crude oil, copper
and bananas have seen price rises, the overall price index has
fallen in the neighborhood of 10-15 per cent in the past six
years.[6] Even these absolute price declines do not present the
entire picture in this respect. At the same time, what is called
the "terms of trade" in economic circles, have moved in a direction adverse to Latin America. That is to say, the unit price
she pays for the things she needs to import—especially the
machinery and equipment needed for more rapid industrializa-

tion—have risen in relation to the unit prices she receives for her own exported raw materials.*

This summary of Latin America's current export-import situation really tells the story of her deep malaise. A relative export decline while most of the world enjoys increases, adverse terms of trade, insufficient foreign exchange to finance needed expansion in the manufacturing sector, punitive capital-draining tax and exchange rates levied by Latin America upon her own chief export industries. . . . All these, combined with the fastest growing and perhaps least productive population of the world, spell out the deepening Latin American tragedy.

As mentioned earlier, the answer does not lie in higher export price umbrellas and quota systems for Latin America's commodities. And yet, at the Inter-American Economic Conference at Punta del Este in Uruguay in September 1961, the United States government promised to join 28 coffee-producing countries in a new international scheme to bolster Latin American income by jacking up coffee prices. The wisdom of this course was sharply challenged in a contemporaneous editorial.[7]

Latin American countries are the world's biggest coffee producers. One of their problems is overproduction. It is forecast that if the present attitude of our State Department persists, an increase of as much as seven to eight cents a pound can be expected by 1963 as the American coffee drinker's contribution to the Administration's foreign-aid program in the southern hemisphere, in addition to the $20 billion to be provided in the "Alliance for Progress" program.

---

*While terms of trade are not as favorable as they were six years ago, still a disparity of 15 per cent need not be disastrous. It depends on costs of production, which have declined, and on volume which obviously has been large. A part of the overall decline is the result of "stabilization" of prices of products which has underwritten overproduction.

This country's policy of paying a bonus above world prices for Cuban sugar failed to halt the spread of communist influence in that country, and there is little to suggest that a similar overpayment for coffee to woo Latin Americans would be any more successful. Aside from that, however, a substantial boost in coffee prices can be expected to do Latin American countries long-run economic harm which will more than offset whatever temporary benefits they are counting on.

They need only refer to our $8.6 billion stockpile of surplus wheat, corn, cotton and other commodities to appreciate how fixing prices at artificially high levels encourages continued overproduction and discourages consumption. If that experience doesn't impress the coffee growers as relevant, they may pause to recall what happened in 1954 when coffee prices went through the roof as a result of heavy weather damage to the Brazilian crop.

It was those high prices that stimulated overplanting of trees and helped generate present surplus problems. American consumers were so irked that they turned to substitute beverages, halting the upward trend in per capita coffee consumption, which has remained barely stable since then.

If coffee producers wish to destroy their markets, high fixed prices are a good way to do it. Spot of tea, anyone?

An even simpler way of analyzing the attempt to pass off a coffee price rise on the American consumer would be to recognize that at some point the cagey housewife on a budget will start to dilute her husband's lunch-bucket coffee. The even more sensitive public eating places give free extra cups when prices are low, use smaller cups and give no refills when the cost is up.

The solution lies *not* in international price fixing, but in export to Latin America from the private sector of the industrialized nations of the free world, especially the United States, of the investment capital necessary to enlarge Latin America's industrial plant. Incentive policies on our part to this end, if coupled with cooperative policies on the part of Latin America herself, could rapidly reduce Latin American unemployment, diversify her exports, restore her competitiveness in world markets, reduce her reliance upon the export of non-processed commodities and upon the resulting importation of finished goods and processed foodstuffs.

Venezuela, a country potentially rich in agricultural products, including dairy output, has nevertheless imported for many years a very substantial quantity of dried milk. Even today, she produces less than 20 per cent of her needed supply, importing the balance. To induce greater local manufacture, she now restricts import permits of dried milk by local manufacturers to a ratio of four pounds of permitted imports for each pound manufactured locally. However, since there is limited internal private capital in Venezuela today, this measure seems more calculated to reduce imports of dried milk than to stimulate a greater local supply.

Venezuela, a rich land nearly half again as large as Texas, with six and one-half million people, normally imports 673,000 hatching eggs weekly and a million eating eggs daily.[8]

This kind of illustration can be duplicated for countless commodities, in the case of nearly every Latin American nation. For example, from 1945 to 1959, Chile imported over $1.2 billion worth of food products. It has been estimated that three fourths of these expenditures for food imports could have been saved by using commodities that can be produced in Chile.[9] Additional incentives on the part of the United States and the Latin American countries are needed to attract to Latin America far more new *private* profit-making capital investments from the United States in order to enhance Latin American development and at the same time to alter her unfavorable trade picture.

The fundamental interdependence of Latin America's foreign trade and her industrial plant is therefore patently clear. And again, the role of our private sector is a dominant one, for just as private United States citizens and firms buy the largest share of Latin America's exports—more than 40 per cent of

her total exports to all of the world—so do our private corporations, firms and individuals own by far the largest foreign-
owned share of her privately owned business and industrial
sector.

These direct long-term private investments in Latin America now add up to $8.4 billion,* around 20 per cent of all total
gross fixed investment in Latin America.

Nearly twice as many United States firms are engaged in
business in Latin America as are listed on the New York Stock
Exchange. Almost without exception, every kind of production, including oil, copper, iron ore, nitrates; every kind of
agriculture and husbandry, including coffee, sugar cane, wool
and beef; every kind of fabrication, including steel, paper,
petrochemicals; telephone, light, heat and power; and mer-
chandising of a thousand kinds is carried on somewhere in the
republics to the south by firms employing private investment
capital of United States citizens. Every United States shareholder of nearly every major and numerous smaller United
States firms—nearly 3,000 firms in all—has a stake in Latin
America.

The magnitude of these investments may be gauged from
the fact that in 1957 alone these *United States private enterprises paid out $1.5 billion in wages and salaries to Latin
Americans.* They employed in Latin America nearly one
million native workers, a larger native work force than
any except Western Europe. Only 2 per cent of all employees

---

*United States Department of Commerce Survey of Current
Business, August 1961. This is the "book value" of all investments in
which the United States share of ownership is 25 per cent or more.
The figure gives effect to depreciation and obsolescence as well as
decline in dollar book value due to local currency decline in relation to the dollar. Market value has been ordinarily regarded as
being far more than the book value figure. But whether it is more
or less now depends on the outcome of the struggle between capital
ism and communism described herein.[10]

were sent from the United States. Our firms paid over $1 billion in taxes to Latin American governments, including more than one-half billion dollars in income taxes. These tax payments by our firms were estimated to represent 20 per cent of all Latin American government revenues.

Approximately $3 billion were spent in that year by our companies in current purchases of materials and outside services in Latin America, which in turn generated substantial additional employment for Latin Americans.

U. S. companies made $38 billion of total sales, including $10.5 billion of export sales, of which $3.8 billion went to the United States. Our firms made 30 per cent of all Latin American exports that year.

In that year, 1957, if one sums up the total paid by our firms for labor, taxes, and locally produced materials and services, it may be deduced that our firms earned and saved for Latin America $6 billion in foreign exchange.

In a more direct balance-of-payments sense, U. S. firms in Latin America exported $3.8 billion of Latin American products to the United States, and brought in about $1 billion of new capital from the United States. These gains to Latin America from our business operations there were offset only by their remittances to the United States of nine tenths of $1 billion in dividends and fees, and by their import to Latin America of $1 billion worth of equipment and components.

After paying Latin American taxes, United States manufacturing firms in 1957 retained and reinvested in Latin America $3 out of every $5 of their net profits.[11]

These are impressive figures and reflect the vital influence our private business operations have on Latin American employment and development. They are quite beyond the scope of any possible government-to-government aid and, furthermore, they generate their own expansion through the repetitive reinvestment of earnings.

Yet in reality, in relation to the size and rate of expansion of our domestic industrial plant, and especially in relation to the capital needs of Latin America, our investments there are pitifully small and are expanding at an even more pathetic rate. For example, in the United States domestic economy we lay down at present, in the way of new plant and equipment alone, nearly $40 billion each year—or about five times as much each year as our total all-time investments in Latin America. Moreover, private U. S. investors just lost, in Cuba, $1 billion of their $8 billion* total Latin American investment, reducing it still further.

Expropriation or outright confiscation; the fear of expropriation; socialism and other brands of statism; inadequate, indifferent and often hostile policies on the part of the United States government toward private investment in Latin America; the imminent danger of more communist victories to the south—all these now are combining to reduce new private investment in Latin America to a trickle.**

This may best be illustrated by the fact that our direct long-term investments, *including reinvested earnings,* increased in Latin America only about 3 per cent in 1960—from $8.098 billion in 1959 to $8.365 billion in 1960 (without deducting the Cuban loss), whereas in the same year they increased by nearly 25 per cent in Western Europe—from $5.323 billion to $6.645 billion.

Overall, new private capital investment in Latin America by United States interests was less than $100 million in 1960. New manufacturing investments especially in Mexico, Brazil,

---

*Book value.

**W. R. Grace & Co. in April, 1962, completed a survey of major investment institutions in New York, Boston, Philadelphia, Washington and Chicago. It found that United States investment sources had "lost confidence in Latin America." Cuba was seen as a major factor, coupled with recent expropriations and other anti-business acts on the part of some Latin American governments. (*New York Times,* Apr. 26, 1962.)

Argentina and Venezuela amounting to $125 million, and other new general investments of $50 million, were offset by the repatriation of some $80 million of funds from mining and oil ventures, especially in Venezuela, Cuba and Peru.[12]

In 1961, United States private interests put $203 million in new money into Latin America. But dividends repatriated (including our firms' branch earnings there) were $3\frac{1}{2}$ times as much—$716 million.[13]

Appraised realistically, from the standpoint of either Cold War or developmental objectives, new long-term United States private capital investment in Latin America has now come almost to a standstill. In fact, it may be going into reverse, with new investment falling below the amount of earnings annually repatriated.

Nevertheless, more purposeful private capital formulation is the weapon upon which we must place our chief reliance in combating the twin problems of communism and underdevelopment in Latin America. Before coming to the remedial measures needed to revive the role of this instrument, however, we must add to this summary of the size and direction of our investments an analysis of their quality and fabric. In so doing we pass from the muscle of capitalism to its conscience and its heart.

From the standpoint of the Cold War between our system of private initiative and communism, the virtual absence of participating native partners or stockholders is, without any doubt, the most harmful aspect of our private ventures in Latin America and elsewhere overseas.

Worldwide, a mere 45 United States corporations have over $15 billion of assets working overseas. These few firms hold more than 50 per cent of all of our foreign business investments. Among the largest 45 are 15 petroleum, 15 manufacturing and 6 mining companies.[14]

Without exception, these firms are widely owned in the United States. Through direct share ownership and indirectly through insurance policies, mutual funds and pension plans, millions of Americans have contributed savings to the capital stock of these 45 firms. Thus they have acquired a personal stake in them. Yet almost without exception, not a single private individual in the host country has ever had a chance to acquire any stake in the operation carried on in his country. To him, these enterprises are actually sealed off against private ownership as effectively as if they were owned by the Soviet.

Our firms doing business overseas operate in the main either through unincorporated branches or subsidiary corporations organized under the laws of each country in which business is conducted. In the first of these situations the branch is a fully integrated part of the United States firm as a legal and practical matter, while in the second the United States parent corporation normally holds, in the United States, 100 per cent of the stock of its foreign subsidiaries.

The choice between these two methods of operating rests upon a variety of considerations, especially the incidence of foreign taxes and United States income taxes. In 1957, our 10,272 foreign establishments were divided between 7,592 foreign subsidiaries and 2,680 branches. Mining, smelting, petroleum, and banking make up the bulk of the branch operations, while manufacturing, processing and utilities account for most of the local incorporations.

In the case of the branch, the denial of local ownership of any part, except in certain limited joint venture situations, is virtually automatic. In the case of the subsidiary the result is the same if, as is ordinarily the case, none of the shares of stock of the local subsidiary company are made available by the United States parent for purchase by local people. In either case we have stripped from our primary instrument of modern, widely shared capitalism its most meaningful attribute: its capacity to provide to individuals of the host nation an opportunity to acquire a personal share in the fruits of capitalism.

In most of Latin America, less than one out of every five of our investments carries a partnership feature of any kind. United States investors have majority control of two-thirds of the firms having local participants, and a minority position in the other one-third.[15]

The absence of local participation in many of our prominent enterprises naturally accentuates the belief that we are engaged in an exploiting rather than a sharing adventure in Latin America. For all practical purposes, no Venezuelan citizen can acquire any interest in our $3 billions of private oil development there. This is substantially true of all Latin America so far as our oil is concerned. No local partners means no local backers. Is it any wonder that state oil development is becoming the rule in Latin America? Can anyone doubt the real political difficulty which Latin American governments face when they, as the owners of the oil under Spanish law and custom, contemplate granting new concessions to United States firms?

"I sit and watch this thing now," a Venezuelan friend recently wrote to me, "and I will say it is just a matter of time. Either you fellows in the United States wake up and find a modern solution or the state is going to take you over."

Ambassador Adlai Stevenson said in *Look* upon his return from Latin America in 1960: ". . . ways will have to be found, such as partial ownership of these companies by local nationals, to integrate American firms into the national economies, so that their continued growth will be welcomed and not provoke more nationalism."[16]

No one in Chile owns a share of Anaconda of Chile. No one in Peru owns a share of Southern Peru Copper, subsidiary of American Smelting and Refining. No one can buy—on the local stock markets or anywhere else in Latin America—a share of General Motors of Latin America or United States Steel or

General Electric or Ford or, in most places, DuPont. The number of United States-controlled local firms, whose shares are listed on all of the stock exchanges of Latin America, can be counted on the fingers of two hands.

To reverse the cards, how long would we—regardless of poverty, illiteracy, underdevelopment or anything else that might beset us—tolerate a situation in which foreigners owned our oil and mines, and controlled such vital industries as explosives, rubber, petrochemicals?

This is meat for the communist grinder and their propaganda advantage is further increased by the fact that our firms do not ordinarily make public their local profit and loss figures, burying these country figures in the worldwide home office accounts which are customarily released here in the United States.

The modern, widely owned United States corporation ought to be the very image of constructive free enterprise in the uncommitted world. How can it be such, however, when the overwhelming majority of United States private operations overseas are 100 per cent owned in the United States by United States citizens? To the local citizen, this is an image of concentrated absentee ownership.

Total foreign ownership and secrecy of accounts hand the communists a huge advantage. Their often unanswered charges that "Wall Street," through our industrial firms, is extracting from the patrimony of the poor, profits so large and indefensible that we are unwilling to reveal them, weigh heavily against us, not only with the socialists and nationalists, but with many average fair-minded people as well.

"You'd be surprised," the head of the United States Chamber of Commerce in Rio said to me, "how many people here in Brazil believe that our business firms—Wall Street—control the United States government and tell the President what to do down here. All of our business practices should be regarded in the light of their opinion that even our own government is helpless to prevent us from exploiting them."

The peoples of the less-developed world are no longer prepared to accept the flat proposition that foreign-owned industry is necessarily a good thing for them, regardless of whether or not they may be permitted to share its ownership. New political and social factors have entered the picture. The simple test of economic soundness in a profit-making, job-producing sense is no longer an adequate measure.

The signs are all around us, growing in intensity. Jose Figueres of Costa Rica pointed to them recently when he said, "The proportion of foreign ownership was entirely exaggerated" in Cuba. Note that he was speaking not of the quantity but of the local ownership "proportion."

According to a recent study of joint or mixed international business ventures conducted by two Columbia University scholars under Ford Foundation auspices, "Before the revolution of 1959 in Cuba, joint ventures probably represented only a minor part of total direct foreign investments."[17]

"Canada shall be for Canadians," said the Prime Minister in 1960 as he promulgated a multipronged program to reduce the domination of Canadian industry by United States interests. United States industry owns over $10 billion of business assets in Canada, a third of all of our private overseas investments. According to Howard W. Graham, President of the Toronto Stock Exchange, foreign investments—mostly American—last year reached a total of 61 per cent of Canada's gross national product, and Americans controlled 44 per cent of Canadian manufacturing. He expressed a widely held point of view when he said there is a "feeling among Canadians that most American parent organizations are inclined to forget their obligation to the Canadian people."[18]

Our closest neighbor to the south, Mexico, has adopted a new mining law to limit foreign ownership of private Mexican mining operations to 49 per cent; the controlling 51 per cent interest is to be passed to Mexican citizens. Administratively, the principle of this law is being applied with respect to some newly establishing non-mining enterprises, and even some existing non-mining firms are faced with the threat that they must divest themselves of control by selling 51 per cent to Mexican citizens. To take control away from the controlling investor is confiscation plain and simple.

Philippine law now provides that foreigners (excluding Americans at present because it is aimed chiefly at the Chinese), cannot hold more than 40 per cent of the shares of any corporation engaged in banking, agriculture, timber, minerals, or national resources. Brazil calls for domestic control for newspapers, radio, television, and aviation companies.

The temper of the times is illustrated by the Ford Motor Company episode in industrial England in 1960. There was a hue and cry in old England when Ford bought its minority British stockholders out of its British subsidiary. The propriety of this large purchase—the total paid to Britishers was about $370 million—was even debated on the floor of the House of Commons. Although Ford had an absolute legal right to buy and the Britishers to sell, the furore surrounding the case reveals a deep-seated feeling at large in the world today that we, as the mightiest capitalistic nation in the world, should find a way to share the fruits of our foreign ventures with ordinary people of the host nation.

We have plenty of lessons from the past in Latin America. Our large privately held oil interests were expropriated nearly 30 years ago with token compensation. These oil discoveries were made as a result of risks our entrepreneurs took with United States shareholders' hard-earned money, and they brought great wealth to Mexico and so we have regarded their nationalization as immoral, to say the least. Yet the fact is that oil is a state monopoly in most of Latin America today, suggesting the need for a new approach on the part of private enterprise.

Unquestionably our Cuban establishments brought wealth, growth and jobs to Cuba. Yet they were nationalized just the same. Suppose for a moment that a way had been found to place a substantial percentage of the more than $1 billion of equity ownership of these enterprises into the hands of a large number of employees and ordinary Cubans, so that most if not all of these firms had had a substantial number of Cuban "partners," instead of being virtually 100 per cent owned by United States citizens.

Would history have been the same? Of course, we cannot know the answer to this question, but the Sears Roebuck story indicates it might have been different. At the time of the Castro seizure, the employees of the Cuban subsidiary—nearly all being Cubans—owned 18 per cent of the stock of the Cuban company through their participation in the profit-sharing plan. The employees resisted the seizure because, as owners of a significant part of the firm, they had a stake in capitalism rather than just a job. Only by threats of force and elaborate promises were the Castro bandits able to take possession of the stores.

Despite the evidence, American business leadership is sharply divided on this question of having local partners. Recently Harlow Curtice, Chairman of General Motors, our very largest firm, said to me, "For my money, we own it 100 per cent or we don't go at all."

The policy of General Electric has been to avoid local participants, whereas Westinghouse has generally operated through license agreements with foreign licensees. Westinghouse ordinarily acquires no equity interest at all in the foreign business.

A somewhat similar contrast is found in the rubber business. B. F. Goodrich Corporation has a number of Latin American affiliated manufacturing companies, while United States Rubber Company generally prefers to go it alone. Firestone and General Tire are amenable to the joint venture procedure, whereas Goodyear generally operates on a wholly owned basis.[19]

One of the Latin American managers of an American rubber firm said to me, "I myself prefer the Goodyear practice because our minority stockholders give us nothing but trouble." Under the laws of certain Latin American countries, the social "reformers" have pushed through such ridiculous laws favoring striker-type stockholders that conflicts with local holders are almost inevitable. For example, in Colombia, as against any minority stockholder, the majority stockholder can only vote 25 per cent of the stock; hence he can only elect 25 per cent of the board of directors even if he owns 60 per cent of the shares. Also, the company has to pay the cost of all minority stockholders' attendance at the stockholders' meeting.

Some United States executives have had their fingers burned by local partners and want none for reasons associated with their own experiences. "We had some minority shareholders in Cuba and where did it get us?" I was told by Langbourne Williams, head of Freeport Sulphur. "Far from assisting us in our relations, they frequently did nothing but complain and make our problems worse." Creole of Venezuela, a subsidiary of Standard Oil of New Jersey, once had a sizeable number of Venezuelan shareholders but they have been buying it back on the open market and nearly have it all again. Now, however, Creole has established a $10 million investment fund to engage in risky partnership ventures in Venezuela. Thus, its oil profits may help light new kinds of lamps in Latin America.[20]

"It doesn't make sense," I was told by Randolph Peters, an American friend who manages supermarkets for a United States concern in Peru, "to pay dividends when you don't have the earnings, but we had to do just that a few years ago to keep our Peruvian stockholders happy.

Henry Gardner, the head of Anaconda's Chilean subsidiary,

puts the case against local participation this way: "Chile is already our senior partner. We pay 75 per cent of our net profits to the Chilean government. A lot of Chileans would like to help us run our business, but when bank savings deposits pay 8 per cent tax-free, who is going to buy common stock of Anaconda of Chile? Besides, if they want an interest in the firm, they can always buy the stock of the parent company on the New York Stock Exchange."

To this can be added the question, where in Chile would sufficient private money come from to buy any significant share of Anaconda's equity? Would it not mainly come from the few Chileans already very rich? And what would happen if, having developed a flock of small stockholders of small means and equally small understanding of capital and risk, you started passing dividends or drilled a lot of dry holes or went broke?

These are hard questions. Yet in the end they merely amount to the defense of a status quo that is failing. Slowly but surely, the opposite view is gaining ground in Latin America. While the top boss in the United States may not discriminate too much in his thinking between the branch in Walla Walla and the one in Sao Paulo, the manager on the front lines does. He can often feel the hot breath of confiscation, and receives the daily shelling from the communists and their claque of fellow travelers.

E. I. duPont de Nemours & Co. in Latin America has favored 100 per cent ownership by DuPont parent, but recently in Mexico they took a minority interest in a new chemical venture, Pigmentos y Productos Químicos.* The balance of its investments in Mexico are wholly owned, as they are in Brazil and Peru as well. Its chemical firms in Chile and Argentina are mixed ventures with a DuPont majority.[21]

---

*Unfortunately, the government of Mexico has the largest piece.

Their Argentina manager, Jorge L. Aguilar, President of Ducilo S.A., a distinguished Latin American with all the gravity, dignity and personal magnetism so prevalent in the Spaniard of all classes, puts it this way:

Sentiment in favor of marketing some of the stock of the local enterprises to local people, and listing it for trading on the local stock exchange, is growing among Latin American managers of United States enterprises. It is no comfort to a local investor that the stock of the parent corporation is owned by hundreds of thousands of United States citizens, or that he himself can buy that same stock on the New York Stock Exchange. Most people in Latin America wouldn't know how to go about buying stock on your Exchange, particularly people in countries with foreign exchange controls or less than full convertibility of their currency. What we want is a chance to own part of the operation physically being carried on here, not some faraway collection of enterprises about which we can know very little.

The most important factor, from the standpoint of our national interests and the future of private enterprise, is that buying the parent stock on the New York Exchange is an exportation of Argentina's private capital, whereas the very thing we need to bolster our growth and defeat the forces of the left is the very opposite—more inflow of foreign private capital and more repatriation of the capital we ourselves have already invested overseas.

The single most significant evidence of the changing opinion is found in Brazil. A group of American businessmen in Sao Paulo and Rio, associated with the United States Chamber of Commerce of Brazil, became alarmed at the unpopularity of United States investments there, which was revealed in Voice of America polls taken among urban Brazilians in 1959 and 1960. To quote from a Chamber release of April 17, 1961:

The committee used as the basis of its study a public opinion survey on the nature and extent of nationalistic feeling that had been completed early last year by the United States Information Service in Brazil. For the most part, the results of this survey confirmed impressions that American companies in Brazil had had for some time:

1. That while nationalistic feeling is quite strong on the part of the general population in Brazil, it is most in evidence among high school and university students.

2. That such groups tend to see United States companies as exploiters of Brazil—and their parent companies in the States as "controlling" the United States government.

3. That it is generally felt that United States companies are strongly opposed to the growth of nationalism in Brazil since it will be a threat to its exploitation of Brazil's wealth.

4. That it is felt, though not quite so generally, that Russia is for stronger nationalism in Brazil because it sees a compatibility with it and socialism and communism, and because nationalism will weaken United States interests in Brazil and alienate the United States from Brazil.

Despite the strong feelings against American companies as evidenced by the survey, significant proportions of the students and of the general public stated that they believe foreign capital investment in Brazil is good—or rather, *could* be good for the country. There is not such complete acceptance of state monopolies as may be thought. Foreign capital is wanted, but with government control and no remittance of profits.

It may be mentioned, incidentally, that in drawing conclusions from the survey, considerable weight was given to student opinion by the USIS* since, in Brazil, as in other countries in Latin America (and unlike the United States), student opinion is a definite factor in shaping the thinking of other population sectors.

The committee proposed, among other measures, that the Chamber go on record as favoring the marketing in Brazil of a portion of the stock of the local operation. The battle to carry this proposal took nearly a year but, finally, in January of 1961, the American Chambers of Commerce for Rio de

---

*The Voice of America.

Janeiro and Sao Paulo in Brazil adopted and later released publicly the following resolution:

Taking into cognizance notable recent instances of new issues of shares which have been freely offered and sold to the public by industrial and public service companies in Brazil, the American Chamber of Commerce for Brazil in Rio and San Paulo commend this practice to all their members, and especially to foreign interests having enterprises in Brazil, because it is believed that the sharing of ownership, wherever feasible, on the basis of a broad distribution of shares among the people, is a significant contribution to the development of modern democracy based on the free enterprise system.

Of course, the public offering of securities is not new in Latin America. The stock exchange in Buenos Aires is 107 years old. In Chile, 5,000 shares of stock of International Telephone and Telegraph of Chile were publicly sold in Chile nearly 15 years ago.

Nevertheless, capital markets as we know them are very small in Latin America.

The Stock Exchange in Mexico City, only a few years old, has some 375 listed stocks. This is a misleading figure, however, since only about 20 are ever traded, and of these only about seven are traded on an average trading day. As for the others, an occasional transaction is "prearranged" to "establish" a price for credit purposes. These are mainly family-owned or very closely held.

Interest in equity shares is also retarded by the fact that most trading is done in bonds, mortgage certificates and obligations of Financiera National, the government-owned industrial complex. What temptation is there to get into risk capital which one government bond is carrying an 8 per cent coupon guaranteed by the central bank, and others yield 10-12 per cent tax-free? Only perhaps 5 per cent or less of the exchange volume is in common stocks.

Another custom that holds down the volume of exchange transactions is the practice followed by banks and financial institutions of maintaining an over-the-counter market in securities. This is particularly true in relation to larger blocks whose sale on the small-volume exchange would depress prices. The exchange desires to prohibit bank trading, as in the United States, in order to strengthen the Exchange and induce more firms to seek expansion capital by public offering of listed securities.

Taking all the factors and even including the small exchanges in Guadalajara and Monterrey, the daily value of Mexican stock transactions could hardly be more than $1 million (U.S.) as compared with $200 million per day on our New York Stock Exchange alone. No more than a minute fraction of this would consist of trading in the very few stocks which represent partnership situations, i.e., significant percentages of both United States and Mexican capital.

Only a few Latin American countries have equity markets even as rudimentary as Mexico's. When I was in Bogotá on the 28th of February 1961, the day's trading included small transactions in the stock of one bank and two beer companies and transactions in two bond issues, one a beer company 12 per cent bond selling just below par. During that period the average daily stock trading would probably not exceed $600,000 (pesos) or about $50,000 (United States) at then current exchange rates.

In Chile in early 1961, stock market activity had declined to 25 per cent of 1955 volume. One reason for this is that Corfo, the government's industrial holding company, had issued 5 per cent bonds legal for use as import payment guarantee deposits. The owners of such bonds were able to lend these bonds to importers at an "override" of 18 per cent, thus producing a 23 per cent yield. Also the banks offer 8 per cent on term deposits of 90 days. Therefore the stock market remained unattractive. The main complaint there, nevertheless, is that foreign firms have no stock available for local purchase. There are only a handful of exceptions—Angla Tierra Nitrate, also listed on the London and New York Stock Exchanges, two companies in which Grace Lines has a majority position, and a tire firm in which our General Tire owns a minority share.

If noise were a measure of volume, the constant babble on the floor of the Buenos Aires Exchange would spell the largest volume in the world. Transactions are made by brokers shouting offers and acceptances as they mill around, confirming details and making entries in small notebooks carried in hand. The exchange, 107 years old, is proud of its illustrious tradition. Over a period of a week nearly 300 stock issues may be traded, and the daily volume of such trading sometimes approaches $10 million (U.S.). Kaiser & Koppers are the two local operations of United States firms whose stock is listed on this exchange.

Trading on the stock markets of Rio and Sao Paulo does not match the Buenos Aires figures, and the Venezuela market is even smaller, ranging daily in the neighborhood of $50,000 (U. S.).

The frailty of these markets indicates how closely held by individuals and families are most indigenous Latin American enterprises. It also discloses how few American firms have seen fit to seek local partners in the public market places of Latin America. Finally, and most significant, this very frailty demonstrates how influential United States capital in Latin America *could* be in leading the way toward a stronger and more widely shared capital base. If policies and programs could be developed for the public marketing of a significant portion of the stock of even 10 per cent of the 3,000 United States establishments in Latin America, the effect on the fabric of capitalism in Latin America, and upon United States prestige as well, would be profound.

Without doubt, currently available statistics do not adequately measure the strong trend on the part of United States and indigenous industry toward the broader dissemination of equity, nor reveal the truly intense interest the ordinary Latin American has in acquiring a piece of what, for most people in an industrializing world, must be the best if not the only practical route to becoming a capitalist.

Say the authors of a Columbia University study: "It is only on the basis of partnership that the economic progress of the less-developed countries can be achieved, and that it will be possible to impart the experience and resources of the more developed countries to nations that want to bridge the gap, without sacrificing national pride and human dignity."[22]

The cynic may be amused to contemplate remote villagers filling out proxies, or head hunters offering motions at stockholders' meetings in paneled board rooms, but the evidence shows that widespread stock ownership in Latin America is no longer a joke.

If one were trying to envision a perfect relationship with Latin America, capitalistically, one carrying a maximum of people-to-people implications, yet realistic in the sense that the unpacified handful still carrying blowguns would hardly be expected to have the necessary status for the affair, he would probably come up with the idea that foreign enterprises in his country, old as well as new, should in substantial degree be widely owned by local people.

Yet in this conception there is buried one deep unanswered problem: Where is the uninvested private indigenous capital in amounts adequate on a broad citizen basis to acquire a significant share of what is there already in foreign investment, and to acquire, as well, an important share of that which must come from outside in order to provide a meaningful external contribution to needed growth? The answer is that much of it is there, in funds that now go into undeveloped land, short-term loans for consumer imports and other relatively non-productive investments, or into cookie jars and mattresses. *Another important share is represented by the $6-8 billion of fugitive Latin American funds now taking a rest in the safer havens of Europe and the United States.*

But in the last analysis sufficient capital is not available locally to fulfill such a concept; and entirely novel measures, to be outlined herein, will be needed. Meanwhile, Latin American citizens of average means are having no difficulty in devouring the offerings that have come their way thus far.

In March 1961, Union Carbide Corporation, one of our country's largest and best-known international corporations, offered 40 per cent of the common stock of its Mexican subsidiary to Mexicans of average means, no individual being allowed to subscribe to more than $3,000 (U. S.) of the issue. Buyers are entitled to pay for the stock on the installment plan, 25 per cent down and 25 per cent per year with a modest interest charge. The offering, which was made through private branch banks all over Mexico, was enthusiastically received by the Mexican people and promptly oversubscribed.*

Now Union Carbide has 1,000 Mexican shareholders—partners from the Texas border to Guatemala, owning listed shares of stock that cost $4 million (U. S.).** Union Carbide in Mexico has moved from a position of exposure into one of collaboration and partnership with the Mexican people.

There is also new evidence of the broadening of ownership of local industries, both among customers and employees.

Teléfonos de Mexico, Mexican Telephone Company, used

---

*As noted earlier in this chapter, high bond and savings account yields in Latin America do undoubtedly retard to some extent the making of risk capital investments. However, the Union Carbide case and others to be mentioned show that the people nevertheless crave an equity position. One reason is that corporate managers necessarily "set their sights" on profit margins higher than fixed yields. Another is that the bond or savings account offers no protection against inflation. A third, I believe, is man's innate desire to carry a part of his country's future growth around in his pocket.

**And shortly rose to $6 million (U. S.) in market value.

to be owned by our International Telephone & Telegraph Corporation and a Swedish firm. Now it is owned by a private Mexican syndicate. Getting a telephone is very difficult, so long has demand been pent up by restrictive government policies, but the monthly charges are low. To get a telephone, you first have to buy at least $3,000 pesos (about $250) worth of telephone company stock. However, the dividends will help you pay your telephone bill. The stock ownership requirement "buys" the company a degree of practical protection against government expropriation.

Under the employee stock ownership plan of the pulp mill in Chihauhau, nearly 70 per cent of the employees have become shareholders. Each employee designates, at the beginning of each year, the amount of stock he wishes to buy during that year. He pays 1/12th down at the first of the year and 1/12th per month, receiving dividends pro-rata during the year. If the employee fails to fulfill the year's purchase, the company takes back the stock and pays back what the employee has paid in, less interest. In his office in Mexico City, financier Carlos Trouyet, who heads the pulp firm, proudly displays a framed letter from the local labor leader ecstatically extolling this plan.

It is not the fault of the United States that Mexico's capitalist system is concentrated. But United States-owned capital in Mexico will continue to be the first target of left-wing elements in the host country unless a drastic change is made. You can find Mexicans from all segments of the economic spectrum who will complain bitterly, for example, that the explosives, tire, and other key Mexican industries are 100 per cent owned in the United States. These complaints against United States industry in Mexico are often made without reference to the fact that concentration of wealth is a hallmark of their society, not ours. Yet how long would we stand still if a foreign firm owned all of our explosives industry?

Corporate executives who favor mixed ownership of foreign ventures can point to several hard-headed factors in its favor. Business risk is obviously reduced when less capital is sunk into each venture, permitting diversification as between areas, countries and industries. Risk of loss from political discrimination is also reduced for there is usually no practical way to express nationalism against a mixed venture. Better access to local management talent, improved public and governmental relations, and enhanced employee morale are also cited.

Celanese Corporation of America, with worldwide operations, has now adopted a positive policy of holding only a minority interest in each foreign venture. Recently it reduced its position in Mexico from a majority of 52 per cent to a minority of 48 per cent in keeping with this doctrine.

Wherever possible, Celanese seeks broad public distribution of the majority ownership in order to gain the widest public support and, in some situations, de facto control through ownership of the most concentrated bloc of stock. In Mexico, where Mexican control is now required by law in certain instances, de facto control for a period of years through the execution of a management contract in favor of the foreign minority is evidently permissible.

Corporate partnerships that cross national boundaries are by no means confined to larger operations capable of public offering. International joint ventures on a smaller scale are also springing up in Latin America. The owner-manager of a small rug firm in Mexico City, René Enríquez, recently concluded he needed to double his capital and acquire more modern equipment and technology to maintain his competitive position. He wrote to Lees, the well-known United States firm. Lees matched the value of the Enríquez company with new equipment and cash, plus a commitment to furnish artistic and technical advice. Enríquez and the United States firm each now owns 50 per cent of the stock and René said to me the last time, "It's a fine arrangement. I'm better financed, more competitive and employing more people."

When I told our then ambassador to Panama, Joseph S. Farland, about this incident, he replied, "If we could get a program to repeat that kind of transaction a few dozen times here in Panama, it would really help develop the country and defeat the Reds."

In Colombia, another technique has been used by an American firm to join hands with people of that country. Colombian Petroleum Company's natural gas venture there is jointly owned by Gulf Oil Company and its Colombian customers. "We decided the best source of support for us, both politically and economically, lay with the Colombians with whom we do most of our business," Geoffrey G. Sowash, assistant manager there, told me.

Still, foreign capital going into Colombia is on the decline. "It's just too risky now," said the manager of one United States firm with whom I talked. Colombia's corporate ownership is highly concentrated—in fact, 71 per cent of all industrial shares are owned by 7/10 of 1 per cent of all the shareholders.

"If our economy is to grow fast enough to give everybody a job and get a little increase in standards of living each year, we are going to have to work everything we have and attract $100 million of new foreign investment every single year besides," said Fernando Carrizosa Herrera, alert and farsighted head of Colombia's industrial association. His hopes for $100 million a year seem quite unattainable under present policies. In 1960, for example, hardly that amount of new private capital went into all of Latin America.

General Tire of United States recently took a minority position in a needed tire plant in Ecuador, providing capital and know-how for its Ecuadorian partners. Ecuador offers special incentives and benefits to United States firms that will "turnkey" a small business and retain a portion of the equity.

This is the way Ecuador hopes to attract new capital and modern technology, thus creating more jobs, reducing imports and improving her international balance. But still the inflow is a trickle, because of uninsured Cold War risks that lie outside the commercial experience of the average United States firm.

Obviously, these risks have not been lessened by the ascendancy to the Ecuadorian Presidency of far-left Vice President C. J. Arosemena, who called for friendlier relations with Castro as he took office in November 1961.*

Sears Roebuck's unique method of operation has done much to spur growth in the Latin American countries in which it does business. In each country in which Sears operates, skilled company officials seek out local fabricators and help train and equip them to manufacture the multiplicity of articles needed to make up the comprehensive Sears stock-in-trade. A very high percentage—from 80 per cent to nearly 100 per cent—of the merchandise carried in the Sears stores in Latin America is locally produced. Furthermore—and this is now a characteristic of nearly all United States-owned enterprises in Latin America—only 2 per cent or less of the employees are sent from the United States and these are ordinarily replaced as soon as local trainees are ready to fill managerial and technical roles. Finally, Sears is helping create capitalists by investing the employees' profit-sharing-plan funds in shares of stock of the local subsidiary. In Mexico, through this vehicle the employees own more than 20 per cent of the company, but in Colombia none at all because antiquated tax and related statutes now render it impracticable there.

W. R. Grace & Company is one of our most active and our most well-regarded firm in Latin America. While approximately two thirds of Grace's operations are inside the

---

*Later on, however, on April 3, 1962, military pressures forced him to sever diplomatic relations with Cuba. (SF Exam. 4/4/62).

United States, chiefly in chemicals, it has more than $75 million working in Latin America, $18 million of this in mixed ventures. Although Grace's major interests are the inter-American steamship line and a one-half interest in the air line Panagra, its joint ventures with Latin Americans are significant.

In Peru, where the Grace enterprise was started as a ship chandlery business by William Russell Grace in 1854, the company has active joint ventures in textiles, candy and crackers and containers. Grace has a majority of the stock of each but local investors own an important share.

Grace has numerous ventures in Chile, Colombia, Bolivia, Argentina, El Salvador, and Guatemala, in which it has local stockholder "partners" in varying degrees. These firms cover a spectrum of local product needs such as chemicals, coffee processing, paints, textiles, sugar, paper, and fertilizer.

In the case of the Peruvian Companias Unidas and the Chilean Tejidos Caupolicán, textile enterprises, a minority of the shares was sold by Grace to the general public.[23]

In his office in New York City, American Smelting and Refining Company's Edward McLanahan Tittman, one of the men responsible for pushing Peru's great Toquepala copper venture into reality, ponders with other top executives the method by which Southern Peru Copper Company can offer an ownership position to a broad section of Peruvians, through a high-yield debenture which the owner, at his option, can convert into common stock. This company, jointly owned by AS&R, Cerro de Pasco, Phelps Dodge and Newmont Mining, spent $250 million in Peru between the first drill-hole in 1942 and the first copper shipment in 1960. The stock offering will enable ordinary Peruvians to share in the fruits of a venture free of the enormous burdens of the long and risky development period.

Cerro de Pasco also contemplates a stock offering of a piece

of the ownership of its Peruvian operating company to the people of Peru. Deltec, the New York firm that successfully
marketed Willys-Overland shares in Brazil, has had under
study the making of a public offering, to Peruvians only, at $5
per share, of a million $5 preferred shares of Cerro, with a
guaranteed dividend of 8 per cent. The shares will include the
right at any time within 10 years to convert them into the
common stock of Cerro de Pasco, the main operating company
in Peru.

The purchase, it is contemplated, can be financed over
a three-to-four-year period, and the number of shares any one
man can buy is to be severely restricted. Since the payments,
technically, would go to the United States parent corporation,
it would agree to reinvest the proceeds of the issue in Peru.
The offering will give thousands of ordinary Peruvians an
almost riskless chance to share Peruvian growth.

There is no doubt that the larger United States firms,
especially petroleum and mining concerns, without local
investors and in that sense without local supporters, are focal
points for communist propaganda. It is well to remember that
under Spanish practice—unlike our own—original land grants
do not carry title to the subsoil. Thus the United States con-
cessionaire is often regarded as having received—and the local
politician often charged with having delivered—a windfall
which, in all justice, should have devolved upon the citizens
of the country.

"Every major company is going to have to walk up to the
question whether it is going to market some of its own stock
locally; we have looked at it several times and doubtless we
will come to it," says Donald Wright, President of General
Electric of Brazil. "But," he adds, "we would want to find a
way to leapfrog over some of the big Brazilian names and get
it into the hands of a lot of people." General Electric is also
thinking of a local employee stock bonus plan, with a require-

ment that no sale can be made for three or four years—to help get people used to hanging onto property.

Esso of Brazil has also been thinking of a local stock distribution. "Underwriting costs are expensive in Brazil," says President Cornelius Griffin, who was also president of the Chamber in 1961 when it pushed across the resolution recommending such action, "and we tend to think that marketing the shares through our own dealers might be a good plan."

Down in Argentina, the Koppers firm has already parted with 48 per cent of its new petrochemical subsidiary. Most of this was privately placed but about 10 per cent—approximately $12 million (U. S.) —was deliberately offered in the La Plata district outside Buenos Aires where the plant is to be located, an area with a strong communist and Peronista flavor. This 10 per cent offering gave Koppers 400 Argentinian partners. Koppers is now one of the few identifiable United States firms listed on the Buenos Aires Stock Exchange.

Until the spring of 1962 when Red-backed Peronista victories at the polls led to a military coup and to the ouster of President Frondizi, Argentina's policies in favor of monetary stability and private enterprise were paying off. She, of all Latin American nations, was attracting large amounts of external capital. Under her laws, new foreign investments were offered attractive incentives, generally consisting of income tax freedom for a period of years and immunity from import levies on original plant and equipment.

The new investments were rapid and impressive, involving fabulous United States outlays in advanced areas of modern industrial technology. Given a chance to mature, they would help push Argentina to a position of regained development.

However, they are also creating enemies and problems. These prominent private investments will continue to be the primary target of the communists, socialists, nationalists and, indeed, of those government officials who have come to look upon development as a state prerogative and who therefore prefer philosophies of growth that edge closer to the socialist road.

Last October, a committee of Argentina's powerful General Labor Confederation declared that the oil field areas, where seven American oil concerns were drilling or completing wells, were being operated as a "United States colony" in which "there is no other law but the will of managers and directors" who are Americans.[24]

On the score of nationalism, it would be only natural if the Argentinians—somewhere down the line—should arrive at the conclusion that too much of their big stuff is owned by foreigners, notably in the United States, and that something ought to be done about it, such as expropriation which, incidentally, is a risk run by our industries in Argentina not covered by the United States Government nor by private insurance policies.

One of our embassy people in Latin America, a man noted for his staunch support of private enterprise, by the way, said to me, "I am beginning to think that anti-Americanism in these countries exists in almost mathematical proportion to the amount of our private investment, especially in oil and other extractive industries."

Doubtless this is too harsh an indictment, but the facts must be faced. A leading oil executive in Argentina told me, "United States industry is getting a reputation for asking too many favors. The government finds it hard to justify some of these special concessions politically, and our local competitors grumble that they are unfair."

If history teaches anything, it is that the gains for private enterprise in Argentina will not be lasting unless new farsighted measures are taken that will enable employees and ordinary citizens in Argentina to share in this private growth. But if such measures are taken, within a framework of political stability, Argentina could become the Latin American prototype of modern capitalism, erected as a free and prosperous contrast to enslaved Cuba.

A pioneer effort in the distribution of subsidiary equity was Kaiser's Willys-Overland of Brazil. A highly successful door-to-door instalment-plan selling campaign produced 40,-000 Brazilian shareholders who now own a majority of the company's stock and at last reports were contented capitalists. This campaign is being duplicated on a smaller scale in Argentina, with respect to Kaiser's auto finance subsidiary, where "jeep teams" tour the hinterland selling stock to remote villagers.

Deltec, Ltd., a New York underwriting firm specializing in the distribution throughout Latin America of securities of United States subsidiaries, as well as indigenous firms, handled the Kaiser placements. Deltec, put together by Brazilian capital with some United States and other Latin American money added, is headed by a tall and furious Peruvian, Manuel Ulloa, whose natural zeal for a warmer kind of capitalism in Latin America happily coincides with his firm's best money-making interests. Deltec has managers in most major Latin American centers, pushing its wares, while Ulloa roams the hemisphere knocking on corporate doors. Deltec is an important force in breaking down the rigid attitudes of yesteryear.

If Deltec pioneered mass instalment-plan stock distribution south of the border, the Rockefellers pioneered the growing pattern of mixed capital ventures. Their efforts go back to the thirties when, one gets the impression, they may have been long on zeal and short on the hard realities of making a profit in a tough environment. Over the years they have learned, as perhaps our foreign aiders will some day, that the way to build for keeps is with the bricks and mortar of capitalism.

Their operations are largely conducted through Ibec, the International Basic Economy Corporation, which owns everything from a resort hotel in Chile to supermarkets in Venezuela. For our purpose here, their most interesting operation is the development of mutual funds along the United States pattern.

"We really have to start from scratch in each country, by persuading the legislature to pass a law regulating our operations," says Richard Aldrich, who heads up this part of Ibec's operations. Now Fundo Crescinco—"Growth Fund"—is established in Colombia, Brazil, Argentina, and Chile. Ibec ordinarily finds some local partners to join in financing the management company, and when the arrangements have been completed they commence selling shares of the fund's stock, directly to the public and through banks and brokers, investing the proceeds in a diversified portfolio of Latin American stocks and, if and when there are any available for local purchase, in the stocks of the local subsidiaries of United States companies.

These operations are giving the lie to those who say Latin Americans are not ready for the age of modern finance. In Brazil, alone, Fundo Crescinco is selling at a rate of $700,000 (U.S.) per month, has over 21,000 shareholders and total net assets in excess of $16,000,000 (U. S.). These are open-end redeemable securities, as are most United States mutual funds, and the buyer can turn in his shares for cash at any time. Fundo Crescinco of Brazil has been able to produce an 8 per cent net return after adjusting for inflation.

These funds are in their infancy there, of course, but the interest in them is revealing. Deltec is starting a fund in Brazil and there are two fledglings in Mexico. Alberto Guido Servente, Manager of the Buenos Aires Stock Exchange, recently came to the United States on a visit. He became fascinated by our funds and wrote a book on how they work, which may become the mutual fund bible of Latin America.[25]

The main complaint of these funds is that so few United States firms make stock available for investors there, because the buyers of the fund's shares like to feel they are backed by a mixed United States-Latin American portfolio, so that each fund share represents a tiny hemispheric partnership in growth. In Mexico recently the fund's managers came around to our embassy and pleaded (to deaf ears, incidentally) that it go on record as favoring the public offering of the stock of United States firms doing business there.

The manager of one of our foreign enterprises in Venezuela said to me, "We can no longer sit back and wait for the local people to come up with advanced corporate thinking. The image of the American corporation is not favorable and only we can change that."

This poor image has alarmed the younger native businessmen into action, because they see it as a threat to all free enterprise. "Of course, the prime target is United States business," says Gilbert Huber of Brazil, who is president of Listas Telefónicas and identified with a large number of other Brazilian enterprises, "but if it goes we'll be next."

There are others like Huber in Brazil; Nicomedes Zuloaga, hijo, Eugenio Mendoza and Gustavo Vollmer of Venezuela; Alberto Samper and José Gómez-Pinzón of Colombia; Juan Bautista Peña, president of the Stock Exchange in Buenos Aires, and Jorge Aguilar; Jorge Ross of Chile; Enrique Pardo of Peru; Fausto Miranda, Luis Legorretta and Carlos Trouyet of Mexico; CEAS of Colombia; IDEAS of Mexico and Argentina; CONCLAP of Brazil. A host of other young men of commerce, industry, and the professions and their organizations are burning candles to the conscience of capitalism.

They are crusading for the adoption of modern corporate doctrines by United States and local business firms—wider distribution of stock, employee stock ownership, final elimination of discrimination in training and pay as between local and United States employees, disclosure of profits.

As a group they have made many trips to the United States at their own expense to plead their case with our top corporate executives here. In 1960, sitting around my desk in Washington's Commerce Department, Vollmer expressed it this way, "We can almost reach in a drawer and pull out the name of the United States firm that will be seized next."

They make a point of showing up at international meetings conducted under government or private auspices, alert to expose the ever-present communist as well as the feudal capitalist of yesteryear. These men are part of a growing group of young intellectual capitalists who, while putting their own company houses in modern order, are battling the forces of reaction and communism with unusual zeal. Their informal "charter" provides:

... a definite program should be implemented to create in Latin America an appreciation of the nature of the democratic capitalist society, demonstrate its virtue and freedoms by comparison with socialistic and communistic doctrines, and reflect the dynamic aspects of private initiative and private ownership at all levels.

Achieving these goals requires a reexamination of the policies which have been followed by the free nations in their postwar aid programs. Emphasis on giving assistance *should shift from a government-to-government relationship to a people-to-people responsibility,* wherein governments backstop the private sector and assume only those roles, which cannot effectively be played by private enterprise, or which complement and assist private initiative. The program must appeal to individuals and governments by stressing the dignity of self-help and self-development and by creating a personal, even intimate, relationship between the provider of financial or technical assistance and the executors of the program. Charity is not wanted but help is. (Emphasis supplied)

From the standpoint of our own national self-interest, Latin Americans of this character represent one of the finest of combatant forces in the Cold War. If we fail to heed their warnings we will, in time, lose all in Latin America and the result will be a hemisphere dominated by the Reds.

MY COMPANY 'TIS OF THEE?

If United States business in Latin America is to free itself of the charge that it has had its time at bat in the Cold War and must yield its place to more and more long-term foreign aid, it must shake loose from the narrow dogmas of the past. Doing business as usual, in the "what-is-best-for-the-corporation" sense, gets a 4-F rating in the Cold War. The milieu in which private firms operate is vastly different from that prevailing only a few decades ago. The attitude of the peoples of the less-developed areas was aptly summed up by G. L. Mehta, Chairman of the Industrial Credit and Investment Corporation of India, Ltd., an important Indian credit institution, in an address at the International Industrial Conference in San Francisco in September 1961.

"In most underdeveloped economies private enterprise is on probation. It will be judged by—and its survival depend upon—its social utility to the economy. This casts a heavy responsibility upon those who sponsor, organize, finance and operate private enterprise."

On the other hand, it is not the purpose of the present book to reheat and serve up again the old public relations lectures for overseas operators, such as:

Having more local people to dinner

Trying not to act rich

Helping form Boy Scout troops

Training local employees for the top jobs

Mixing with the people

Avoiding racial snobbery

Learning the language

By and large these mandates are being carried out—and well—and this is important.*

---

*Raymond W. Miller in his *Can Capitalism Compete?"* (Ronald Press, New York, 1959) did a fine and influential piece of work in this area.[26]

Colombia, in its labor code, requires firms with more than 10 employees to have Colombians in 80 per cent of the executive and specialized positions, a requirement which can be lowered temporarily while Colombians are being trained.[27] Contrary to communist and nationalist claims, however, the average United States firm in Latin America beats this percentage already. Department of Commerce figures show that only 18 per cent of the supervisory, professional and technical people in our enterprises in Latin America, and only about one out of 400 other employees, are imported from the United States.[28]

Capitalism in Peru is probably as old-fashioned as it is anywhere on the globe, yet evidence of their striving for modernization is nevertheless quite visible. Nowhere have more marvels of training been worked by private enterprise.

United States firms in Peru are doing a great deal to make the average Peruvian a participant in modern capitalism. Seventy-five per cent of the executive staff of International Petroleum, a Standard Oil operation, is Peruvian.

At the great Toquepala copper mine of American Smelting and Refining Company, a village of modern homes in the sky has been created by the company, and 4,000 Indians have been taught advanced mechanical skills. A committee of United States businessmen, called North Americans for Peru, is assisting on many welfare projects, including the furnishing of one-frequency radios to the Catholic priests for educational programs in remote areas.

In Río recently, the United States Chamber of Commerce made an effort to develop a composite profit and loss statement of United States corporate operations there in order to prove that our firms there are not, as it is widely alleged, "siphoning" huge profits out of Brazil in dividends paid to the United States parent company, as well as in payments to cover home-office overhead, know-how, patent rights and research.

The Chamber sent a detailed questionnaire to 300 firms there. Only nine responses were received. This is a shocking failure since excessive repatriation to the United States of profits is perhaps the most successful of all of the communist propaganda claims, one which could be easily refuted in most instances.

"United States firms here are going to have to publicize their financial information in their own defense," I was told by the president of one of our largest establishments in Brazil, "but in that case our local Brazilian competitors should do so too, since we are working the same markets, customers and suppliers." It is submitted here that Cold War considerations cannot tolerate United States business waiting around in the wings like a poorly trained stand-in until Brazilian corporate feudalism breaks down of its own accord, perhaps centuries later, whereas we could be taking a vigorous lead in pointing the way to modern practices.

The plain fact is, however, that no amount of good feeling or public relations is adequate to stem the tide now running against our private sector in Latin America. Only a thorough *restructuring* can save the day and justify the assignment to our private foreign capital operations of an expanded role in the continuing struggle.

*   *   *   *   *

These observations naturally inspire the question, what is the United States government doing in policy and program to protect, nourish and expand modern democratic capitalism in Latin America? The answer is: substantially nothing. Of course, this may be technically an overstatement, but not in substance. Existing programs to promote free enterprise are more in the nature of lip service than anything else. They are, in fact, dangerous because they lead some to claim and many to believe that third base is covered when it is not.

The so-called investment guarantee program is our best illustration. In theory it enables our investors in Latin America to pay a premium and obtain an insurance policy against confiscation, war and currency inconvertibility—risks not covered by private insurance companies. In practice, however, the program is practically inoperative in Latin America. One of the reasons is that under present law a treaty of understanding between the United States and the host government is a prerequisite to providing the coverage. Then each and every covered investment has to be approved in advance by Washington and the host government under the treaty.

Latin American governments, because of anti-United States political pressures or socialist inclinations, are in the main unable or unwilling to sign such a treaty. In other words, we have put the foreign government (Cuba, for example) in charge of determining whether we can protect our own foreign enterprises and they have decided we cannot. The damper this puts on new capital flow to Latin America under present conditions, especially in the wake of Cuba, is virtually total.

Furthermore, even if the necessary treaties were to be signed, the program would still be so inadequate as to be almost ridiculous. No way, for example, exists under present law for any *existing* facility to be protected. Presumably, in other words, only new investments are worthy of protection. One Latin American executive complained to me, "We could give half of the company to the peasants and still not be able to get protection against Cold War risks for the other half."

Further, a new investment, if it should become entitled to coverage, could not be disqualified by any kind of conduct however bad, just as there is no kind of conduct on the part of an existing enterprise, however salutary, that can entitle it to protection. As a matter of principle, it would seem that all United States private enterprises overseas—new or old—should be entitled to obtain protection against Cold War risks, but at the same time it appears to be extremely doubtful that any of them should today be entitled to sovereign protection from the United States government without paying a "price" in conduct that is specifically relevant to America's Cold War objectives, a "price" to be spelled out more fully hereinafter.

In any case, the so-called investment guarantee program is now inapplicable in fact in Latin America because, as a nation, we have placed our natural right to issue the guarantees beyond our power by requiring that the host government approve our issuance of them in advance. As a result, so-called U.S. war-risk-insurance coverage is unavailable everywhere except in Panama; expropriation risk guarantees are unavailable in Argentina, Brazil, Chile, Colombia, Mexico, Peru and Venezuela—95 per cent of Latin America in economic and population terms. Furthermore, convertibility risks, while covered much more widely due to the fact that Latin Americans do not want to take any chance of placing their own overseas investments out of bounds, are not available in Argentina, Brazil, Colombia, Guatemala, Mexico, Panama, or Venezuela.[29]

None of the $1 billion Cuban seizure was covered, although the investment guaranty legislation was enacted in 1954, five years before Castro.

In 1961 the Administration proposed and the Congress enacted a miniature expansion of this virtually non-existent program.[30] Political risk guarantees against loss of our private overseas investments continue to apply *only* if the host government approves, although the specific requirement for United States subrogation rights was softened. No procedure was included for covering existing investments under any conditions of conduct. The overall limit of coverage remains at $1 billion—a mere 10 per cent of what we already have in Latin America alone, and perhaps 50 per cent of the amount of new private long-term capital investment we should be laying out in Latin America alone, *annually,* to make a meaningful impact.*

All-risk guarantees may now be offered in special situations where government might want to "seed" some of its foreign aid with a little private money, up to an overall cumulative aggregate of $180 million worldwide.

The text of the "Role of American Private Enterprise," the 10 pages of 189 devoted to this subject in the Congressional presentation of the foreign aid program, is filled with warnings, reservations and qualifications about the capacity of private enterprise in these weighty matters. It speaks volumes about the composers' attitude toward our private sector. The theme is that private industry must fit strictly into the aid planners' total development plan, and must repress any idea that government aid is temporary or in any way replaceable by private enterprise.

"The contributions of United States private enterprise," the document states sternly, "must be regarded as an important complement to publicly funded economic assistance, but not as a substitute for them."[31]

In 1960, the Congress showed considerable interest in the enactment of a tax measure to make investment in Latin America more attractive. This legislation[32], which came to be known as the Boggs bill, was passed by the House in a whittled-down version but failed of passage in the Senate and now appears defunct. More recently, the Kennedy Administration has, unfortunately, sought a revenue measure which would retard rather than enhance new investment in Latin America. This deeply isolationist measure, which in its total impact goes far beyond the issues under consideration here, puts new dampers on the flow of U.S. investment to Latin America. In

---

*Sixty per cent, or about $600 million of this total $1 billion is already used up, most of it for coverage of investments made in Western Europe before that area was withdrawn from the program.

several respects the bill (H.R. 10650) increases U.S. taxes on Latin American earnings. This means that Latin American investors would have to bring more earnings home to maintain the same level of dividends. By the same token it will discourage the making of new investments. By thus draining Latin America of private capital, the administration's tax proposals actually violate an existing act of Congress, i.e. the provision in the 1961 Act for International Development which calls for the elimination of barriers to the "free flow of private capital" to Latin America.

There never have been any proposals, of which I am aware, to induce new private capital to go into Latin America through an application to foreign investment, in the less developed countries, of the Victory Loan concepts of World War II.

In consequence it can be said with conviction that there is not now in existence, or in prospect, any significant United States government program to induce more private capital to go to Latin America, or to do so more constructively, or to support and protect that which is already there.

Yet Latin America needs, most of all, a vast increase in remunerative jobs for her people. From the standpoint of individual freedom as well as compatibility with our society, these should be jobs in privately owned and widely owned establishments. Achieving this goal means a large step-up in private capital formation, preferably in industries having a relatively high labor-to-capital ratio. Most of this is going to have to come from Latin America herself in the way of greater productivity, harder work, repatriation of idle capital. But we can supplement her effort to perhaps a crucial extent by a foreign economic policy calculated to induce United States private capital to flow to Latin America, not only on a greatly increased scale but also on terms that will demonstrate in Latin America the strength and justice of modern capitalism.

These few concepts point to the way in which we can, if but we will, enlist our real strength in the Cold War struggle.

CHAPTER VII

REFERENCES

1 Journal, Stanford Research Institute, Menlo Park, Calif. 2nd quarter, 1961, Vol. 5, p. 41.

2 "U.S.-Latin American Relations," 86th Congress, 2nd sess., Senate Document 125, 1960, p. 120.

3 Economic Report of the President, January 1961, Government Printing Office, Washington, D.C., p. 212.

4 Survey of Current Business, OBE, Department of Commerce, September 1960, pp. S-20 to 22.

5 *Supra,* Note 2, p. 94.

6 *Ibid.*

7 *Chicago Tribune,* Sept. 21, 1961.

8 *Wall Street Journal,* Sept. 11, 1961.

9 "Developing Better Managers," An Eight Nation Study, National Industrial Conference Board, New York, 1961.

10 "Survey of Current Business, OBE, Department of Commerce, August 1961.

11 "U.S. Business Investments in Foreign Countries," Pizer and Cutler, Department of Commerce, Washington, D.C., 1960, p. 7.

12 *Supra,* Note 10.

13 Survey of Current Business, OBE, Department of Commerce, March 1962, p. 22.

14 *Supra,* Note 11, p. 6.

15 *Ibid.,* p. 101.

16 *Look* Magazine, Nov. 22, 1960.

17 "Joint International Business Ventures," W. G. Friedmann and G. Kalmanoff, Columbia University Press, 1961, p. 29.

[18] *San Francisco Examiner,* June 14, 1961.

[19] *Supra,* Note 17, p. 70.

[20] Harry A. Jarvis, "The Changing Role of the American Business-man in Latin America," Proceedings, 1961, Inter-American Industries Conference, Chicago Association of Commerce and Industry, p. 131.

[21] *Supra,* Note 17, p. 68.

[22] *Supra,* Note 17, p. 274.

[23] *Supra,* Note 16, p. 541.

[24] *New York Times,* Oct. 22, 1961.

[25] "Sociedades de Inversión," Servente, Tipografica Editora Argentina, Buenos Aires, 1959.

[26] Raymond W. Miller, *Can Capitalism Compete,* Ronald Press, New York, 1959.

[27] *Supra,* Note 17, p. 200.

[28] *Supra,* Note 11, p. 122.

[29] Investment Guarantees Handbook, July 1960, and Supplement for period ending Dec. 31, 1960, International Cooperation Administration, Washington, D.C.

[30] Public Law 87-195, 87th Congress, S. 1983, Sept. 4, 1961.

[31] "An Act for International Development," Department of State, June 1961, p. 102.

[32] H. R. 5, 86th Congress.

Policy and Program: The Exportation of Successful Capitalism

Our own brand of modern, widely shared democratic capitalism dispels the communist myth that private initiative and private ownership are inconsistent with the common good. Indeed, these personal prerogatives are among the fundamental freedoms protected by the concept of limited government.

It can hardly be denied that there were many unjust aspects of 19th century capitalism in the United States, just as there are elements of injustice in what we have referred to here as the post-feudal remnants of capitalism in Latin America today. Political democracy cannot bring freedom unless it is coupled with *economic* democracy, a social responsibility on the part of the chiefs of enterprise. It was the weakness of the latter quality in the capitalism of a century ago that gave momentum to the theories of Marx. Now we reject the philosophy of Marx because it is easy enough to see that there is no freedom when all men are slaves of the state.

At the same time, as clearly pointed out by Mortimer Adler in the Kelso and Adler "Capitalist Manifesto," there has grown up a widespread and erroneous belief that the way to ameliorate the harsher aspects of old-fashioned capitalism is to adopt parts but not all of Marx's socialist policies. This is a fundamental fallacy because an economy heavily socialized by government ownership, intervention and master planning creates a "society . . . in which there is sharp class division between the rulers who are, in effect, the owners and the workers who are economically as well as politically enslaved."

Now we can plainly see that it is not the intrusions of socialism into our United States capitalism that keep it free of communism, but rather the widespread enlargement of capitalism's primary attribute: private ownership. Thus it is "socialism, not capitalism, which is essentially incompatible with democracy."

It is the principles of capitalism itself upon which we must build, rather than progressive or "creeping" socialism, say Adler and Kelso, because "partly socialized capitalism is an unstable mixture of conflicting principles, a halfway house from which we must go forward in one direction or the other."[1]

These concepts are even more vividly applicable to the nations of Latin America and our relationship to them. We have seen the heavy layer of socialism which they have engrafted upon their backward capitalism. The resulting frictions have led to their present unstable and frustrated societies. *All of Latin America is now at a critical point in history from which its nations will either proceed through rapidly progressive socialist stages to communism or, reversing their course, will turn in the direction of modern capitalism. They cannot do both and the choice will be decisive.*

In the words of Sir Oliver Franks, Chairman of England's great Lloyds Bank, it "cannot be just assumed that the development of the underdeveloped peoples will take place in the historical way through the methods of private enterprise. An alternative is on offer, the alternative of the communist system in which governmental decisions determine all the workings of the economy. . . . It must be a matter of high policy and hard work to lead the developing peoples so that they *wish* their economies to grow in freedom, in a broad way on lines similar to our own."[2]

If Latin America chooses the course on which they are now

launched in the main—a compromise with ever heavier doses of socialization—the arrival of communism is near. If they elect the opposite, more time will be needed, for the road to modern capitalism is long, but it will triumph in the end.

At this juncture, the kind of influence we bring to Latin America through our foreign economic policies is critical. Unfortunately the message we bring today is more government-to-government aid, government intervention, government planning, government ownership—policies that can do nothing except push Latin America faster down the road to communism. It is believed that the proposals outlined herein would not only help Latin America get on the road to successful capitalism, but would, in the process, clarify our own national intentions.

In essence, in the Cold War, capitalism and communism are engaged in a struggle to prove which is the more efficient system. Latin America starts with a capitalistic structure, but must now be deemed "uncommitted" in view of Cuba and the fact that a probable majority of her peoples favor Castro communism.

Thus each side now has important advantages and the influences each brings to bear will be decisive. That we sense this as a nation is evidenced by the Act of Bogotá, the Alliance for Progress and the Congressional acquiescence in the increased levels of government support—in the case of Latin America, to regions in the neighborhood of $1.5 billion per year. But the evidence that we fail to sense the qualitative aspect of the struggle lies in the fact that no significant attempt is being made to enlarge private capital flow to Latin America, nor to make our private contribution more relevant to the struggle.

This is all the more surprising in view of the fact that private person-to-person transactions are part of our very stock in trade, whereas the communist society is so structured as to be literally incapable of engaging in a single one. This gives us an arsenal of weapons not possessed by communism, and creates what might be called its Freedom Gap.

There is no way in which any individual Russian can enter into any personal relationship with any Latin American, either as partner, employee, co-owner, seller, buyer, principal or agent. Not a solitary Russian can be a co-venturer in a Latin American firm. None can emigrate to Latin America and take a job in a private establishment, nor be a private tourist, nor export anything from Russia to anyone in Latin America, nor buy a single article from anyone in Latin America—unless, of course, the Russian government elects to do these things for him. There is no way in which a Russian can invest in the future of Latin America.

All of these things each of us can do if we so desire, without exception and without interference from our government, whereas the communists' very system requires that every transaction with Latin America be a government-to-government transaction.

How do we harness these inherent advantages and put them into practical action in Latin America? First, if we want capitalism to prevail, it seems rather obvious that we should start by creating more capitalists, by finding ways to carry a person-to-person capitalistic message to Latin America. Secondly, since the poverty of Latin America stems immediately from joblessness, the creation of more private jobs in more private plants must be a key objective.

What we are searching for is a way to enlist our private sector in the Cold War, while diminishing and ultimately eliminating the government-to-government outlays which "copy" the limited weaponry of the communists and wreck our own balance of payments.

While the major role is to be a private one, obviously government must play an important financial part in the attraction of more new private investment capital into combat in Latin America, since Cold War conditions there have created a situation inimical to the normal flow of investment funds from the United States private sector to Latin America.

The channeling of new investment by government policy is not a new experience for us. In World War II, our government gave advantages in the way of fast tax write-offs to industry to enable it to construct plants—say, to make gas masks—that would not have been economical in peacetime. In the absence of some such government incentives, it was correctly assumed that special risks—such as an early end to the war or a surprise shift in military needs—might make investment in a gas mask plant unattractive when tested by conventional investment criteria.

In order to expand our industrial capacity to meet high war demands, our government also guaranteed Victory Loans, made by our private banks to private companies, so that they could make enlargements that might have been imprudent in a peaceful world. Also, of course, the government issued insurance against war risks, because private insurance firms could not reasonably cover them since they had insufficient experience upon which to base a rate structure, and the risks taken would be too cosmic in character.

In endeavoring to apply the lesson of these policies to Latin America we should not be blind to the significant differences between an all-out military conflict and the present Cold War. In World War II the government took virtual control of our economy to direct it into the military effort. Prices and wages went under control and the War Production Board attempted to wield vast powers in the way of planning and organizing production, waiving the antitrust laws and allocating supplies and materials among manufacturers.

The need for developmental private capital to flow into Latin America on a vastly increased and more purposeful basis is in every respect as urgent, from the standpoint of winning the Cold War, as was the channeling of production into military items in World War II. Some, indeed, have urged that this government machinery of World War II be reestablished to marshal our attack on the development problems of Latin America.

Leaving aside the fact that price and wage controls were largely ineffective in World War II, there is, in any case, a controlling difference between the two situations. We have become prepared to accept, in a shooting war, the abrogation of many civil liberties and a high degree of government intervention. But the very necessity of the Cold War struggle is that capitalism, while operating freely and unfettered, prove its inherent economic superiority over statist philosophies.

It is the very essence of our contention that free institutions operating within the framework of political democracy will inevitably prevail over a regimented society. If we succumb to regimentation or to what, in effect, is its equivalent—assignment of the economic development role to the government—we accept the system of our enemy and confess the inadequacy of our own.

Hence, in all that is to be recommended, the role of government should be confined to the creation of the climate in which private institutions, operating freely, can take hold of the development job. In due course, government can then make an orderly retirement from a field of battle where it is sorely out of place, and confine itself to the conventional activities for which it was created.

A FINANCING FOR FREEDOM ACT

The Congress of the United States, in order to induce more private capital to invest in job-creating facilities in Latin America and to encourage compliance—by existing as well as new investments—with purposeful criteria specifically relevant to the Cold War struggle, should enact a comprehensive new measure, to be known perhaps as the Financing For Freedom Act.

Under the Act, the United States government should insure United States investors, in Latin America and other less developed countries, against all political or non-commercial risks, including expropriation without compensation, riot, sabotage, exchange controls and war. This insurance should be written by private United States insurance companies, banks and other financial firms which would collect a premium to be remitted to the Treasury Department. The insurance against expropriation should cover "creeping" expropriation as well as outright physical seizure, as does the protection the West German government now offers its foreign investments.

United States government-backed coverage against political risks is now offered through private banks and insurance companies to our exporters who sell abroad on credit, and there is no apparent reason why analogous protection cannot be extended to United States investments made overseas.

The insurance protection should be automatic in the sense that no treaty with or other acquiescence by the foreign government would be required as it is now. In the Cold War the placement of new private development capital in hostile or risky environments is the very thing desired. There is no justification for placing such investments beyond our own protection. Places into which our private investments will not naturally flow without special protection are often the ones in which actual demonstrations of our private system at work are most needed, from a Cold War standpoint. The features of present law which require a treaty with the host government, and approval of each new investment as a prerequisite to coverage, should be repealed. So also should the present $1 billion aggregate ceiling, and the feature of present law making insurance coverage unavailable to existing investments. The political-risk coverage should be available to any *existing* United States enterprise in Latin America, upon compliance with the same criteria as those applicable to *new* investments.

At the central core of the program outlined herein lies the

concept that the mere making of private investments in Latin America, regardless of the risk entailed, is not an adequate justification for government insurance. In order to qualify for this political-risk insurance, therefore, our foreign enterprises should be required to adopt specific measures to widen their ownership and modernize their employee practices on the subject of profit sharing and training.

First, such insurance should not be made available to any United States enterprise in Latin America unless and until it has committed itself to offer to sell to the people of the host country at least 35 per cent (or some other percentage to be fixed by the Congress in the enabling legislation) of its ordinary common shares. Such commitment should contemplate the offering of the shares for sale to the public in small lots, and on the instalment plan where necessary, in order to avoid the acquisition of preponderant amounts of these new share distributions by the few Latin Americans in whose hands a large amount of the wealth is already concentrated. The method of financing such instalment sales by government-backed Cold War Victory Loans is covered subsequently herein.

Evidence of the actual subscription of the specified percentage of the stock, by the minimum number of local investors specified in the commitment, would have to be produced within a specified period or the political risk insurance would lapse. No attempt should be made, however, to restrict normal transfers of the stock once issued in a bona fide transaction.

Furthermore, such insurance coverage should not be available until the enterprise has committed itself to establish an employee profit-sharing plan providing a suitable mechanism for employee acquisition of shares of stock in the enterprise. Among other things, the criteria set forth in the Act should guard against illusory plans, such as those requiring high employee matching ratios that are unrealistic under Latin American wage and salary practices.

Having regard especially for smaller firms not ordinarily accustomed to public offering of shares, the adoption of an employee stock-ownership plan could be accepted as an alternative to such public offering, provided the operation of the plan would within a given period satisfy, through employee ownership, the above mentioned requirement that at least 35 per cent (or other percentage fixed in the Act) of the shares of the enterprise be owned by local citizens.

Finally, such insurance coverage should be available only to firms which commit themselves to employee-training programs having a basic educational and vocational content. The specific criteria, to be developed by the Congress after hearings, would presumably call not only for vocational education pertinent to the operation of the company but also for the teaching of reading, writing, arithmetic, and English, together with the basic ideals of western Christian capitalistic society.

Through this measure, United States enterprises in Latin America would become a key instrument in (1) reducing the literacy gap, (2) increasing Latin American productivity and (3) offering educational opportunities free from the usual communist indoctrination. There should, of course, be no objection to many firms combining to provide these facilities.

A failure to honor the commitments undertaken by the insured enterprise would nullify its insurance coverage.

The limiting of the availability of the political-risk insurance to situations in which, perforce, there will be a body of local citizens and employees motivated by a desire to protect the enterprise, automatically puts the risk in far lower key than has been the case under present law. The commitments described will act as automatic risk-reducers, taking a major part of the exposure off the shoulders of Uncle Sam. Yet at the same time such protection—against all risks save the ordinary commercial risks of the market place—would attract new flow of private income and job-producing investment to Latin America.

No United States concern preferring to proceed *without* the coverage would be obliged to purchase it, nor to conform to its requirements. In other words, any firm believing its own policies to be adequate to protect its shareholders against these risks without insurance could go happily ahead without it. Yet it seems probable that a large number of investments, new and old, would *want* to bring themselves within the coverage since its requirements would, in a sense, be an expression of a national purpose to bring our private enterprises overseas into purposeful combat in the Cold War.

No United States government official or master-planner would pore over each investment, trying to decide whether it fit certain "priorities" of his pet 5- or 10-year plan. So far as the United States is concerned, reliance would be rested solely on the market place, that is, the judgment of the experienced investor on the question whether the investment would make money, and, in consequence, create jobs and savings and wealth.

Needless to say, no squad of United States government officials would be asked to go along to "administer" the investment.*

Such a political risk insurance program would doubtless attract substantial amounts of capital to Latin America that would not otherwise go there. Doubtless, also, a considerable number of our existing firms doing business there would want to qualify by marketing the requisite portion of their shares in Latin America, and complying with the other facets of the plan.

It may be surmised that the marketing in Latin America,

---

*In Chile, a small country, we had 55 people serving in our foreign-aid office in April 1961, compared to 45 in all of the rest of our embassy, including political, economic, consular and military attaches and Voice of America. Both figures exclude clerical help and local employees. This was before the Alliance for Progress got into swing.

among employees and the public at large, of a significant portion of the equity stock of new ventures being established there and of existing wholly owned enterprises, would in due course —and perhaps rather quickly—absorb and draw into productive investment most of the rather limited amount of available private equity capital in Latin America.

Accordingly, unless some method were developed to finance additional local equity purchases, the very requirement for local stock participation might operate to retard the desired increase in capital flow to Latin America, especially into mass ownership. To meet this obstacle, as well as to stimulate an ever greater investment flow to Latin America, under the constructive criteria applicable to the political-risk insurance plan, a program of government guaranteed all-risk credits should be offered, through our private lending institutions, to investments meeting such criteria.

The World War II Victory Loan procedure is closely analogous. Under that program the United States government, chiefly through private banks and lending institutions acting as agent for the government, guaranteed up to 90 per cent of the face amount of loans made by the banks and institutions to enterprises willing to go ahead with designated categories of needed industrial expansion. In return for the guarantee, the borrowing enterprise paid a small premium which was remitted to the United States Treasury to defray the costs of the program, and as a reserve to cover any losses. Billions were loaned in this fashion, but the premiums more than covered the losses so that neither the United States Treasury nor the taxpayer suffered loss.

Applying the principle of that program to the present circumstances, any United States private lending institution willing to lend long-term capital to a United States investor in Latin America would, providing the investor were prepared to comply with the conditions of the political-risk insurance plan, be entitled to obtain a United States government guarantee against all risks—commercial as well as political—up to 85 per cent of the face amount of the loan, or some similar percentage to be fixed in the enabling legislation. In no case should any such guarantee exceed the dollar amount of the minimum percentage of common stock of the enterprise required to be sold to Latin Americans in order to comply with the plan. Through this latter limitation, the exposure of the United States under the all-risk guarantee would be specifically equated to the expansion of private equity ownership in Latin America.

The United States guarantee in favor of the United States bank or insurance company or other lending institution would cover all risks (up to 85 per cent or other fixed percentage of the loan), rather than merely political or so-called Cold War risks since, in essence, the loan would enable the enterprise to complete its capitalization at the outset and at the same time to satisfy the local ownership requirement, by selling shares on the instalment plan and using the instalments to reduce the loan.

The commercial soundness of the venture would still have to stand the test of the market place since the United States investor would be uninsured commercially on at least 65 per cent* of the total equity investment and the United States private lending institution would be unguaranteed on at least 15 per cent (or some lesser percentage) of the amount of its loan to the enterprise.

The political-risk insurance plan would take the real scare out of Latin American investing today. The requirement for heavy popular partnership participation locally would reduce risk and spread the fruits of capitalism. The Cold War Victory Loan program would add substantially to the finances

---

*If we assume the minimum percentage of the equity stock required to be sold in Latin America is fixed at 35 per cent by the Congress.

presently available for expansion in Latin America and, not only that, would provide a way to finance a portion into the hands of employees and purchasers of limited means. The profit-sharing plan and training programs would make the employee an advocate of private enterprise and an adversary of communism. These would be capitalism's modern weapons at work.

It is never quite possible to predict with accuracy the effect incentive programs will have. It is probable that Congressional hearings on these proposals would develop the need for added inducements. In the field of taxation the principles of the Boggs bill should be enacted so as to permit deferral of tax on income earned in less developed countries regardless of whether operations are carried on as a branch or as a foreign subsidiary, so long as the requirements of the political-risk guarantee program are observed. The tax laws should make it possible for either foreign subsidiaries or foreign branches of United States firms to comply with the conditions of the plan, without incurring United States taxes additional to those now incurred.

One more modification of our tax laws or policies appears essential to the effective working of the plan. It is common practice for developing countries to offer exception from their own income taxes, for varying periods of time, as an incentive to attract new foreign investments—either generally or in specified industrial fields. Frequently, however, these incentives are frustrated by the application of our own income taxes since, generally speaking, our income tax rate is 52 per cent, less credit for taxes paid to the foreign country. The foreign country's investment incentive is destroyed if we simply collect the tax it has foregone.

To avoid this consequence it is necessary that the United States government enter into so-called "Tax Sparing" treaties with the foreign governments concerned, under which the United States government would agree to forego the same percentage of tax as that foregone by the host government, and that such treaties be approved by the Senate. At the present writing, no such treaties are in effect. A number are under consideration, but the only one completed, in the case of Pakistan, has not met with Senate approval.

It would seem unlikely that the benefits of the program should be extended to any investment by a United States citizen or firm which is less than 25 per cent of the total enterprise. In other words, the program is not intended to cover mere foreign portfolio holdings of United States citizens.

It should be definitely contemplated, as an important implicit aspect of the program, that it could be used to finance the purchase and resale to the public at large in Latin America and the United States, of those business firms and establishments now held in government ownership in Latin America. In this respect, as well as the others outlined, the program seeks to make a qualitative contribution to the cause of capitalism. The excuse now frequently offered by Latin American governments for becoming partners in industrial and business enterprises is that insufficient capital is available in the hands of the public at large. Within the past year the government of Venezuela has taken 50 per cent of the equity stock in the aluminum venture being developed by our Reynolds Aluminum Company there, and the government of Mexico is taking 51 per cent of the stock of Du Pont's new chemical pigments operation in that country. The program under discussion would, in effect, outlaw this excuse.

The influx of substantial amounts of new United States private capital to Latin America would inevitably make available *local* government funds, formerly channeled into industry, for needed infrastructure items such as schools, roads, dams and other non-revenue-producing public works. As necessary these funds could be supplemented by long-term loans for like purposes from private lenders, the World Bank and other international lending institutions. Then the United

States government could get out of the business of "federal
aid to schools," "federal aid to roads," "federal aid to what-
not" in Latin America.

The aims and goals of the Financing For Freedom Act
would be:

►To stimulate personal identification of the local population
with the economic, social and political rewards of a privately
developed society.

►To enlarge educational standards and purchasing capacities
of indigenous people.

►To counter the tendency toward state ownership of productive and business facilities, thus working against the
Soviet objective.

►To discourage expropriation and discrimination.

►To offer the best chance for private versus socialized economic development.

►To supplant balance-of-payments drains in the way of foreign aid.

The results in terms of jobs and development could be
very striking. Our enterprises own $8 billion of assets in
Latin America now, and they employ a million people. This
means there are $8 thousand of private U. S. capital invest-
ment behind each job. Many of our Latin American investments were made when costs were at lower levels. But on the
other hand, much of the present investment is in petroleum,
an industry with an extremely high capital-to-labor ratio.*
Hence it would not seem inappropriate to assume that today
$8 thousand of capital expenditure for new plant or equip-
ment would be required to create one new job in Latin

---

*As an illustration, Venezuela derives over $1 billion a year from
her oil, accounting for more than 90 per cent of her foreign-exchange
earnings, 60 per cent of her government revenues, and 25 per cent
of her gross national product. Yet the oil industry employs only
40,000 people out of a work force of 2½ million—less than 2 per
cent of the working people.[4]

America. Hence if United States investors invested $2 billion per year, and the Latin Americans invested $2 billion more in new mixed-ownership enterprises or expansions of existing ones, this would create one-half million new jobs each year, a fantastic contribution on our part to Latin American development.

The effect of the climate that could be created by such a program is not to be overlooked. It is very probable that investment in Latin America by the other capital exporting nations of the world, Western Europe and Japan chiefly, would be similarly enhanced. The noted international banker, Dr. Herman J. Abs, general manager of Germany's Deutsche Bank, has long advocated the adoption of a multinational program to guarantee the investments of the capitalist nations against political risks, in the less developed countries, on a uniform basis. It might be that the exercise of bold leadership in this field by the United States, as to its own citizens' investments in these areas, would lead to an international program of this character.[3]

The possibility of a $2 billion new annual United States private capital flow to Latin America does not seem exaggerated when it is remembered that $2 billion is only about 5 per cent of the nearly $40 billion expended by industry each year for new plant and equipment inside the United States.

And evidence collected from observation and personal interview in several countries of Latin America, as well as at home, indicates that new development and growth under such a plan would be substantial.

In the first place, the recent public offerings made by Willys Overland in Brazil, Union Carbide in Mexico, and Koppers in Argentina demonstrate that Latin Americans are hungry to acquire a share in United States subsidiary companies doing business in their homelands.

Then, too, the emerging mutual fund industry is pleading with United States industry to make some of its stock available

locally. "One of our main problems," says William R. B. Atkin,
a young Britisher who runs Ibec's Fundo Crecinco in Chile,
"is that only two or three local stocks of United States firms
are on the market here."

"Your plan," he told me, "would bring a lot of new capital
to Chile, and the public offerings would strengthen the capital
market."

Our charge d'affaires in Chile at that time, William L.
Krieg, speaking of the treaty requirement of present law, said
to me, "Even a president of Chile who is favorable to private
enterprise and increased foreign investment, as is President
Alessandri, cannot succeed in making a treaty against expropriation because the political forces of the left are too strong."

"Specifically," he said, "I know of a number of plans for
expansion and new investment that are not being undertaken
here because some such plan is not in effect."

Victor Algrant, the commercial attaché of our embassy in
Chile, fluent in four languages and deeply schooled in the
economics of Chile, told me that in his opinion this plan would
definitely attract needed private capital that would not otherwise come. "Chile is a small country, hence offers a small
market, but many small businesses could succeed here if the
product to be manufactured is not now being made here and
is not a luxury item—things like pharmaceuticals, special
chemicals, agricultural processing and small machinery fabrication."

While I was in Colombia, José Goméz-Pinzón, formerly
Minister of Public Works and one of the leaders of CEAS,
the organization working to stem communism by an increase
in private initiative, education and political action, told me,
"The plan is intellectually sound because it would bring a
modern conscience to capitalism in Latin America. It avoids
the extremes of private wealth concentration on the one hand,
and state control and ownership on the other."

When I discussed the plan in detail with Arturo Gomez

Jaramillo, head of the coffee association there—a slim, restless man of 40 who told me he doubled the wages of the association's employees the day he became president, he said to me, "Of all the whole spectrum of suggestions about industrial development, this is the clearest and most needed."

The plan was enthusiastically received by Fenalco, the Colombian Chamber of Commerce, and its chairman, Pablo Cárdenas Peréz. With a twinkle in his eye, he got off a typical dry Spanish witticism. "Business is never going to be suspected of left-wing tendencies," he said, "and therefore it should be the one to sell modern capitalism."

Dr. Misael Pastrana, present Minister of Public Works of Colombia, expressed great enthusiasm for the plan. He and two Colombian senators had been working on a bill, then still in preparation, to give special incentives to foreign investors who have Colombian co-owners or partners. "There is not the slightest doubt," he told me, "that the enactment of the plan in the United States would induce Latin American nations to enact compatible incentive measures, giving income-tax or other advantages to mixed enterprises."

"Industrial jobs are the only answer to the hordes coming down from the Andes," I was told by our charge de'affaires in Peru. There are such jobs now, but the jungle of human poverty and filth that rings the beautiful city of Lima testifies that there are not half enough. Peru's exports, heavily concentrated in cotton, copper, sugar, iron ore, and fish meal, were $500 million in 1960, exceeding imports by $90 million. There is great opportunity, given the right incentives, for growth and diversification in this vast land, which has every kind of climate and terrain known to man, is larger than Texas, California, and New York combined, and has a population of only 12 million people. As things are now, however, Peru's imports include many things that could be produced there under conditions conducive to new capital formation.

As noted previously, Mexico has adopted a law in the

mining field, and a policy in some other situations, designed to force foreign investors to vest control in Mexican interests. In a sense, this Mexican law already responds to the plan outlined herein, but unfortunately, it appears to be more an expression of nationalistic attitudes than a program for the attraction of needed capital. Indeed, its rigid control requirement does not conform to the realities of investment practices and policies which turn on a multiplicity of variable factors, not the least of which is frequently the possession of the patents or advanced technology. Regrettably, it is a fair assumption that the law will tend to repel rather than attract foreign capital, in which case a further increase in government financing and government ownership may be expected. An even greater flaw is that the law contains no feature for the dispersal of capital ownership and, until it does, one may expect that the controlling 51 per cent will fall into the hands of the few wealthy groups in which so much Mexican industrial capital is now already concentrated.

Suppose the United States government adopted the policies advocated here. What influence would they have on indigenous Latin American enterprises in which United States citizens have no interest. The direct influence would be very great, in the opinion of David Beatty, official in Brazil of Deltec, Inc., the New York underwriting firm that specializes in the distribution of Latin American stock offerings to Latin Americans. Beatty, a World War II pilot in Brazil, who stayed on and makes his home there, talked far into the night with me about the various aspects of the plan.

"I believe," he told me, "that pride and competitive factors would have the effect of inducing many Brazilian companies to take parallel action, meaning more generous practices in the way of pay, training, profit sharing and stock offering."

That our own local managers in Latin America are well aware of the need for change is amply evidenced by the resolutions favoring local offering of stock adopted, after a year of internal disagreement, by the membership of the United States Chamber of Commerce in Rio de Janeiro and Sao Paulo.

The overwhelming majority of informed Latin Americans, in and out of government, with whom I have talked believe that our foreign-aid programs tend to sponsor socialism. "The thing I like about your plan," said Dr. Otero Monsegur, distinguished deputy chief of the Central Bank of Argentina, "is that it finds a way for growth on a people-to-people basis. Let equity growth belong to individuals and let governments build the roads, borrowing for this purpose from the World Bank or the Inter-American Bank if need be."

In Venezuela, there are 800 card-carrying communist students in the engineering school of the university. With communists being manufactured almost like cookies, it is high time capitalism came up with new techniques to create more capitalists. Venezuelan industrialists like Eugenio Mendoza and Gustavo Vollmer are doing everything in their power to alleviate the harsh conditions that prevail in Venezuela. They and their associates have established modern polio clinics and nurseries for children of working parents. They have developed, publicized and financed ingenious low-cost self-help housing plans. Business firms, they told me, are getting behind the Catholic Church in its Fe y Alegria program in the slums. Privately owned land in Caracas is being donated for a new private university to offer high quality instruction free of communist influence. A young Caracas lawyer, Nicomedes Zuloaga, hijo, is taking the lead in forming a Venezuelan chapter of "Ideas," chapters of which exist in Mexico and Argentina. "Ideas" fights communism on the intellectual and practical level, enlisting professors, priests, businessmen, lawyers, doctors, political figures and other community leaders. On the action front, for example, to help counteract the Cuban invasion fiasco, "Ideas" was at that very moment pushing frequent radio spots dramatizing Castro's executions without trial and his refusal to hold elections.

These men are strongly in favor of the plan outlined herein. In fact, they had summarized it in a brief brochure being distributed throughout Latin America. "This is the kind of thing we need, not handouts," one of them said to me.

My wife and I visited at the home of C. Allan Stewart, then serving as First Minister of our embassy there, in company with Emil Rieve of our AFL-CIO. After reviewing the various aspects of this plan, Stewart told us he believed it "would be great for Venezuela." Rieve expressed the opinion that "more than all else these nations need entrepreneur capital."

While in Venezuela last, I had the pleasure of presenting this plan to the board of directors of the United States Chamber of Commerce in Venezuela, whose chairman is a personable entrepreneur named William Hinkle, founder of an industrial gas firm there. Other special guests were present including Gerald Maxfield, Venezuelan partner of Price Waterhouse & Company, and head of the North American Association in Venezuela. The group went on record in favor of the plan, the chairman describing it as the "freshest approach heard yet."

In the absence of some such plan, politicians in Venezuela are going to continue to be lured, or even driven, to state ownership. Dr. Rafael Caldera, head of Copei, the Christian Democratic party, told me that state intrusion into private industry will always be necessary when the private sector does not come up with the necessary funds. Thus does a capital vacuum favor communism.

The new Reynolds Aluminum enterprise in Venezuela will be owned one half by the government. It is entirely probable that if a plan of this character had been in effect when that transaction was being arranged, this 50 per cent of the stock could have been financed into widespread private ownership, and a good blow struck against state socialism.

As we left Venezuela, Teodoro Moscoso from Puerto Rico

would be coming in a few days to commence serving as our ambassador there.* Already the left-wing press and communist propagandists were threatening and denouncing him as an "imperialist," a citizen of a "subjugated colony" of the United States. They seemed determined to destroy the man whose Operation Bootstrap attracted huge amounts of new private capital to poverty-stricken, illiterate Puerto Rico, and made her the showcase of the Caribbean.

Puerto Rico is a prosperous testimonial to the proposition that the road to successful democratic capitalism in Latin America lies along private pathways rather than government aid. This small island in the Caribbean, largely mountainous, 100 miles long and 35 wide, Spanish-speaking, has enjoyed a unique status under our law since 1952 as an entirely self-governing commonwealth, freely and voluntarily associated with the United States.

She is one of the most densely populated areas in the world. With about 683 inhabitants per square mile, there is little to distinguish her from other republics of Latin America. Indeed, most Latin American nations are immensely rich in natural resources as compared to Puerto Rico, and for generations she languished in poverty, ignorance and disease. As recently as 1940, Puerto Rico was still a poverty-stricken colony, and even in 1950 conditions were little better. The big sugar companies were wholly owned in the United States. The concentration of investment in sugar necessitated heavy imports of foodstuffs.

Today, Puerto Rico has one of the highest standards of living in Latin America. Under Operation Bootstrap she has established more than 600 new factories, and has greatly increased agricultural production, transportation and communications facilities, electric power, housing and other industries. Puerto Ricans now own most of the sugar mills,

---

*Now serving President Kennedy as aid administrator for Latin America.

once wholly owned on the mainland. Many new United
States-owned firms welcome local partners, and all are desirous
of employing Puerto Rican managers and technicians whenever obtainable.

But Puerto Rico had to learn the hard way, had to actually
experience the failure of government ownership and government intervention in development. In the words of Ambassador Moscoso:

Initially, the government set out to operate five factories
making cement, glass containers, paperboard, structural clay
products and shoes. Wartime shortages helped float these public enterprises; but with the postwar slump in rum sales, our
plants to make glass and paperboard for packaging were too
big by the time we got them going. Next, the shoe plant priced
itself out of the market by trying to produce too many styles
in uneconomical short runs. The cement plant had been
purchased by PRIDCO as a going concern from the federal
government's relief agency and was profitable from the outset.
But price setting and wage negotiations were complicated. A
government-owned factory had other government agencies
among its largest customers. Its employees also were con-
stituents. Take my word for it, that is one of the most difficult
ways to "meet a payroll."

During this early period the Development Company did
prove, however, that it was possible for Puerto Rico to produce
something besides hand needlework and sugar. But at the
end of 1947, five years after its establishment, the company had
invested most of its capital without denting Puerto Rico's
problem. Not only was unemployment as high as prewar, but
when renewed competition from Japan and the Philippines
killed off contract home needlework, it got worse. The mere
hope of an industrial or construction job drew farmers into
the cities to swell the rolls of unemployed. Although the Development Company had created 2,000 jobs, at least 200,000
were needed. The company's investment was generating perhaps $4,000,000 of new income per year when we needed $1
billion.

Those first five years convinced us in Puerto Rico that

government capital and government know-how were entirely too scarce and too limited to meet our people's needs. It was also becoming evident that existence of government-owned plants made the promotion of private ventures more difficult. So we resolved to use government funds, not as a principal ingredient, but as a catalyst. We sold the Development Company's plants to a private buyer and organized ourselves for a different kind of development effort.

To attract new capital and the production and sales know-how that goes with it, we enacted tax incentives which had to be equitable to existing industry and to business and labor interested in the U. S. Puerto Rico has no voting representation in the U. S. Congress and U. S. Federal taxes do not apply in the Commonwealth.* The exemption is from our own taxes on corporate income and property and is for ten years. We also enacted minimum wage laws. To all this we gave the name "Operation Bootstrap" to emphasize that the success of our plans literally depended on lifting ourselves up by our own bootstraps. In the five years before Operation Bootstrap was started Puerto Rico established 19 factories, or an average of about four per year. The next five years saw 169 new factories added, or about 34 a year. In the plan's second five years, now ending, we have established 350 more plants, or an average increase of 70 plants a year.[5]

Operation Bootstrap carries a lesson to every Latin American country for, as its creator says, "Risk capital is the crying need of every one of them." The Puerto Rican experience provides a clear prophecy that the billions in government-to-government aid we now are contemplating would not make a "dent," to use his word, in the Latin American development problem.

We must now establish in our national mind the proposition that our primary policy, in the development of these

---

*Hence, it may be noted, "tax sparing" was automatically effective in Puerto Rico, unlike the case of other Latin American countries. See page above.

underindustrialized nations, is the advancement of free and private ownership and jobs. Then the roles of government and business can be clear and constructive and mutually supporting. All the rest will flow from that.

The very key to our helping Latin America start down the road to more successful capitalism lies in offering United States government benefits or incentives to our industries operating in Latin America, *in exchange for* business conduct that serves constructive national purposes. The result of our failure to have done so, politically, is that we do not now offer, in any significant sense, either the needed incentives for expansion or protection from risk to our exposed enterprises in Latin America, and the foreign expression of our dynamic and democratic capitalism either lacks clarity of expression or is downright hurtful to us.

As a nation we must make these hard and realistic choices if we would put the horses of free enterprise ahead of the carts and tumbrels of communism, thereby offering to the uncommitted people and underdeveloped lands the promise of strength and freedom which is our own heritage.

AN ACT OF BOGOTA FOR PRIVATE ENTERPRISE?

It would be foolhardy to assume that United States policies and programs for stimulating a large and sustained flow of private risk capital to Latin America could succeed without the cooperation of the Latin American governments themselves. Furthermore, it may be questioned whether our national interest would be served by an undiscriminating offering of these sovereign benefits with respect to nations that refuse to foster a climate favorable to private enterprise in general and new private investments in particular, any more than it is served by the giving of foreign aid to neutral, non-aligned or hostile nations.

Accordingly, in enacting the Financing for Freedom Act, and as a part of it, the Congress of the United States should declare certain principles to be essential to the effective operation of these policies and programs:

► Honest elections and honest governments. Without them, no measures for economic development can succeed and the fruits of progress fall into the hands of crooked politicians and their cronies.

► Repatriation of Latin American capital resting overseas. It is positively immoral to suggest that we should take unusual measures to export our capital to risky Latin America without insisting that the $5 to $10 billion of their own that has taken refuge in the United States and Europe should be brought home and invested in development in their own countries. This was a key measure required by our Bell Commission on the economic reconstruction of the Philippines following World War II.

► And, finally, the fostering of a climate conducive to widespread ownership of enterprise, including the reduction of state proprietorship of productive facilities.

Violation of these fundamental principles would entitle our government to terminate the further availability of the credits and guarantees otherwise applicable.

Through these measures, we will channel our resources into those nations truly desirous of pursuing a course toward modern democratic capitalism—rather than dissipating them without discrimination among those who court or openly espouse economic and political philosophies alien to our own.

CHAPTER VIII

REFERENCES

[1] Louis J. Kelso and Mortimer J. Adler, *The Capitalist Manifesto,* Random House, New York, 1958, pp. X-XVI.

[2] Sir Oliver Franks, "World Economic Growth: The Outlook," Stanford Research Institute, National Industrial Conference Board, Menlo Park, California, 1961.

³ Dr. Herman J. Abs, address, Commonwealth Club of San Francisco, Sept. 15, 1961; and see Marcel A. Demonque, president of Aments Lafarge, France, "Problems the West Faces," Stanford Research Institute, September 1961, who advances the idea of international reinsurance for bilateral political guarantees.

⁴ *Supra,* Chapter V, Note 3, p. 121.

⁵ Teodoro Moscoso, "Puerto Rico Chooses Free Enterprise"; *Private Investment: The Key to International Development,* McGraw-Hill, New York, 1958, pp. 142-47.

The Ultimate Test: A Unity of Interest

From Benjamin Franklin's time to the present day, the cardinal rule of United States foreign policy has been that it must stand the test of national self-interest. Not, to be sure, must it serve our own ends in any narrow nationalistic or materialistic sense, but it must achieve consistency with our most humanitarian ideals: self-reliance; personal initiative; what we mean when we say "the land of the free and the home of the brave."

In the preceding pages, we have tried to show that a foreign economic policy based on massive government-to-government aid, rather than on the expansion of enlightened private entrepreneurship, cannot serve our national interest well.

Such a policy places us in alignment with the Left in most places in Latin America. For example, we thereby espouse the social democratic school which believes, in an extreme way, in a full service state with the government as the active director of all economic policy. Between them and private industry, which they distrust, there exists at best an uneasy truce.[1] Inevitably, we thereby give a kind of economic and political endorsement to officials all over Latin America who have virtually turned off the tap of new private expansion and opened the spigot of state development.

Such a policy means we pay our aid money to further the nationalism and eclecticism of those countries who reprimand us sharply if we attach conditions to our grants, and who actively court the Soviets and decline to denounce Castro.

Thereby we espouse the socialist cause and discourage those who attempt to escape from it. Such a policy drives us to grant money to governments to expand state-owned enterprises. Government-to-government aid to education in many areas can only mean the beefing up of communist indoctrination. Granting aid to left-wing development agencies can only mean more state ownership and intrusion into the private economy.

In practical terms, our choice of government-to-government aid as our major instrument means, as to most Latin American areas, that we are banking on the far left, in some form or other, as representing our best chance to develop these nations economically and to save them from communism. It seems certain that the average United States citizen would be shocked to be told that he had made any such choice, or that such a course serves our best national interest.

This is not to say that diplomatically and in other respects we should not support any particular lawful popular government of the moment, but rather that long-term, string-free government aid necessarily implies an untenable degree of adherence to the economic philosophy of the recipient.

There are other significant respects in which current policy works against our best interests. One is our international balance of payments. The United States has had an adverse balance of payments during most of the postwar period. In nearly every year our gross receipts from exports, remitted foreign earnings and other payments from overseas have been less than our out-payments in the way of imports, new foreign investments and other outflows.

Beginning with 1950, the United States balance of payments have shown a deficit every year except 1957, but the situation did not become serious enough to attract widespread public attention until 1958. The deficit reached $3.8 billion in that year, slightly more than $4 billion in 1959 and approximately $3 billion in 1960. While the deficit declined to approximately $2.5 billion in 1961 the drop was attributable chiefly to short-term factors, such as lowered European interest rates, unusually high exports to Europe and lowered imports from Europe. The drop does not presage any relief from continued large imbalance.[2]

The problem remains very serious because upon our maintenance of a reasonably balanced set of international accounts over the years rests the preservation of an adequate gold reserve, the stability of the United States dollar, its acceptability as a primary world currency.

Leading United States economists, financiers and government officials are, with few exceptions, united in their opinion that the continuance of balance-of-payments deficits at anything like the 1958-1961 level would be quite intolerable. In "Foreign Deficit of the United States, Causes and Issues," it is said:

The foreign deficit of the United States has led to deep concern at many levels of American society regarding domestic and foreign economic policy. It is clear that the very large deficits of the past two years (1958-59) cannot be allowed to continue unabated, and still less can the deficit be permitted to grow.

For if this were to happen, the outlook would be for a continued dwindling of United States gold holdings, the final means of settlement for international obligations. At some future point this process would almost certainly result in a large-scale loss of foreign confidence in the dollar as a world currency. In turn, this would lead sooner or later to large conversion of foreign dollar balances into gold, with the result that the U. S. gold holdings might rapidly evaporate. Such an eventuality would require drastic surgical corrective action whose effects might well shake the entire Free World economy to its very foundations. It is the avoidance of this kind of catastrophe in the future which places added stress on reasonable and wise corrective steps now to adjust the U. S. foreign deficit.[3]

While there is virtually unanimous agreement on the seriousness of the deficit, there is no such consensus when it comes to choosing the remedies. When the acuteness of the payments problem became apparent, government officials and others with a "vested" intellectual interest in the continuance of our foreign-aid policies, correctly assumed that foreign aid might be attacked as a free-loader in the balance-of-payments affair. So they went into action to enshrine foreign government aid as a constructive member of the team—as not being a drain at all or hardly at all from a balance-of-payments standpoint.

First, it was said, a high percentage of our aid results in the purchase of United States commodities; and, to the extent our aid creates such exports, it does not produce a balance-of-payments drain. On this score the government presentation to the public and Congress in support of the aid program for the fiscal year ending June 30, 1962, states:

It is often not understood that the preponderance of United States economic assistance funds are, and always have been, used directly for the purchase of goods and services in the United States. For example, it is estimated that during the past five calendar years the proportion of gross economic assistance funds (including surplus agricultural commodity program) used directly for the purchase of United States goods and services has not, in any one year, fallen below two-thirds of the gross foreign economic aid provided, even at times when more liberal policies were in effect governing procurement.[4]

In other words, the idea is that as long as we give away United States *things* instead of United States *dollars* to foreign nations, there is no impairment of the strength of the dollar. While this is true as a matter of strict balance-of-payments accounting, it reduces itself to an absurdity as a matter of substance since it implies that we could actually overcome a payments deficit by our government giving away to foreigners products purchased with tax receipts. If all of our $20 billion of annual exports were given away rather than sold to foreign buyers for dollars, the effect on the strength of our currency would be immediate and disastrous. The fact that we only give away 20 per cent of our exports merely makes the adverse effect less apparent and less immediate.

Despite this imposition on the public mentality, the aid apologists nevertheless have to concede *some* drain occurs as a result of foreign aid and they admit that "disbursements of funds under the new program are expected to contribute in the range of $300 million to $400 million to the balance-of-payments deficit. . . ."

As to this admitted drain, the comforting argument is advanced that our aid is going to make the foreign recipient so strong economically, in time, that its citizens—by then enriched by our foreign aid—will buy a lot more of our goods and we will get back more than we gave.

A chart accompanying this part of the presentation shows Western Europe's purchases from us are far higher than Latin America's, per capita, and depicts what our exports to Latin America would be if they were the same, per capita, as those of prosperous Western Europe. Since we gave aid to Europe following World War II, the argument goes, all we have to do is repeat the performance in Latin America and then sit back and reap the benefits.

But is Latin America really like Europe—a highly educated, urbanized, and industrialized society temporarily devastated by war? Is it not desirable that our imports from Latin America exceed our exports, as they do—aid in the form of trade? In Marshall Plan aid days our export balance was so unfavorable to Europe, they finally screamed for help. "Trade not aid," they pleaded, meaning "buy our goods instead of giving us money to buy yours." Can we really predict what our future export-import relationships might be with a highly developed, low-cost Latin America?

Independent authorities do not share this view that our aid outlays have little if any adverse impact on our balance-of-payments and the international position of the United States dollar. In his last Economic Report to the Congress (Economic Report of the President, January 1961), President Eisenhower wrote: "By and large . . . the deficit has reflected the postwar economic comeback of Western Europe and Japan, together with continued large expenditures for defense and foreign aid which the United States has made in discharging its international responsibilities."

In "The Patchwork History of Foreign Aid," the Felix and Lorna Morley study, the authors state: "The issue of whether the United States can afford to continue its foreign-aid program on the scale already developed has now come sharply to the fore. President Kennedy's campaign proposal for an even larger aid program must be measured against the economic exigencies of our international balance-of-payments deficit and consequent loss of gold. Subsidies to other countries, *in whatever form conveyed,** become part of the international balance of payments."[5]

"The chief weakness in the U. S. balance of payments," says the First National City Bank of New York (Monthly Letter, December 1960), "stems from the vast overseas expenditures of the U. S. Government. These expenditures . . . have reached the staggering total of close to $110 billion over the past 15 years. Of this total, more than four fifths has been in the form of cash military outlays abroad and military and economic grants."[6]

Said the 1959 Report of the Joint Economic Committee of the Congress on "Employment, Growth & Price Levels," page 60: "Rising government expenditures abroad have contributed substantially to the balance of payments deficit, and explain a considerable part of the large deficit this year."[7]

---

*That is, whether free goods or free dollars.

Says the Stanford Research Institute Staff study above referred to (page 28): "A large and generally rising volume of U. S. government dollar transfers abroad has been a significant factor in the development of overall deficit in the U. S. balance of payments."[8]

The illusion that foreign aid is a means of halting communism and helping our balance of payments was recently assailed by one of the world's most eminent authorities on the subject. Eugene R. Black, president of the International Bank for Reconstruction and Development, the world's largest multinational development lending agency declared:

"We have been sold foreign aid as an emergency measure to stop communism, as a necessary tool to 'make friends and influence people' in the underdeveloped world, as a 'must' to expand our export trade.

"Yet none of these so-called objectives has been achieved.

"Soviet influence remains at high tide; our dispensations of money have won us neither gratitude nor affection, but more often grumbling dissatisfaction; and our balance of payments position has worsened, not improved."[9]

Recently, a high official of the Kennedy Administration, Undersecretary of State George Ball, writing in the Department of State Bulletin for April, 1962, declared, "The causes of this (balance of payments) deficit are unique in history. It does not result from the failure of the United States to compete in world markets; our annual commercial balance continues to be in surplus in the amount of *several billion dollars*. It results *purely and simply* from the fact that we are carrying an extraordinary burden of effort for the defense of the free world and for assistance to the less-developed nations."

It is probably a safe assumption that the net dollar drain attributable to the enhanced government economic aid programs now projected, worldwide and excluding military expenditures, will be in the neighborhood of $4 billion per year, including as much as $1.5 billion in the case of Latin America.

There would be only two principal ways we could offset this governmental drain on our balance-of-payments in the case of Latin America—either by exporting more to them than we import from them or by repatriating more in income from our private investments in Latin America than we add in new investment there, or both. But either measure would be injurious to Latin America and hurtful to our own self-interest. We cannot do the first because our citizens need most of the things they buy from Latin America and, in any event, the Latin Americans cannot now buy much more from us than they do because they do not now generate the foreign erchange to do so. The second course of action—a net withdrawal of private capital from Latin America—would retard Latin America's growth and withdraw job-creating wealth. It would plunge Latin America deeper into economic desolation, leaving no alternative save more Soviet and United States government aid.

Yet such are our national policies. We put on drives to expand our exports in order that we can create an export surplus to "finance our aid," whereas we should be doing so in order to be able, without injury to our balance-of-payments, to buy more from Latin America. Whereas we should be pushing expanded private investment in Latin America, because this would strengthen Latin America and ultimately pay for itself in remitted earnings, we move steadily in the direction of more non-remunerative foreign aid instead, a primary factor in our unsatisfactory balance of payments.*

---

*And, recently, aid protagonists have taken to attacking our foreign private investments as a balance-of-payments villain, in a further attempt to enshrine our foreign aid. On its face, the attack is centered on our investments in developed areas such as Europe. Using the device of taxing unrepatriated foreign earnings, which would make our foreign enterprises more valuable to a foreigner than to a United States citizen, the Administration seeks to restrain new foreign private investment. This would temporarily aid our

Far from being one of the balance-of-payments culprits, private investment overseas can be the best ultimate answer to our balance-of-payments problem, especially in reference to the less developed nations. Private investment can create brick and mortar establishments that produce repetitive income and permanent jobs. It will, if anything can, finally displace one of the main causes of our balance-of-payments problem—our huge outlays of direct government aid. As we strengthen the economies of the underdeveloped regions and raise their standards through methods keyed to our own traditions, we provide them with continually increasing resources with which to buy our exports and create new jobs for us.

Yet unfortunately the trend for the past several years is in the opposite direction.

President Eisenhower's last Economic Report to Congress shows that of the $13 billion of capital flow from the United States alone to the less developed countries, including Latin America, over the period 1956-1959, $9 billion was in government aid and $4 billion in private lending and investment. This highly unsatisfactory government aid/private investment

---

balance of payments and provide temporary funds to give away, but it would be ruinous in the long run, since it would ultimately displace our position in foreign markets. In other words, as new capital outflow dwindled, remittances from previous investments and liquidations of old ones under the tax "hammer" would increase and thus temporarily contribute more to financing our aid programs. In 1959, for example, United States interests made new direct private long-term investments overseas to the tune of $1.5 billion. But they repatriated $2.5 billion in that year, as sent-home earnings from all previous such investments overseas. And this is more or less the picture today. Most of this surplus comes from the developed areas where our private investments are the most mature. The surplus helps finance new jobs in the United States as well as Latin America. A Commerce Department survey in 1961 showed Congress that earnings from our ventures in Europe flow "crosswise" into Latin America in significant amounts, even in relation to the amounts which move directly from the United States to Latin America.[10]

ratio has since worsened materially. In 1961 the Congress approved government economic aid to the less developed countries, including Latin America, in amounts approaching $5 billion per year—at least a 50 per cent increase over the 1956-59 period. At the same time private investment has been retarded by Cuba and other blows.[11]

This unhappy trend is worldwide. Government statistics show that the *private sector's* share of the total flow of financial resources from the developed countries (including the Soviet bloc) to the less developed has declined from 45 to nearly 30 per cent—a 50 per cent decline, while the Western governments' share has climbed from 47 to nearly 60 per cent of the total. The Soviet bloc's share has climbed from about 9 per cent of the total in 1956 to an estimated 14 per cent in 1960.[12]

The trend is even worse in Latin America than it is worldwide. As noted previously, because of Cuba and other unstabilizing factors, our private flow of capital to Latin America has gone down to a trickle. Even the Administration spokesman at Punta del Este, in predicting a $2 billion annual flow to Latin America from all free world sources, prophesied that only $300 million would come from our private sector as against $1.5 billion in United States government aid, a ratio of 1 to 5.

Another unfortunate aspect of these worsening ratios lies in the fact that most of the percentage increase in government funds flowing from the Western developed countries to the underdeveloped ones is attributable to the United States aid. Government figures show that our developed allies, Western Europe and Japan, still rely upon private investment to a much heavier extent, relatively, in making their financial contributions to the less developed.

This will mean, unless the trend is reversed, that they will "do the business" while we hand out the aid.

The following announcement by the government of West Germany on March 30, 1962, dramatically illustrates the tragic difference between the attitudes of Washington and those of our powerful Western allies:

> The German Cabinet has decided to go ahead with a Development Corporation designed to assist small and medium-sized German industries to go into business in the developing countries.
>
> The Corporation will be financed from the Bonn Government's aid funds and will enter into temporary partnerships with those German enterprises lacking the financial resources to face the risks of setting up subsidiaries in the developing countries.
>
> In other words, Government money will be used to lessen the risk faced by the individual investor and to tide him over the period when no profits can be expected. It is planned that once this initial period is over, the Development Corporation will part with the holding, making funds available for ventures elsewhere.[13]

Paradoxically, on April 2, just three days after the West German Government announced this plan to guarantee the profits of infant German industries going into risky environments, the Secretary of the Treasury in Washington appeared before the Senate Finance Committee and pressed for the imposition of new and increased United States taxes upon the earnings of American enterprises in Latin America and other under developed regions of the world.[14]

The president of a large United States firm in Brazil said to me while we were there, "Everybody will tell you that the competition in these markets is tough. The Italian, German and Japanese traders and investors are moving in here in force." His firm, he told me, expects to put another $20 million down there. "We can't see much profit in it," he said, "but we have a lot at stake and are trying to keep our position in these markets."

The recent precipitous decline in the flow of our private capital to these areas, both absolutely and in relation to government dollar outflows, is a calamitous consequence of our enshrining of foreign aid as a "sacred cow" and our refusal to stand behind our private enterprise system overseas.

It has also been suggested by some of the protagonists of government aid that an enlarged flow of private capital to Latin America would be an "export" to jobs because it would take away money that would otherwise be invested in plants in the United States to provide needed new jobs here. In the first place, if this argument is valid then the foreign aid ought not be given away to foreigners but rather to U. S. citizens or left untaxed in the hands of United States citizens for expenditure and investment here at home. No one doubts the need for more rapid creation of jobs in the United States, especially in view of the persistent unemployment, but it is not true that increasing foreign aid, while retarding foreign *private* investment, would help achieve that result.

Personal and institutional savings in the United States are at record highs, and there is no dearth of available credit or equity for the undertaking of any profitable venture. A freeing of the economy from government intrusion probably points the way to faster growth in the United States rather than a return to isolationism through retardation or inhibition of capital flow—now already unduly retarded to Latin America because of increased political risks and fears of Fidelismo.

The most fundamental cause of the phenomenon of continued high unemployment despite widespread prosperity, seen in the United States in recent years and at the present time, lies in the highly excessive allocation to labor of the joint production of capital and labor, resulting in an abnormal spur to labor-saving research and technology—a phenomenon once called technocracy, now commonly referred to as automation. Retarding foreign investment would not significantly affect this misallocation, which has resulted from a government-labor coalition against the owners and managers of private capital.

From the longer point of view, Latin America represents a huge and potentially profitable market for our goods and services, provided she remains in the capitalistic column. At the present time, however, Latin America is seething with joblessness, poverty and communism. She needs to industrialize rapidly to eliminate her imports of some consumer products. This does not foreshadow a decrease in our exports but a shift in degree from consumer to capital goods. The surest way to insure our export of American equipment and technology into a developing Latin America is through expanded investment on the partnership basis herein advocated. Her shift away from consumer products will be temporary since as she grows in wealth and strength, imports of consumer luxuries and the great innovations of the American product developers will again be permissible.

As for Latin American exports to the United States displacing United States jobs, recent Commerce Department surveys show that even United States investments made in the highly developed Common Market of Europe are, with negligible exceptions, made to capture a market no longer available through United States exports rather than as a haven from which to slip back "cheap labor goods" to the United States.[15] This is even more true of Latin America. Except in the case of raw materials we lack, our industrial investments in Latin America are not made for the purpose of exporting commodities to the United States. Our investments, unlike foreign aid, return a profit to us and provide repetitive jobs and earnings to the host country. That which we import from Latin America—coffee, copper, bananas, oil—stokes the needs of our own economy.

But the real criticism of government-to-government aid in lieu of more—and more purposefully directed—private effort is not in the final analysis its adverse effect on our budget or our balance of payments, grave as those effects may be.

Nor is it the alleged inefficiency in the administration of our aid programs. While in Latin America, we were besieged with illustrations of the inefficiency and inadequacy of our foreign aid. The dried milk was being used to mark soccer field boundaries, it was said. We were told that only 20 per cent of our earthquake aid to Chile ever reached its destination; that our grants of wheat to Brazil unfairly displaced potential wheat exports from Argentina. Most of our aid finds its way into the hands of the wealthy and influential, we heard repeatedly. We gained, from reliable sources, information to the effect that our Food for Peace stocks were being diverted from their original goals and sold at black market prices, indeed at such high prices in Bolivia that for a while a flourishing export market from neighboring countries to Bolivia grew up in the same aid commodities. Our aid is insufficient, we often were told. The notion that our aid programs are not motivated by generosity but by cynical purposes to unload our own surplus food, or to gain economic control, was pressed upon us. Grants are not wanted. Pay us more for our coffee and other commodities and it will reduce your aid, we were told.

Yet the plain fact of the matter is that giving never has managed to be and never was intended to be an efficient operation, and in any event efficiency surely is not a skill possessed by government. The books about the "inefficiency" of aid, its "poor administration," and the so-called "Ugly Americans" who deliver it have all been written and this is not one of them. Aside from their unfairness and inaccuracy, those treatises serve chiefly to detract from the central fact: our interest lies not in carrying *gifts* to the underdeveloped countries but replicas of successful capitalism. Since we believe in our system's merit, we must believe it to be in Latin America's interest too.

We need to stimulate United States private investment in Latin America because the only alternative, government-to-government aid, contradicts the very system upon which our own economic strength is based. The exportation, the re-creation abroad, of the fact of what we are is bound to serve best the common interests of our own citizens and our fellow Americans to the south. The time when we place all of our national resources behind that kind of an effort will be the start of a golden age for all the Americas and the demise of communism in our hemisphere.

CHAPTER IX

REFERENCES

1 Nathaniel Weyl, *Red Star Over Cuba,* Devin-Adair, New York 1961, p. 141.

2 Economic Report of the President, January 1961, Government Printing Office, Washington, D.C., and Survey of Current Business, OBE, Department of Commerce, March 1962, p. 22.

3 William B. Dale, "Foreign Deficit of the United States, Causes and Issues," Stanford Research Institute, Menlo Park, Calif., 1960.

4 "An Act for International Development," State Department, 1961.

5 Felix and Lorna Morley, "Patchwork History of Foreign Aid," American Private Enterprise Association, Washington, D.C., April 1961.

6 First National City Bank of New York, Monthly Letter, December 1960.

7 "Employment, Growth & Price Levels," Joint Economic Committee, U.S. Congress, 1959, p. 60.

8 *Supra,* Note 3, p. 28.

9 Eugene Black, President of International Bank for Reconstruction and Development, as reported in *San Francisco Examiner,* Oct. 18, 1961.

10 Report, U.S. Department of Commerce to Hon. Wilbur Mills, chairman of the Ways and Means Committee, House of Representatives, July 22, 1961.

[11] Economic Report of the President, January 1961, Government Printing Office, p. 115.

[12] "The Flow of Financial Resources to Countries in Course of Economic Development," 1956-9, Organization for European Economic Cooperation, 1961; Dr. Paolo N. Rogers, "Patterns for Private Participation in Developing Economies," address, International Industrial Conference, San Francisco, September 1961, Stanford Research Institute, Menlo Park, Calif.

[13] As reported in the *London Financial Times*, Mar. 30, 1962.

[14] H.R. 10650.

[15] Pizer & Cutler, "U.S. Investments in Foreign Countries," U.S. Department of Commerce, 1960.

Appendix

A Common Super-Market For Latin America

Considering how much the Latin American republics have in common in the way of language, temperament, culture and commercial experience, not to mention the three centuries during which all were held under colonial domination by the Iberian powers, Spain or Portugal, the tiny volume of their inter-country trade is truly astonishing.

In 1960, all of the private trade between all of the twenty republics (including Cuba) amounted to a trifling $695 million dollars. This is less than 10% of the two-way trade between them and the United States alone, and it is only slightly more than 4% of their total trade with the world (Yearbook of International Trade Statistics, 1960, United Nations, Page 18).

The principal reasons for this seeming paradox are readily discerned. For centuries Latin America was a raw-material world in which the growth of manufactures and inter-regional trade was either neglected or actively discouraged by colonial authorities. The wars of liberation brought in their wake an intense nationalism, which still persists. More recently many of the countries, in an effort to build more diversified economies, have erected tariff walls against each other in order to protect industries which are often uneconomic when viewed against the tiny population and consumer capacity of the particular nation. These manufactured products have not been able to compete in world markets with similar facilities outside Latin America, because of limited capacity and high unit costs of production. These factors emphasize Latin

America's reliance upon primary products, which account for over 90% of her exports to the outside world.

Thus we see a gigantic population of more than 200 million people, now coming to be larger than ours and possessing great consumer potentiality, going to waste as it were through an uneconomic proliferation of resources and through trade restrictions and tariff walls which have stifled expansion and growth.

Now, however, the "common market" concept is beginning to gain a foothold in two different Latin American groupings. One is the Latin American Free Trade Area (LAFTA) which has been stimulated by the examples of the European Community of six and the European Free Trade Area. In 1957 at the economic conference of the Organization of American States (OAS), a resolution was adopted declaring the advisability of establishing, gradually and progressively in a multilateral and competitive form, a Latin American regional market.

On February 18, 1960, representatives of seven Latin American republics (Argentina, Brazil, Chile, Mexico, Uruguay, Perú and Paraguay) signed at Montevideo a treaty instituting the Latin American Free Trade Association. The treaty went into force in 1961, and later in that year, Colombia and Ecuador also acceded to the treaty. On December 12, 1961, the first series of intra-area tariff negotiations were concluded, all of these countries except Colombia and Ecuador taking part. It was estimated that the total volume of the trade concessions then agreed upon exceeded by a substantial amount the required level of reduction set forth in the Treaty of Montevideo, although few concessions were granted on items particularly sensitive to competition from other sources within the area. The new rates which went into effect January 1, 1962, apply mainly to items already figuring significantly in intra-area trade. Subsequently, a special negotiation was conducted between the group and Colombia, and another with Ecuador is in prospect.

Like the Common Market of Europe, each country will retain its own tariffs on imports originating outside the free trade area. Unlike the Common Market of Europe, which provides for automatic annual reductions on non-agricultural products between member countries, in LAFTA the reductions must be negotiated periodically on a product-by-product basis. The freeing of intra-area trade is to be accomplished over a twelve-year period as follows: First, annual negotiations to establish schedules of concessions each member country is to give to the others, these schedules to result each year in reductions equivalent to not less than 8% of the weighted average of duties and charges applicable to outside countries; and then at three-year intervals, a common schedule of products on which the member countries agree eventually to eliminate duties is to be expanded so that the aggregate value of the free trade among member countries will be raised to 25% during the first three years, 50% during the second, 75% during the third, and to substantially all of the trade during the fourth and final three-year period.

LAFTA is an important beginning. However, the Treaty of Montevideo is fraught with safeguards and exceptions which could result in preferences within the free area as well as against non-signing countries. Also, neither Venezuela nor Bolivia has subscribed to the agreement because of special problems, including their overwhelming reliance upon a single export commodity: oil in the case of Venezuela and tin in the case of Bolivia.

At various times it has been suggested that the United States should join this or an even more expanded hemispheric common market. At the present time, however, it appears that neither their interests nor ours would be served by such a move. An elimination of restrictions and duties as between the United States and these Latin American nations would be injurious to the latter and open them to competition in their markets which they are ill-prepared to receive. If we desire to help Latin America through trade and investment rather than through foreign aid, we should strive to reduce our restrictions and tariffs relative to Latin American products without asking compensation in like reductions of the perimeter tariffs of LAFTA.

The second promising movement in the direction of Latin American regional economic integration had its beginnings in 1951 when the five republics of Central America established committees and institutions to deal on a regional basis with such matters as technical assistance, industrial research, electric power, housing, highways, and customs nomenclature. Later, on June 10, 1958, these five (El Salvador, Guatemala, Nicaragua, Honduras, and Costa Rica) signed a multilateral treaty on free trade and Central American economic integration, providing for the establishment within ten years of free trade within the countries for a limited and specified list of commodities. Unfortunately, this treaty has not yet been ratified by Costa Rica and has not come into force because its ratification by all five countries is a prerequisite.

In a separate move in 1959, the Ministers of Economy of the five countries signed two additional agreements: one providing for the application to outside countries of uniform tariff rates of those commodities exempt from duties in the intra-area trade; and the other extending a tariff preference of 20% on the importation of all goods produced within the area. The first of these agreements has been ratified, and negotiations to establish a common external tariff are making progress.

Then, in 1960, El Salvador, Guatemala and Honduras signed a treaty of economic association calling for the free circulation of persons, goods, and capital within their territories. Going far in the direction of a complete customs union, this agreement subjected to immediate free trade among the three all save a limited number of products originating in their territories. Even most of these exceptions are to be free after scheduled periods of five or six years.

Later in 1960, Guatemala, El Salvador, Nicaragua, and Honduras signed another major instrument, The General Treaty of Central American Integration, now in effect in the first three states. It provides for immediate free trade among the signatories in all but a limited number of specified products, the latter to be generally free within five years. Thus, in two years' time, the movement toward Central American integration evolved from a limited free trade area to a nearly complete customs union in at least three of the five Central American states.

Free trade within Latin America offers the most important spur to her development, surpassing the influence of any conceivable amount of foreign investment or aid. For the first time in history each nation would have to compete with all others in political and economic stability, in the restraint of their wild inflations and currency gyrations and, finally and most important, in productivity. Uneconomic and subsidized industries, many of them state-owned and operated, would feel the pressure of competition in a huge free market. They would have to reduce their costs, through modernization, wage and price restraint and otherwise, or else yield to their more efficient competitors in other countries. Each industry in each country would inevitably be driven to that which it could perform most productively and efficiently.

One of the main reasons for present high rates of economic growth in the Common Market of Europe, at their present stage of free internal trade coupled with continuing political separateness, lies in the very fact that each Government is under pressure to follow political, fiscal, monetary, and balance-of-payments policies which create the kind of stable environment in which their industries can compete with those of other member nations. Their industries, while offered a vast new free market, face new competition against which they have no weapon except greater productivity. It is doubtful that Western Europe would be as competitive or grow as fast economically if she were politically unified at this stage of development.

The United States is the world's greatest common market, with our federal Government guaranteeing free trade among our fifty states and providing political and currency unity. We have prospered largely by trading with ourselves, in our own vast market. Our foreign trade in volume and value is the largest in the world, but it is one of the smallest as a percentage of our internal commerce. Now, however, with the emergence of the European Common Market, freer world-wide trade and more intense competition, our Government must face the same severe fiscal, monetary and balance-of-payments disciplines to which each Government of Europe is now subject. If we continue to respond with budget and balance-of-payments deficits and inflation, we will enter an era of economic decline and stagnation. But if we face and surmount them, we will owe a debt of gratitude for the pressures placed upon us by world competition, especially from Europe.

The urgent necessity that the Latin American republics move rapidly to a position of free internal trade with responsible political separateness is thus apparent. They will be the chief beneficiaries of their own huge internal market, unrivalled in the world in size, resources, and potential strength. Through perimeter tariffs, they can protect their new supermarket against undue external competition during their years of full development. The retention, at least during this stage, of political separateness will force each nation to compete with all others for the kind of political stability without which their dreams of economic development can never come true.

INDEX

A

Abs, Dr. Herman J., 197

Act of Bogotá, 77, 184

Adler, Mortimer, quoted, 182-183

Agri-Business, 33

Agriculture: answer to agrarian problem, 40; capital needs, 38; decline in food production, 80; destruction of rural culture, 29; diversification of output, 40; divorce of industry from, 28-29; early agrarian society, 25; farm village, Brazil, 28; food imports, Latin America, 141; Fresno County, California, 32-33; leadership failures, 40; local solution to unemployment, need for, 28; low productivity in, reason for, 38; modern attributes, 31-33; population of, in Latin America, 34; post-feudal in character, 25; pro-Castroism in, 29; responsibility of local community leaders, 39; seizure of farms, 29-30; United States investment in, 41

Aguilar, Jorge L., quoted, 154, 171

Aldrich, Richard, 170

Alessandri, President Jorge, 4, 64, 198

Alliance for Progress (see Foreign Aid)

Altos Hornos, 54

Aluminia del Uruguay, S.A., 62

Aluminium, Ltd., 62

American Smelting and Refining Corporation, 31, 43, 147, 165, 174

Anaconda Copper Company, 31, 147, 152-153

Angla Tierra Nitrate, 158

Anti-trust laws, 47

Argentina: development in, 62-63; Dinie, 63; highlight elements favoring Reds, 11; inflation, 46; Land Reform program in, 36; neutralism, 6; new investment capital, 63-64, 167-168; railway deficit of government, 51; sale of state industries, 62-63; stock exchange, 158; taxation of grain, 34

Arosemena, President C. J., 164

Atkin, William R. B., quoted, 198

B

Ball, George, Undersecretary of State, quoted, 215

Balance of payments, 210-220

Bananas: Colombia, 4; decline in trade, 78

Bauer, Peter T., quoted, 126

Beatty, David, quoted, 200

Beltran, Dr. Pedro G., Prime Minister of Peru, quoted, 57

Benton, ex-Senator William, quoted, 85-86

Berle, Adolph A., quoted, 125

Bethlehem Iron Mines of Chile, 64

Black, Eugene R., quoted, 215

Bolivia: highlight elements favoring Reds, 11; inflation, 46; neutralism, 6; petroleum, 67; Soviets do business, 123-124; tin, 50, 70, 78

Brandt, Professor Karl, quoted, 33, 34

Brazil: aid to, 52; coffee policy, 79-81; Conclap, 127; Export-Import Bank aid, 53-54; expropriation of United States utilities, 51-52; farm village in, 28; favellas, 2; government-owned steel, 54; highlight elements favoring Reds, 12; inflation, 46; Juliao, peasant leader, 20; neutralism, 6-7; opinion of United States capital, 10; slums, 2-3; stock exchanges, 158; taxation of coffee, 34

British Guiana: aid claims, 14-15; communism by election, 4; East German aid, 123

Brizola, Governor Leonel, 51

Brozen, Professor Yale, quoted, 80-81

Byington, Albert, Jr., quoted, 127

C

Caldera, Dr. Rafael, 202

California Packing Corporation, 41

Canada, protests against foreign ownership, 149

Capitalism (see also United States Private Investment, Communism, Socialism, Cold War) : abandonment of, as instrument of United States policy, 123; brainwashing against, 118; competition of government banks, 51-57; conscience of, 39; craving for stock ownership in Latin America, 160 and infra; dispels communist myth in United States, 22; double standard, 71; fabric of in Latin America, 11-14; failing in Latin America, 22; farm answer, 40; flight of capital from Latin America, 45, 160; Indians want, 42-43; industrial feudalism, 47; limited entrepreneurship, 44; modern, in United States farming, 31-32; "Needles-eye" variety, 28, 44-45; Otavalos prepared for, 42-43; personal stake in, 146-148; socialism incompatible with democracy, 182; stock exchanges, 156-159; United States concern in 50; yield requirements, 44-45; how viewed, 9

Cárdenas, General Lazaro, 14, 37

Cárdenas Perez, Pablo, 199

Carrizosa Herrera, Fernando, quoted, 163

Castro, Fidel (see Communism, Cuba)

Catholic church: Fé y Alegria, 201; role in early agrarian society, 27; school by radio, 96-97; slums in Venezuela, 1-2

Celanese Corporation of America, 162

Cerro de Pasco Corporation, 29, 165-166

Charitable activities: business action, 201; Fé y Alegria, Venezuela, 1-2

Chase International Investment Corporation, 56

Chile: Alessandri, President Arturo, 4; callampas, 2; Corfo, 64, 157; election of Communists, 12; expropriation platform, pref. vii; government industries, 64-65; government-owned steel, 54; highlight elements favoring Reds, 12; imports of food, 141; inflation, 46; inquilinos, 40; landowners attitude, 40; neutralism, 6; slums, 3; small business, 198; stock exchange, 157

Cities: Bogotá, Colombia, 157; Buenos Aires, Argentina, 91, 158; Caracas, Venezuela, 1-2; Córdoba, Argentina, 97; Guanajuato, Mexico, 49; Lima, Peru, 2; Mexico City, Mexico, 2-3, 90; Montevideo, Uruguay, 60, 62, 91; population statis-tics, 104; Rio de Janeiro, Brazil, 2, 158; Sao Paulo, Brazil, 106, 158

Coffee (see also Commodities) : Colombia, 4; over-reliance, 40; price and production control, 139-140; production and prices, 77-79; price hike as aid, 76; synthetic, 82; United States help in controlling, 77

Cold War: capitalism's advantage, 184-185; development struggle related, 135; Hitler, Lenin methodology, 112; Latin America "uncommitted", 184; loss of confidence in free enterprise, 117; need to prove efficiency of capitalism, 127; Pavlov, experiments, 110-111; psychological factors, 110-131; risks, 41

Colonial revolutions, effect of, 26

Colombia: Committee for Education and Social Action (CEAS), 65, 171, 198; compulsory sale of government steel stock to public, 55; government-owned steel, 55; highlight elements favoring Reds, 12; natural resouces, 4; stock exchange, 157; Technological Institute in agiculture, 38

Colombian Petroleum Company, 163

Committee for Education and Social Action (CEAS), 65, 171, 198

Committee for Economic Development (CED), 77

Commodities (see also particular commodity, Trade) : decline in trade, 78-80; international price and production controls, 75-83, 139-141; Latin American complaints, 75-76; overdependence on few, 40

Common markets, Latin America: Central America, 228-229; European market, analogy, 230; general, 225-230;; Latin American Free Trade Area (LAFTA), 61, 226-228; United States market, related to, 230

Communism (see also Socialism, Capitalism) : capture of popular revolutions, 9; Castro admission of, 6; Castro, as front man, 127; Castro-type revolution, outmoded, 4; commercial successes, 124; Communist Party, 16-17; Costa Rica (1948), 20; critical point in time, in Latin America, 183; election of Communists, 3-4, 12; emigration due to, 3; farm penetration, 20; freedom gap of, 184-185; impact of Cuba in Latin America, 5-8; labor organizations, 17, 30; Mao Tse-Tung, 3-4; Marx, Karl, 4, 21-23, 25-26, 31, 50; Peace Conference in Mexico (1961), 13-14; percent in Chile, pref. viii; promoting land seizure, 29-30; promotion of land reform, 40; publications and press, 17-18; public opinion, 18; students, 2, 19-20; teachers in Venezuela, 2; universities, 90-94; use of Cuban embassies, 9; victory at polls, 15

Companhía de Mineracao Novalimense, 54

Compañía Fundadora de Fierro y Acero de Monterrey, S.A., 54

Companhía Telefónica Nacional, 51

Competition, 46

Concentration of wealth, 4

Conclap (Brazil), 171

Consumers, 45-46

Copper: export increase, 78; political pressure in Chile, 64-65

Corn Products Company, 41, 61

Costa Rica: communist seizure, 20-21; cost of living, 46

Cotton, 81-82

Creeping capitalism in U.S.S.R., 69

Creole Corporation, 152

Cuba: Castro, armed revolt, 3; diplomatic relations with, 5; Dorticos, President Oswaldo, touring Red China, 16; importance worldwide, 5; increase in pro-Castroism, 7-9; land reform in, 37-38; proportion of foreign ownership in, 149; Soviet aid policy, 122

D

Deltec, Ltd., 166, 169

Development: job for private capital, 186-187; local responsibility, 39, 40; private capital, key to, 134; quality of United States contribution, 22; reliance upon aid, 129; shift from government to private, 172; time required, 22

Dictatorship of left, 58-59

Dillon, Douglas, Secretary of the Treasury, quoted, 77, 125, 128, 219

duPont, E. I. de Nemours, 148, 153

E

Ecuador: farm seizure, 30; highlight element favoring Reds, 12; Jivaros, head shrinking by, 43; neutralism, 6

Education: Bologna system of, 89, 93; business role in, 95-98; Chambers of Commerce, 96; communism in, 19-20; freedom and literacy, 86-87; general, 85-98; in earlier agrarian society, 27; literacy, 27, 85-88; politics, campus, 2; program recommended, 94-98; Red bias, 89; seizure in Cuba, 93; United States and Latin America compared, 85, 87, 88; universities, student control of, 89-94

Eisenhower, ex-President Dwight D., 114, 214, 217-218

England, protest against foreign ownership, 150

Enriquez, René, quoted, 162-163

Esso de Brazil, 167

Export-Import Bank of Washington: aid amounts, 128; competition with private finance, 56; domestic pressures,

57; financing of government ownership, 53-56; government guarantee requirement, 55-56; roads financing, 39

Expropriation (see Government Ownership, Communism, Capitalism, Financing for Freedom Act)

F

Feudalism of middle ages, compared, 25

Figueres, José, quoted, 21, 149

Financing for Freedom Act: aims and goals, 196; business obligations under, 188-190; cooperation of Latin America, 206-207; effect of, upon Latin America, 200-201; effect on government ownership, 195; effect on jobs, 196-197; general, 187-198; government-guaranteed all-risk credits, 192-193; insurance against expropriation and other Cold War risks, 187-192; multi-national guarantee program, 197; opinions concerning, 197-205; taxation features, 194-195, 205

Firestone Tire & Rubber Company, 151

First National City Bank of New York, 214

Food for Peace, 42, 128

Ford Foundation, 91, 149

Ford Motor Company, 148, 150

Foreign Aid: Act of Bogotá, 184; aid to expropriated enterprises, 52, 68-69; agencies, 56-57, 68, 76, 126, 129; Alliance for Progress, 5, 29-30, 76, 128, 130, 184; amounts, 5-6, 120-121, 128-129, 184, 215; balance of payments, effect on, 210-220; Bolivia, 11; contradicts United States economic system, 222-223; Food for Peace, Bolivia, 70; government planning of development, 124-127; inefficiency, 222; Marshall Plan philosophy inapplicable, 106-108; patchwork history of, 129; railroads, to, 71; ratio of, to private investment, 217-218; Truman doctrine, 107; unhinged from American experience and character, 126-127; United States adoption of Soviet approach, 120-131; United States and Soviet aid compared, 120-123; vanishing dollars in Haiti, 130; Venezuela, 68

Foremost Dairies Corporation of San Francisco, 41

Franks, Sir Oliver, quoted, 183

Freeborn, James, 97

Friedman, Milton, quoted, 126

Frondizi, Arturo, 62, 67, 167

Fundo Crescinco, 170, 198

G

Gardner, Henry, quoted, 152-153

Garner, Robert L., quoted, 126

General Agreement on Tariffs and Trade (GATT), 80

General Electric Corporation, 148, 151, 166

General Foods Corporation, 41

General Mills Company, 41

General Motors Corporation, 147, 151

General Tire Company, 151, 158

Gomez Jaramillo, Arturo, 198-199 Gomez-Pinzón, José, quoted, 171, 198

Goodrich, B. F., Corporation, 151

Goodyear Tire Company, 152

Goulart, President Joao of Brazil, 12, 52

Government ownership: Argentina, 63; billion dollar confiscation in Cuba, 7; character of, in Latin America, 49-50; Chile, 4, 64-65; Colombia, 65; Congressional disapproval, 52; discourages capital, 62; expropriation "going in," 53-54; general, 49-71; "import license checkmate" method, 53; India, Ceylon, 122; Marx doctrine, 4, 21-23, 50; methods of achieving, 50-54; Mexico, amount in, 13, 66; nationalization of industry, Bolivia, 11; oil, 66-68; oil in Mexico, 13, 50; payment for through United States aid, 52; pressure for in Chile, 65; "retroactive tax" method, 52-53; reversals in Australia, England, Germany, 70-71; "squeeze-out" technique, 51; squeeze in Colombia, 65-66; steel, 53-55; tin in Bolivia, 50; uneconomic, 54; United States policy toward, 51-52; utilities "squeeze-out," 50-51; works for communism, 58

Grace, W. R. & Company, 144, 158, 164-165

Graham, Howard W., quoted, 149

Griffin, Cornelius, quoted, 167

Guarantee program (see Financing for Freedom Act, United States Foreign Policy)

Guatemala, Land Reform Program in, 35

Guevara, Ernesto "Che", 7, 127

Gulf Oil Company, 163

H

Haiti, foreign aid to, 130

Head shrinking, discipline of, 43

Heller, Dr. Walter, quoted, 107

Herrera, Alberto Luis, quoted, 62

Herrera, Felipe, quoted, 73

Hinkle, William, 202

Huber, Gilbert, quoted, 171

I

IDEAS (Venezuela), 171, 201

Indians: capitalistic propensities, 42-44; comparison to United States, 27-28

Inflation: depreciation account, 46; general, 44-46; "squeeze-out" of utilities, 50-51

Inter-American Development Bank, 56-57, 76, 201

Interest rates, 44

International Bank for Reconstruction and Development (World Bank), 126, 129, 195, 201

International Basic Economy Corporation (IBEC), 169-171

International Business Machines, 62

International Finance Corporation, 56, 126, 129

International Monetary Fund, 129

International Petroleum Company, 174

International Telephone and Telegraph Corporation, 51, 156

Iron ore, 53-54

J

Jagan, Prime Minister Cheddi, 14

Jarvis, Harry H., quoted, 96

Joblessness (see Unemployment)

Joint ventures (see Partnership Ventures)

K

Kaiser of Argentina, 158

Kellogg Company, 41

Kelso, Louis, quoted, 183

Kennedy, President John F.: aid

to expropriated enterprise, approval of, 68-69; inaugural address, 31, 117; interview in Izvestia, 14-15; joint communiqué of April 4, 1962, 52

Koppers Company in Argentina, 158, 167, 197

Krieg, William, quoted, 198

Khrushchev, 114, 127

L

LaBouisse, Henry R., quoted, 124

La Piere, Professor Richard, quoted, 86

Labor: communist influence in, 17, 30; International Labor Organization (ILO) meeting in Buenos Aires, 17; productivity, 73-75, 105-106; wages, 5; welfare legislation, 72-74

Lahey, Edwin A., quoted, 130

Land reform (see also Agriculture, Commodities): Alliance for Progress, 30; Argentina, 36; Bolivia, 69; capitalist solution, 33; Chile, 30, 40; Chinese-type revolution, 30; communist farm failures, 33; Cuba, 37-38; cutting up farms, 33; failure in Latin America, 35-38; food and farm product processing, 40; Guatemala, 35; land grant policy, need for, 39; Mexico, 36-37; modern corporate answer, 31-33; pitfalls of, 30-41; political attempts in United States, 31; statistics, erroneous, 34; tax

penalties on farm produce, 34; Uruguay, 35-36

Latapi, Luis, 44

Lead and zinc, decline in trade, 78

Legoretta, Luis, 66, 171

Lenin, method of victory, 21, 111, 112

Liddel-Hart, B. H., quoted, 112

Listas Telefónicas, S. A., 171

Littlefield, Edmund, 43

Local self-government, absence, 38

Lopez, Jacinto, farm "parachuters", 29

M

Machado Gomez, Alfredo, quoted, 66

Marshall Plan, 106-108

Marx, Karl: collapse of capitalism, 31; Europe at time of, 25-26; theory as applied to Latin America, 4, 21-23, 50

Maryknoll fathers, 42

Mateos, President Lopez, quoted, 6, 36

Maxfield, Gerald, 202

Mazzaferri, José, quoted, 63

McLellan, Father Dan, 42

Meat, market loss, 81

Mejía Palacio, Jorge, quoted, 76

Mendoza, Eugenio, 95, 171

Mexico: costs of money, 44-45; ejido system, 36-37; farm seizure, 30; government-owned steel, 54; government ownership trend, 66; highlight elements favoring Reds, 13; Land Reform Program in, 36-37; limits on foreign investment, 149-150; Mexicanization of industry by law, 53; mining law, 53, 149, 199-200; National Financiera de Mexico, 66; neutralism, 6-7; petroleum, 13, 50; population growth, 100; power and light "squeeze-out", 51; slums, 2-3; stock exchanges, 156-157

Minerals, original government title, 49

Miranda, Fausto, 171

Monsegur, Dr. Otero, quoted, 201

Morley, Felix, quoted, 129, 214

Morris, James, quoted, 3

Moscoso, Teodoro, quoted, 202-205

Mutual funds (see Partnership Ventures)

Myrdal, Dr. Gunnar, quoted, 119

N

National Industrial Conference Board, 76

Neutralism: growing tendency, 6-8; new kind in British Guiana, 14

Newmont Mining Company, 165

Nixon, ex-Vice President Richard, 19

Non-violent revolution, 4

North American Association (Venezuela), 202

O

Operation Bootstrap, 202-205

Organization of American States, 6

P

Panama, highlight elements favoring Reds, 13

Panama Canal, 13

Pardo, Enrique, 171

Partnership ventures: customer participation, 163; importance of, 147-175; instances of, 151-172; public offerings, 154-175; mutual funds, 169-171; small business, 162-164; stock exchanges, 156-158; underwriting in Brazil, 169; United States Chamber of Commerce in Rio and Sao Paulo, action by, 154-156

Pastrana, Dr. Misael, 199

Paternalism of the soil, 42

Patterson, Albion W., quoted, 90

Paz Estenssoro, President, Bolivia, 69

Peace Corps, 123, 128

Peña, Juan Bautista, 171

People's capitalism, 108

Peru: access road to Andes, 39; American society in Peru, 97; barriadas, 2; business in education, 96; capitalistic Indians, 42-43; farm seizure, 29; government-owned steel, 54; inflation, 46; opportunities, 199; private credit unions, 42; slums, 2

Peters, Randolph, quoted, 152

Petroleum: Argentina, 62; Colombia, 4; exports, 78; government ownership, 66-68; original government ownership, 49; over-reliance, 40, 82; taxation of, 82; trade, 78, 82; Venezuela, 67-68, 82

Phelps Dodge Copper Company, 165

Philippines, limit on foreign ownership, 150

Philips Lamp of Holland, 61

Pigmentos y Productos Químicos, 153

Pinedo, Federico, quoted, 30

Political instability, 15

Population: birth control, 102-103; Colombia, 4; concentrating in large cities, 104; experience in Japan, 104; farm, in United States, 31; growth and composition, 100-106; Indians in Peru, 3; Mexico City, 3; percentage on farms, 34

Post feudalism, 25-48

Price Waterhouse & Company, 202

Public offerings (see Partnership Ventures)

Puerto Rico, 203-205

Punta del Este, 5, 77, 128

Productivity, 11

Q

Quadros, ex-President Janio, of Brazil, 12

R

Rangel, Alberto Domingo, 8

Ravines, Eudacio, quoted, 8

Reconstruction Finance Corporation, 56

Reston, James, quoted, 108

Reynolds Aluminum Company, 202

Rieve, Emil, quoted, 74, 202

Rockhill, Victor E., quoted, 56

Ross, Jorge, 171

Rusk, Secretary of State Dean, quoted, 118

S

Samper, Alberto, 171

Savings, 44

Sears Roebuck & Company, 46, 151, 164

Servente, Alberto Guido, 170

Silvert, H. K., quoted, 8, 90

Slums (see Urban Slums)

Socialism (see also Government Ownership): communism no longer distinguished, 50; creates unstable society, 182-183; foreign aid fosters, 126; Inter-American Development Bank, receptivity, 56-57, 125; orthodoxy of the Left, 58-59; running communist campaign, 4;

social legislation, 71-75, 152; social reform, meaning, 105; Uruguay, 59-62

"Soft Six", 6

Southern Peru Copper Company, 147, 165

Standard Brands Corporation, 41

Standard Oil of New Jersey, 152

Stanford Research Institute, 76, 215

Stevenson, Ambassador Adlai, 18, 147

Stewart, C. Allan, 202

Stokes, Professor William S., 70

Sugar: Colombia, 4-5; Cuban subsidy, 81; decline in trade, 78

Swift & Company, 60

T

Taxation: local power, absence of, 39; punitive agricultural and mineral policies, 40, 59, 82; Revenue Act of 1962 (H. R. 10650), 178-179, 216-217 (footnote), 219

Teléfonos de Mexico, 160

Tin: Bolivia, 50, 70; decline in trade, 78

Tittman, Edward McLanahan, 165

Tomlinson, Edward, quoted, 60-61

Trade: dependence on few commodities, 40-41; internal, in Latin America, 225-226; Latin American decline, 79; terms of trade, 41, 138-139; United States-Latin America, 136-141

Trouyet, Carlos, 135, 161

U

Unemployment: Caracas, Venezuela, 1-2; fundamental problem, 15, 83, 179

Union Carbide Corporation, 160, 197

United Fruit Company, 30

United Nations Technical Fund, 38

United States Business (see United States Private Investment, Financing for Freedom Act)

United States Development Loan Fund, 68

United States foreign policy: alignment with Left, 209-210; Boggs bill, 178, 194; channeling of capital flow, 186; guarantee program, 175-178; incentives in exchange for business conduct, 206; person-to-person capitalistic message, 185; reformation, 130-131; role in education, 98; taxation, 178-179, 216-217 (footnote), 219; Victory Loan approach, 186

United States private investment (see also Partnership Ventures, Financing for Freedom Act): agricultural, 41; amount and character, 142-175; annual goal, 129; Argentina, 61-64; communist propaganda, 10-11;

decline, 144-145, 217-220; export of jobs argument, 220-221; government support, lack of, 175-180; inducement, lack of, 179; job-creating capacity, 106; publication of foreign financial data, 174-175; public offerings, 154-175; public opinion polls, 9-10; ratio of, to foreign aid, 217-218; Revenue Act of 1962 (H.R. 10650), 178-179; scapegoat for ills, 135; showcase sample, 135; significance, 135-138; social responsibility, 173-175; taxation of, 178-179; widely-owned United States corporation, as image of constructive capitalism, 148

United States Rubber Company, 151

United States Steel Corporation, 31, 147

Urban slums: barriadas, Lima, Peru, 2-3; callampas, Chile, 2; favellas, Rio de Janeiro, Brazil, 2; Mexico D. F., Mexico, 2; migration to, 3, 42; ranchitos, Caracas, Venezuela, 1-2

Uruguay: Land Reform Program in, 35-36; new private investment, 61-62; socialistic, 14; taxation of grain, 34; welfare state, 60-62

Utah Construction and Mining Company, 31, 43

V

Venezuela: aluminum, government ownership, 65; annual

loss, government enterprises, 54; communist teachers, 2; flight of capital from, 45; government-owned steel, 54; highlight element favoring Reds, 12; imports of food, 141; inflation, 46; North American Association, 97; petroleum, 67-68, 82; population splurge, 100; ranchitos, 1; slums, 1-2; student politics, 2, 92, 94; unemployment, 1-2

Voice of America, pref. vii, 9, 50, 119, 155

Vollmer, Gustavo, quoted, 171-172, 201

Volta Redonda, 54

W

Ways, Max, quoted, 126

West Germany, incentives to industry, 218-219

Westinghouse Electric Company, 151

Willys-Overland of Brazil, 166, 169, 197

Wright, Donald, quoted, 166

Y

Yugoslavia, aid to, 57-58

Z

Zuloaga, Nicomedes, Hijo, 171, 201